A HISTORY OF
ARCHITECTURE IN ITALY

The dramatic entrance portico to Bernini's centrally-planned S. Andrea al Quirinale, Rome (1658), shows the curved motifs and boldly modelled forms typical of Baroque.

A History of ARCHITECTURE *in Italy*

T. W. WEST M.A.

UNIVERSITY OF LONDON PRESS LTD

SBN 340 06926 0 Boards
SBN 340 09431 1 Paper

University of London Press Ltd
St Paul's House, Warwick Lane, London EC4

Printed and bound in Great Britain by
Cox and Wyman Ltd, London,
Fakenham and Reading

CONTENTS

LIST OF LINE DRAWINGS

LIST OF PLATES

ACKNOWLEDGEMENTS

The author and publishers thank the following for permission to reproduce photographs: Fototeca Unione, Rome (plates 1a, 1b, 3a, 6b, 7a and jacket, 8, 10a, 12, photos by Alinari; frontispiece and plate 2, photos by Anderson); The Mansell Collection (plates 3b, 4b, 10b, photos by Alinari; plates 4a, 5b, 7b, photos by Anderson); F. A. Mella (plates 5a, 6a, 9, 11, 13, 14b, 15); The Royal Institute of British Architects (plate 14a).

To Jane

who helped so generously

PREFACE

GUIDES to the architecture of England and Scotland have already appeared in this series, but *A History of Architecture in Italy* is the first devoted to the architecture of a European country beyond these islands.

The British have been accused of insularity, not through a propensity to stay at home, for as traders, colonizers, and travellers they have an unbeatable record, but rather because of a natural resistance to foreign influences and a disinclination to think internationally. But times change and in a shrinking world, without an empire that paradoxically carried their insularity across the globe, the British are more conscious than ever before of their European connection. Already powerful economic pressures are bringing about the integration of the different sovereign states of Europe into a community of which Britain will soon become a member. And beyond that there are those who see an even closer political interdependence.

It is against this general background of an increasingly European consciousness, the vast boom in continental travel since the Second World War, and the growth in popular interest in the visual arts that this series of introductions to the architecture of Europe has been written. It is intended to be informative not only to students of all ages but also to the intelligent modern traveller who has no time to read longer books on the subject but who nevertheless wishes for a comprehensive account of the architecture of a particular country presented in a balanced and up-to-date manner. This is by no means a mere catalogue of buildings. The characteristics of each style are described, the most important and representative works of each period are briefly analysed, and the contributions of the outstanding architects related to the evolution of western architecture as a whole.

Even those who are not at present contemplating a visit to Italy should find this book useful if they are at all interested in British architecture. A distinguished precedent for this situation was set by Sir Christopher Wren for, though he was never in

Rome, St Paul's Cathedral owes much to Italian Renaissance sources. Indeed Britain has large numbers of classical buildings dating from the seventeenth century onwards, perhaps nearly as many as exist in Italy today – vernacular excepted of course – and it is impossible to understand or appreciate them properly without some knowledge of the origins of classical architecture and the diverse forms into which it was evolved by Italian architects from the Early Christian period to the Baroque. To name but a single instance of cross-fertilization, Andrea Palladio was one of the great formative influences on British architecture. And long before this the basilican form of the typical medieval church and later revivals, with many of its features, was gradually evolved – though not exclusively – in the Early Christian and Romanesque architecture of Italy.

Italy seems the obvious choice to begin with, partly on account of the intrinsic importance and nobility of the Italian contributions to European architecture, and partly because of the special appeal which the land and art of Italy have always had for the British. From the time of the virtuosi and the Grand Tour, when Dr Johnson remarked that 'a man who has not been in Italy is always conscious of an inferiority', successive generations have felt the same attraction encouraged by the enthusiasm of the Romantics and men and women of letters as diverse as the Brownings, Henry James, and D. H. Lawrence, to say nothing of J. A. Symonds and Ruskin – despite the fact that the latter condemned Renaissance architecture as pagan and impious, preferring instead Venetian Gothic. Even political interest played its part when liberalism championed Italy's cause in her struggle for freedom and unity at the Risorgimento and thereby earned the undying gratitude of patriots like Mazzini and Garibaldi.

If two world wars put an end to tourism for a time they took many thousands of British and American servicemen to the ancient towns and cities of Italy; now it is the turn of unequalled numbers of holidaymakers – over 20 million each year – to benefit from the new opportunities created by more leisure and unprecedented affluence. The tourist industry plays a very vital part in the Italian economy and though many visitors are attracted to scenery as diverse as the Dolomites, the northern lakes, the hill-top towns, and the torrid littoral of the south the majority are still drawn by the fabulous art treasures of the great historic cities, finding stimulus for their imaginations and senses in the extraordinary variety of the architecture of the peninsula.

Rich though the main centres of Italy are in noble buildings, there is hardly a town in the remotest province that has nothing of architectural interest, an arcaded piazza, some graceful houses, some monuments of note, to show the receptive traveller; and only the traveller with some interest in the cultural history of Italy can enjoy much of the experience that this land of such great charm has the power to give. No longer is it necessary to be rich to enjoy European architecture and in Italy the student enjoys many privileges such as the *case dello studente* (inexpensive students' lodgings like the Casa Internationale at the Palazzo Salviati, Rome) or the International Youth Hostels Federation's houses. Thus it is the particular aim of the book to try and arouse the interest of the younger traveller in an important part of his European heritage and to satisfy some of his curiosity.

INTRODUCTION

THE Italians, though racially very mixed, with the most striking differences between north and south, are essentially a people of quick and lively intelligence to which is coupled a remarkable instinct for creating and appreciating works of art. There is too, throughout Italy, a strong awareness of and sympathy with the past and the products of the past. It is apparent in the many festivals and processions – Corpus Christi, the Palio horse races at Siena, the marriage of the sea at Venice, and many more – besides the expense and care lavished on the great art collections and works of architecture, many war-damaged examples of which have been so carefully restored. (St Mark's, Venice, receives a government grant equivalent to £25,000 annually for its maintenance.) Italian high achievement in painting, sculpture, and music is paralleled in architecture, which though it has sometimes served as a setting for the other arts, is yet greater than them because it is so much more inclusive. As Vasari says in his famous *Lives* it is 'the most useful, universal, and necessary' art to men; it is that for which the others exist to adorn.

Despite high ideals of government, the beneficial legacy of its laws, and its noble literature, the character of Roman society may not in all its phases be attractive to twentieth-century man; but its importance in shaping the course of western civilization is indisputable. Today the brooding relics of Imperial Rome are as rich a symbol of this fact as they were to Gibbon two hundred years ago, while the incredible reality of resurrected Pompeii enables us as never before to experience the 'feel' of Roman life. And in the background are the relics of the Greek colonists, the Doric temples like ghosts of an earlier, more refined and intellectual ethos.

After the 'grandeur that was Rome', when the rest of Europe was groping in the mists of barbarism, the now Christianized and more spiritual culture of Italy continued to flower, if intermittently and somewhat less gorgeously than the exotic blooms of Byzantium which had become by the early fifth century the greatest city of the Christian world – juridically Roman but culturally Greek – exerting its influence particularly on the north-east.

Two hundred years of Lombard occupation was followed by Italy becoming part of the Holy Roman Empire and for the next three hundred years, from the time of Pope Gregory VII until the death of the Emperor Frederick II in 1250 the struggle between pope and emperor dominated the political life of the country.

If the Babylonian Captivity, when the Pope was at Avignon, and the Great Schism, when there were two popes, was a period of weakness for the papacy in the fourteenth century, the Middle Ages generally were a great era for the city-states of Italy – whether oligarchies or tyrannies – which grew powerful on international trade; until their power began to dwindle towards the end of the fifteenth century when the importance of Rome began to increase as, under masterful popes, it became the political and cultural node of the peninsula.

The early medieval period was also a great one for Italian literature when, through the genius of Dante Alighieri, the *Divine Comedy* showed how the vernacular language could supersede Latin as the medium of high art as well as express the spirit of a nation that, whatever its political divisions, was increasingly conscious of itself as heir to the ancient civilization of the Romans.

When one comes to the Renaissance – the springboard of the modern world which began in quattrocento Florence – the output of art of genius and exceptional talent, to descend no lower, from what was by modern standards so small a population, is staggering, even for a people who at most periods of their history have contributed to the arts as prodigally as the Italians.

Yet art was not divorced from daily life as so often in the modern world. The same pulse beat through it as through the thriving commerce of the communes, and the princes and merchants were men of real not factitious culture as well as men of power. The fact that the population was so fragmented, however, was probably in the favour of art since political and commercial rivalry was also expressed by competition in architectural works, often generously subsidized by the commune or local tyrant. There is too an astonishing breadth to this burgeoning of the human spirit at the Renaissance for besides the architects there were scholars, men of letters, painters, sculptors, and musicians too numerous to mention yet whose names are household words – a dazzling spectrum of achievement by any measure.

The least energetic period of Italian history is perhaps the eighteenth century when much of the country was not only divided but subject to the indignity of foreign rule by Spaniards and Austrians. It is here, therefore, after the Counter-Reformation and later Baroque, that there is least to plot on the historical map of Italian architecture; yet even then there were great works like the royal palace at Caserta. The work of Tiepolo in painting and Vivaldi in music were not isolated cultural phenomena by any means.

Italy has been a united country for only a century now. Metternich could still call her 'a geographical expression' in 1815. Before that, as we have seen, she was a collection of independent or occupied states. The nineteenth century was an age of political passions when under the driving force of men like Cavour and Mazzini she was bent on recreating the unity which Roman government had given her more than two thousand years before and making good her position among the nations of modern Europe.

Of all these nations Italy has, not surprisingly, maintained the strongest classical tradition in architecture. It was not even severed during the barbarian invasions when the Ostrogoths proved susceptible to it nor was it forgotten during the late Gothic period of the Middle Ages. At the Renaissance it was at its strongest; and if one uses the term classical to mean more than the system of orders or even antique culture, then it may be claimed that the spirit of rationalism that permeated the so-called modern architecture of the first half of the twentieth century was really a reincarnation of classicism reduced to its essentials.

Within this classical tradition there is a considerable variety of mode and feeling. What could be more different in aspect and significance than a Doric temple in rural Sicily and a Baroque church in the heart of the Eternal City? Against the northern sympathies expressed by the buttresses and the hundred and thirty thrusting pinnacles of Milan Cathedral may be set the opulent blend of Byzantine, Islamic, and Norman at Palermo and Monreale. To the four-square magnificence of the Renaissance palaces the elegant space-age structures of P. L. Nervi are the perfect foil.

If there are qualities common to the various styles of Italian architecture – as distinct from the ancient Greek monuments in

Italy – they are a certain Latin breadth and clarity, an intellectual articulation married to a rich sensuous feeling for plastic forms and vivid decoration. Sometimes the first quality is dominant as in the Early Renaissance, sometimes the second as in Baroque. Perhaps the High Renaissance masters like Bramante and Raphael achieved a brief but perfect balance between the two.

If there is one shortcoming of Italian architecture and decorative art, at any rate to the differently nurtured northerner, it is the opulence that sometimes spills over into excess. But even this has its attractions to one accustomed to a more inhibited norm; and Italian architecture is never extreme in the way that Spanish sometimes is.

Italy is traditionally a land of churches and it is true that nowhere else is there to be found such an abundant variety of ecclesiastical architecture of all periods. But there is much more than churches, splendid as so many of these are. There are the medieval fortresses of the north and south and much interesting civic architecture from the Middle Ages onward; and even commercial buildings from as long ago as the twelfth century. There are the sumptuous Renaissance palaces, sophisticated Mannerist villas, powerfully conceived Baroque monasteries, colleges, and theatres. As we approach nearer to our own time so the diversity of building types increases until today when Italian architecture seems more fertile in solutions to modern building problems than most other continental countries. More than this, her designers have sustained the national reputation for artistic creativity by expressing the latest in social needs and technology in forms of considerable aesthetic originality and imagination. As in the days of the *pax Romana* and the glory of the Renaissance the rest of Europe has much to learn from architecture in Italy.

'In one region of the world again are
not half so many strangers as in Italy . . .
more for knowledge and pleasure than for
curiosity and lucre.'

An English traveller in 1549

CHAPTER ONE

Prehistoric, Greek, Etruscan

THE earliest known peoples in the Italian peninsula were Neolithic peoples who arrived from North Africa *c.* 2500 B.C. Like other groups of similar culture their dwellings, if they were not conveniently discovered caves – only recently some 15,000 modern cave-dwellers were rehoused at Matera – did not amount to more than round or oval wattle-and-daub huts sunk beneath ground level to a depth of about three feet and roofed with timber above a central clay hearth.

Some five hundred years later Bronze Age migrants entered from the north as so many subsequent invaders did. They came from the region which is now Switzerland and introduced pile dwellings, such as they had already adapted to the shallow waters of the Swiss lakes, into those of north Italy. Another version – the terremare, constructed on dry land – was introduced some hundred years later by the ancestors of the Romans who originated in the Danube basin.

Some of the most interesting early structures are the groups of trulli of Apulia (e.g. Alberobello), a trulle being a sort of corbelled beehive building, circular in plan with stepped profile, a form of very great antiquity found at Mycenae in southern Greece.

These 'Proto-Italic' peoples were followed later by the Villanovans, also from the north, whose dominance extended down to

TRULLE, APULIA

the Iron Age when the Etruscans arrived, apparently from western Asia Minor, *c.* 800 B.C. These are the first people who occupied the territory we now recognize as the Republic of Italy whose building works warrant the term architecture. But before considering their few remains and their interesting relationship with their successors, the Romans, it is better to look first at the Greek architecture of southern Italy and Sicily.

GREEK

The Greeks with their genius for trade and an expanding population were great colonizers and there grew up in southern Italy and Sicily from *c.* 800 B.C. a number of Dorian settlements collectively known as Magna Graecia – Naples was one, for example, 'the new city'. They were to produce some of the most admirable temple architecture ever built, and many important remains are still to be seen there.

The constructional system of the Greeks was a simple one called variously a trabeated, post and lintel, or column and beam system in which upright members gave support to horizontal ones. It was a system which, because of its inherent limitations, made for simplicity in design to which was added a simplicity of function, for the Greeks unlike the Romans did not go in for civic or utilitarian buildings and put almost the whole of their architectural instinct into temple structures. But since the Greeks were a people whose intellectual and aesthetic gifts were highly developed in applying them to architecture they produced powerfully conceived buildings which have never been surpassed for clarity, precision, and refinement.

The Greek temple was designed as an isolated structure, almost in a sculptural sense, in which the exterior effect was more important than the interior. It consisted of a rectangular stylobate or three-stepped platform in the middle of which stood a naos or walled sanctuary chamber, containing a statue and perhaps a treasury, and surrounded by a colonnade or peristyle carrying a continuous horizontal entablature. The building was covered with a timber ridge roof of shallow pitch, tiled with marble slabs and ending in triangular-shaped pediments with very obtuse apices. At the three angles of these pediments were placed carved blocks called acroteria. Where the roofed colonnade extended beyond the naos, porticos were formed at both ends of the temple through one of which the square-headed entrance was reached. There were no windows and light entered only through this doorway, unless there was some form of top-lighting. Orientation was usual, as in later Christian times.

The Greek temples of southern Italy and Sicily which follow this general description differ in their use of materials. Whereas in Greece itself a highly polished hard white marble was usual the Greeks in Italy had to make use of creamy travertine, a rather coarse hard limestone; but they simulated a marble finish by coating it with a fine cement stucco. Unfortunately this has weathered away giving them an unwonted appearance of coarseness. Blocks of stone fitted exactly and were unmortared, though metal clamps were sometimes also used.

It was the Greeks who invented the three basic orders of classical architecture: the Doric, Ionic, and Corinthian. Each order, the unit of a colonnade, consists of its characteristic column, with base below and capital above, supporting its appropriate entablature of three parts: architrave, frieze (the widest part) and the projecting cornice above. The proportions, mouldings, and formalized ornament of the three orders are all varied to form a basic vocabulary of design which was later to be taken over and developed by the Romans as part of their more complex architectural system.

One of the best preserved of Greek temples, better preserved than the Parthenon on the Acropolis of Athens, is the temple of Poseidon at Paestum near Salerno, dating from 450 B.C. Technically, in the terminology of Vitruvius, the Roman writer on architecture, this is a peripteral hexastyle temple, which is to say that it has a surrounding colonnade or peristyle with a six-columned portico at both ends. Interesting features are the inner colonnades which support smaller ranges above upon which the higher part of the roof rested. This was the usual way the need for internal support was met in larger temples, though superimposed columns were never used externally in Greek architecture.

The order employed, as in most Greek temples in Italy, is the Doric order, a noble placid order, the first one to be evolved over several hundred years and consisting of a sturdy tapering fluted column without a base but with a plain moulded capital of curved echinus and square abacus above, and an entablature the frieze of which is divided into triglyphs or three vertical channels alternating with metopes or square panels, often carved.

The columns of the Temple of Poseidon, Paestum, are 28 ft high in relation to the basic dimensions of the building (198 × 80 ft) and there is an absence of the sculpture that was a common feature of the tympanum of the pediment, though it had the usual acroteria which stood up from the three corners. When it was employed, the beautifully conceived and executed ideal figure sculpture of the Greeks was wonderfully integrated with its architectural setting.

The evolution of Doric is well displayed at Paestum and some hundred years earlier in the so-called 'Basilica', on the same site, another large fifty-columned Doric temple with its rare nine-columned portico and single inner range of columns down the centre of the naos. Early Doric features are the widely projecting capitals, reducing the lintel's span, and the pronounced 'entasis' of the columns. This is the usually very slight swelling of the column about its middle to correct the optical illusion of its

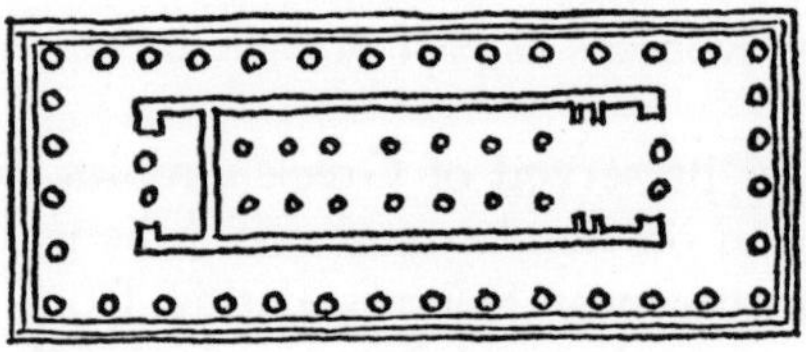

TEMPLE OF POSEIDON, PAESTUM

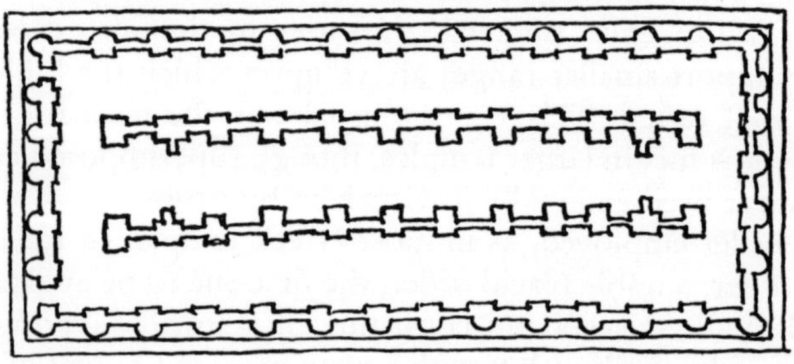

TEMPLE OF ZEUS OLYMPIUS, AGRIGENTO

BASILICA, PAESTUM

being convex, as would appear if the sides were exactly parallel. This is an example of the intellectual (since mathematically calculated) and aesthetic refinement which the Greeks brought to their temple architecture; but it was only one of a number of similar optical corrections which they made. Another is the slight upward curve they gave to horizontal features to eliminate the apparent distortion of sagging towards the centre. Moreover, if the Greeks found no appeal in structural experiment their temples were subtly modelled to exploit effects of sunlight and shadow.

Ornament was delicately restrained and simple and mouldings were finely contoured; but probably Greek architecture looked less 'pure' and austere originally than it now appears since there is evidence that polychrome effects were obtained by fresco painting on a fine cement base that has long since been eroded.

A third temple at Paestum is that of Demeter, also sixth century B.C. and the smallest of the group, and there are ruins at Metaponto between Naples and Taranto. South of Bari a single pillar at Capo Colonna – hence its name – is all that remains of the former 36 columns that were once part of the Doric temple of Hera. More important are the temples of Sicily. At Selinunte, within the ancient acropolis jutting out into the Mediterranean, are the remains of no less than seven sixth- and fifth-century B.C. Doric temples. Temple 'B' is an example of a prostyle tetrastyle, i.e. a small structure without a surrounding colonnade and only one portico. The biggest is dedicated to Apollo (540 B.C.). But larger still is the Temple of Zeus Olympius at Agrigento dating from *c.* 470 B.C. Over 300 ft long and 140 ft wide this was the second largest temple in the Greek world – bigger than the Parthenon – and it was designed by one Theron who is the first architect we can name working in Italy. It is pseudo-peripteral septastyle, i.e. its columns are not free-standing in the usual Greek manner but engaged half columns, a practice later adopted by the Romans. There are two more Doric temples of about the same date at Agrigento, and one at Egesta.

At Siracusa was the fifth-century B.C. Temple of Athene, the 30-ft columns of which have been built into the cathedral and there are remains of two more temples, one the Temple of Apollo, with many columns. Here also are the remains of a theatre of about 400 B.C. The importance of drama in the religious and social life of the Greeks is well-known and it is to them that we owe the prototype of the theatre – an auditorium representing two-thirds of a circle of tiered seats which was excavated out of a hillside. At the centre was an open space (orchestra) for the chorus, which played an important role in the drama, and beyond was the stage itself with a tiring room behind. Unfortunately this and the theatre at Segesta were both remodelled by the Romans, so there is no Greek theatre in Italy in its original form. Segesta also has a fine Doric temple.

No Greek domestic architecture has survived but we may deduce the appearance of larger houses of the Hellenistic or late Greek period from what has survived at Pompeii if we imagine them without the atrium or colonnaded court which the Romans added and remember that Greek houses were of one storey only.

To sum up, Greek architecture in Italy as everywhere else was an eminently rational architecture. But it was in no sense mechanical, being the product of a remarkable aesthetic sensibility. If sculptural and static it is never inert but enlivened from within by the vitality of the relationship existing between its various carefully-balanced elements and their parts; and the execution of the design shows a sophistication of craftsmanship which was essential to its total harmony. Though it was to form one of the principal elements in Roman architecture it was not to be known again in Europe, not even at the Renaissance, until the eighteenth century when once again scholars and architects like Winckelmann and Wilkins appreciated its noble simplicity and calm grandeur. As late as our own century it could contribute to the War Memorial, Milan, to the dead of the First World War.

ETRUSCAN

A good deal more is now known about the Etruscans and their religion, art, administrative, and technical skills than formerly when it was customary to attach to them the epithet 'mysterious'; but there is still much that is not known about them and this includes their architecture.

As already said, they seem to have come from Asia Minor in the ninth century and they occupied central Italy (part of which, Tuscany, still bears their name) until *c.* 300 B.C. by which time they had been largely absorbed by the Romans. Nothing of their building works has survived that is earlier than the sixth century B.C. but there is good reason for supposing that their architectural achievements were not without significance. The hostile Romans did much to erase from history the real memory of their predecessors but there appears to be little doubt that it was from the Etruscans that they learned the art of constructing arches, vaults, and domes that were to play so important a part in their own architecture.

Etruscan masonry, unmortared and laid in alternate courses of 'headers' and 'stretchers', is incorporated in the lower part of the Arco d'Augusta at Perugia, restored by the Romans. Composed of large blocks, like those of the walls at Alatri, it is of the variety known as cyclopean. The earliest Etruscan 'arches' are corbelled ones, each course of stones projecting beyond the one below until they meet, as in their tombs, but they were the first people to use the true arch in Europe. The best preserved is in the gateway at Volterra called Porta all' Arco.

An Etruscan temple has been reconstructed from Vitruvius's description. It is the Temple of Juno Sospita, Lanuvium, fifth century B.C. with its portico of four rather stumpy widely-spaced Doric columns and clumsy overhanging pediment obviously derived somewhat rustically from Greek architecture. The naos on its low podium is divided into three parallel cells with separate openings and is approached up a short flight of steps between flanking walls. The latter feature is not found in Greek architecture, however, and yet was to become a characteristic of Roman temples.

In the garden of the Villa Giulia, Rome, is the recreated small single-celled Temple of Alatri of the third century B.C. It has a portico of only two Doric columns approached by a low ramp.

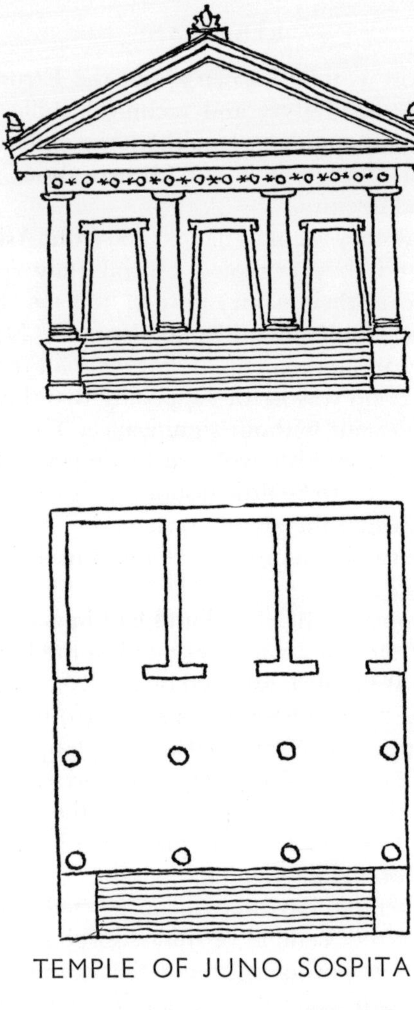

TEMPLE OF JUNO SOSPITA

Both temples have timber roofs of low pitch and coverings of terracotta tiles. Their pediments are heavily moulded and ornamented with acroteria in the Greek manner. The effect is highly individual and suggests a blend of Greek and Roman styles, though it was antecedent to and one of the main sources of the latter.

As with that of the Greeks, no Etruscan domestic architecture has survived and what it was like can only be a matter of conjecture bearing in mind the Vitruvian descriptions. Etruscan houses seem to have been generally constructed of sun-dried brick and timber with a tiled roof. There was a plain windowless front with a larger ornamental doorway in relief facing the street. The door itself was small and led through a passage to a small court or central room, the living-room of the family, with a central fire and louvre overhead. This was the atrium, derived from the Greeks and later adopted by the Romans in their houses. Beyond there was sometimes a garden. At Marzabotto near Bologna are the remains of a residential quarter laid out with a rectilinear street pattern, public buildings, water supply and drainage systems, thus showing that the Etruscans were capable of urban planning before the Romans.

The many Etruscan tombs which have been discovered with their rich contents also offered clues as to their domestic architecture, particularly rock-cut examples such as those at the necropolis of Cerveteri, north of Rome, which exhibit many architectural features carved in the soft tufa. Such rock-tombs resemble houses in some ways. At Bieda there are 'ridge' beams and imitation rafters carved on the roof and false windows and benches carved on the walls. Sometimes these houses of the dead are arranged in streets with doors opening on to them as at Castel d'Asso. Other impressions of their ideas in building may be gained from the remains to be inspected in the Vatican Museum and the Etruscan Museum, Florence. Their practice of sealing away in tombs such beautiful works of art and craftsmanship is a 'wastefulness' difficult for the modern mind to comprehend.

CHAPTER TWO

Roman I

ROME was founded as long ago as 753 B.C. but the Roman conquest of Italy did not begin until the middle of the fourth century B.C. and their surviving architectural works are mostly from the first century B.C. onwards.

The Romans combined the trabeated system of the Greeks with the forms that the Etruscans introduced: the arch (always semicircular), the vault, and the dome, the use of which they were to develop enormously. The result was buildings that were structurally more complex and ambitious than those of either. Their bold robust effects, great size, variety, complex imaginative planning, and grouping – usually symmetrical – were all new tendencies related to the materialistic development of Roman life and civilization and the desire of the extrovert Romans to find a forceful expression of the political power of the state. Solemn and magnificent, the best Roman buildings have a proud vitality quite different in feeling from Greek.

Moreover the Roman architects did not confine themselves to temples and houses. They brought in a whole new range of building types – public, domestic, utilitarian – that have no parallel in the architecture of the Greeks. And though their basic ideas derived from elsewhere what the Romans did through their theory and practice was to build up a body of technical knowledge and a system of designs, a complete 'language' of architecture in fact, that like Latin was bequeathed to Western Europe and the world. Only recently has the last of this capital been spent.

Marcus Vitruvius Pollio lived during the reign of the Emperor Augustus in the first century B.C., the great Augustan age of Virgil, Horace, and Livy. In his distinguished work *De Architectura Libri Decem*, a treatise in ten books on materials, methods, building types, town planning, military engineering, and the training of architects, he attempted the first classification of orders on the basis of Greek authorities and his own observation and practice.

To the three orders invented by the Greeks he added the so-called 'Tuscan' order representing Tuscan Doric, though it was largely of his own devising, with its less sturdy, often unfluted columns, and its base. The Composite order which combines the capitals of the Corinthian and Ionic was a fifth and later arrival on the scene. In the Corinthian order Roman practice differed from Greek in that the acanthus leaf decoration was carved from a different species of the plant and the columns were sometimes unfluted. To give columns greater height the device of raising them on pedestals was frequently adopted. The Romans standardized and systematized the proportions of the orders in a more rigid way

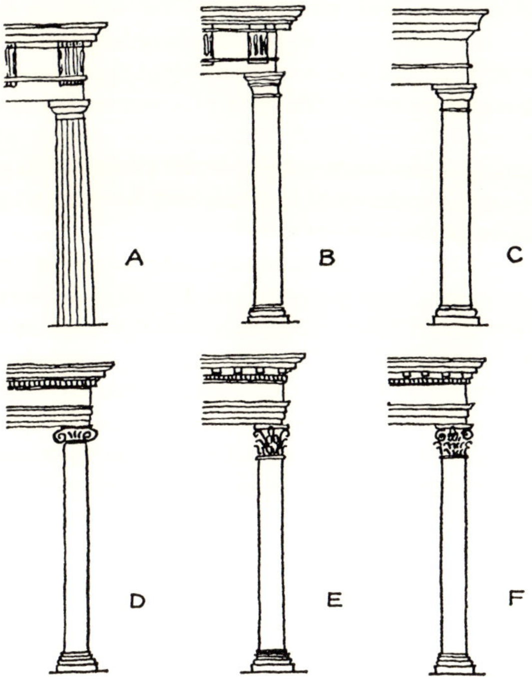

ORDERS

A GREEK DORIC
B ROMAN DORIC
C TUSCAN
D ROMAN IONIC
E ROMAN CORINTHIAN
F COMPOSITE

than had previously been attempted, and consolidated and extended their function as the basic grammar of classical architecture. As a classical system it was also 'modular', one in which proportions and relationships were carefully calculated (a module being a half or whole diameter at the base of a column). The various parts of a building were thus arranged in a harmonious and symmetrical way and related to the scale of the human figure. It was a conception to be eagerly revived by the architects of the Renaissance.

One of the chief ways in which the Romans developed the use of the orders was to apply them to what were basically arcuated rather than trabeated structures. That is to say they used them superficially, often with arches, to face structures that were built on the pier and arch system. This was not entirely to serve a decorative purpose for the orders were carefully placed and adjusted so that they contributed to the scale and proportion of the whole design, and in this way, in buildings of several storeys, they were superimposed externally in a way never attempted by the Greeks.

The Romans constructed walls using a traditional stone technique, but they also developed a lime mortar and invented a very hard cohesive pozzolana cement from the volcanic ash found at Pozzuoli, near Naples. This proved an ideal material, not only for making the core of the concrete and rubble walls to be faced in different ways with finer stone, brick, and marble attached with bronze or iron cramps, but also for constructing vaults, arches, and domes and semi-domes; especially as the concrete could be made economically in large quantities with unskilled labour and masons' rubble. These were very important technical innovations: The earliest concrete dome is that of the second-century B.C. Stabian Baths, Pompeii; the earliest large vault that of the Tabularium, Rome, dating from a century later and showing also the first use of half-columns decoratively.

Vaults and domes were cast *in situ* making them very strong with little thrust. Sometimes brick arches were embedded in them and their bare concrete surfaces were covered in a variety of protective or decorative materials, the latter including painted stucco and mosaic. Exedrae or semi-circular apses were covered with semi-domes while the vaults were of the tunnel type or cross, or groined, vaults which originated from the intersection of two tunnel vaults. Both vaults and domes were frequently coffered, both for decorative effect and to lighten the structure.

Doorways in these walls were straight or round-headed and received more decorative emphasis than hitherto; windows were semicircular or segmentally headed, often with two mullions; and a feature of interior walls was sometimes the niche with an architectural frame of columns and pediment known as the aedicule.

The Romans of course were great town builders and their belief that the plan of a town should reflect a universal order established by the gods and to which man should be properly related is reflected in the closed rectilinear or 'grid-iron' arrangement of streets which they confined between square or polygonal defensive walls punctuated by square towers set within covering fire of one another. Roman town planning is seen best, however, not in Rome which grew up irregularly but in the Augustan towns of Turin and Aosta. They have the characteristic orientated rectilinear street system with wider intersecting main thoroughfares running north–south (the Cardo) and east–west (the Decumanus); and at the centre was the town square or forum. The plan of their military forts was a miniature version of this arrangement.

Of the walls of Rome with their towers, gates, and posterns, twelve miles survive to give some idea of the formidable defences of the ancient city. The finest section was the third-century Aurelian Wall, massive, very high, and provided with a crenellated parapet and gallery, square and half-round towers and fine round-arched gateways of which the Porta Tiburtina, the Porta Appia, and the Porta Pinciana still impress. Verona was the great Porta de' Bosari.

The centre of the Roman town was always the forum, a public meeting place, market cum civic centre, that represented a development of the Greek agora. With their surrounding public buildings such as temples and basilicas, shops and commercial buildings, their necessary shady colonnades and peristyles, sometimes of two storeys, and their public monuments they are among the earliest examples of urban design. Rome had several fora, the oldest being the Forum Romanum, the largest the Forum of Trajan (A.D. 98).

Adjacent to the forum were the principal temples. The type was basically Greek but shorter with sometimes wider intercolumnia-

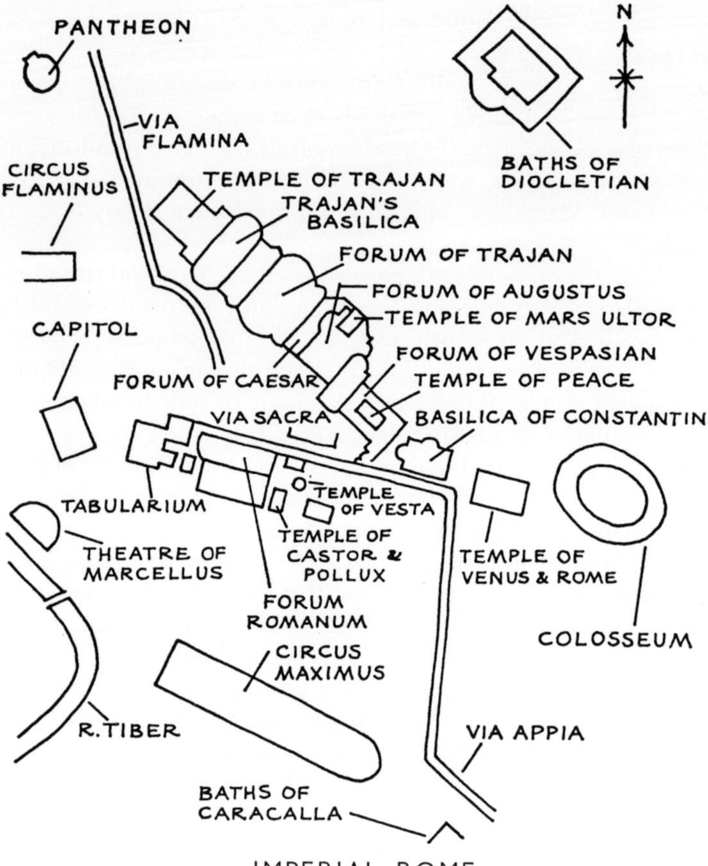

IMPERIAL ROME

tions and placed on a podium or base. More importance was given to the entrance front, a deep prostyle portico of Etruscan type approached by a flight of steps between side walls. More than peripteral temples with freestanding columns the Romans preferred pseudo-peripteral designs with non-structural attached columns, as already noted in the Greek Temple of Zeus at Agrigento. Roofs were of timber and covered with tiles of terracotta, marble or bronze. Sometimes ceilings were vaulted. Roman temples were not orientated.

A better idea of one than can be obtained anywhere in Italy may be had from the Maison Carrée, Nîmes; but among the grandest in

Rome itself were the very large Temple of Mars Ultor in the Forum of Augustus (14 B.C.) with its nearly 60-ft Corinthian columns. The favourite order of the Romans was the showy Corinthian; the richness of its fluting and ancathus capital admirably suited to their predeliction for rather florid decorative forms.

The cella of the Temple of Mars had both columns and pilasters (flat engaged columns) and one of the earliest apsidal recesses. In Rome there are remains of three other Corinthian temples of note. That dedicated to Castor and Pollux (A.D. 6) also dates from the age of Augustus and is sheathed with white Pentelic marble which was imported from Greece to supplement that from Carrara

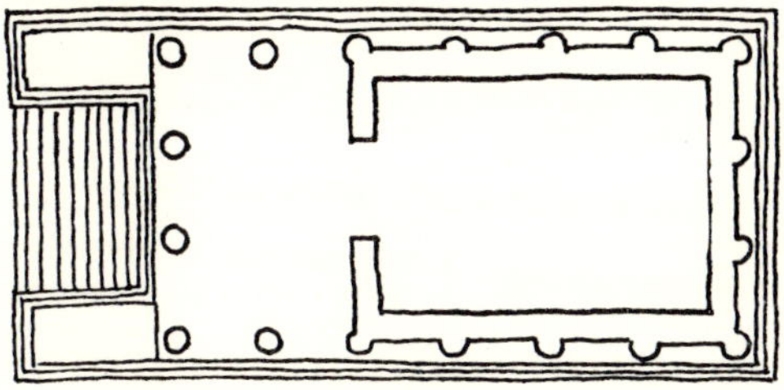

TEMPLE OF FORTUNA VIRILIS

TEMPLE OF ANTONINUS AND FAUSTINA

TEMPLE OF VESTA, ROME

which came into use about this time. Augustus, it was said, found Rome a city of brick and left it a city of marble.

The Temple of Venus and Rome (A.D. 123), by Apollodorus of Damascus who planned the Forum of Trajan, was a very large one raised on a wide colonnaded platform; inside there were two cella, their apses at the centre placed back to back. The Temple of Antoninus and Faustina (A.D. 141) was a prostyle hexastyle converted to a church in 1602. At Assisi is the Corinthian Temple of Minerva (40 B.C.).

The Ionic order with its voluted capitals, derived from the Greek architecture of Asia Minor, was little used in Roman temples but among those in Rome are the tiny Temple of Fortuna Virilis (40 B.C.) – a good example – and the Temple of Saturn (A.D. 284), a late rather debased type with typical angle volutes on the capitals of its 40-ft columns.

All these are rectangular temples but the Romans also built a number of smaller circular and polygonal ones, a plan which goes back through the Etruscans to the Greeks, the Tholos of Epidauros, for example. The Temple of Vesta (A.D. 205) in the Forum Romanum was the most revered in Rome where the Vestal Virgins tended the sacred hearth-fire, symbol of the family, the foundation of Roman society. It consisted of a circular podium and cella surrounded by a Corinthian peristyle and was probably capped with a low domical roof.

Earlier circular temples, Augustan examples and both Corin-

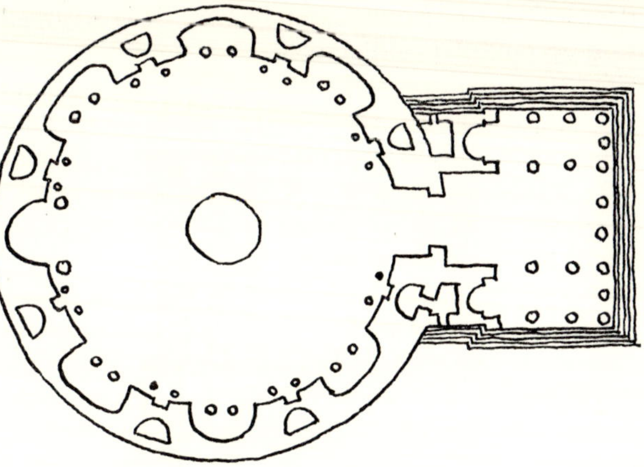

THE PANTHEON, ROME

thian also, are the Temple of Mater Matuta, Rome (now S. Maria del Sole), where the peristyle rises from a circular stylobate, and the Temple of Vesta, Tivoli, with shorter and more thick-set columns.

The Pantheon (A.D. 120), now a Christian church, S. Maria Rotunda, is quite exceptional among circular temples for its size, magnificence, and state of preservation. Indeed it is the best preserved Roman building which has come down to us. Tradition ascribes it to the Emperor Hadrian who was it seems an able dilettante architect and student of building, as his famous Wall in Britain testifies.

The Pantheon is a design of remarkable unity and simplicity but quite un-Greek in its 'plasticity'. Fundamentally it is a very large rotunda or drum-like structure roofed with a hemispherical dome and its proportions are based on a sphere, the walls being equal in height to the dome's radius. To it has been added an immense rectangular portico with unfluted granite columns and Corinthian capitals of Pentelic marble, originally part of Agrippa's Temple.

A podium of travertine, a stone much favoured by the Romans, forms the base for the 20-ft thick concrete wall of the rotunda. Originally its exterior was faced not with the present bands of brick and tile but with Pentelic marble to the first-floor level and above that with stucco, its attic storey being pilastered.

Internally the wall is treated sculpturally or plastically in a manner typical of late Roman architecture. It is scooped out into alternating rectangular and semicircular semi-domed exedrae or recesses for statues of the gods, framed or screened by Corinthian columns supporting an entablature. The piers between the exedrae have niches set in aedicular frames (pairs of small columns supporting miniature entablatures and pediments) and these are repeated on the level above. There was lavish use of ornamental marbles and porphyry for facings.

Between a ribbed framework which is the basis of its structure the vast dome is coffered with optically adjusted mouldings and is pierced centrally with an unglazed circular 'eye' which gives ample, even top-lighting to the solemn but serene space beneath. There is no feeling of heaviness from the dome which, despite its great size, seems to hover overhead. But the Romans left it to the Renaissance architects to develop the full potentialities of the dome as an external feature and that of the Pantheon is low and shallow when seen from outside. It was once covered with bronze roof tiles, gilded, in the manner of important buildings, as were the surviving bronze doors. Originally too there was a great bronze relief in the pediment and statuary on the attic storey.

One of the most important buildings adjacent to any Roman forum was the basilica, a large public hall serving as a town hall, law court, or commercial exchange. Probably derived from the Greek temple or stoa it was usually a rectangular building with a high central nave separated from two or four lower flanking aisles by colonnades. So far the description resembles the internal arrangement of a Christian church and this is not accidental since the latter owed a good deal to the Roman basilica. However, the colonnades of the latter were usually continued across the nave at both ends as well, which marks a difference. The upper walls of the nave supported on the main colonnades were pierced with clerestory windows and, above the aisles, were sometimes galleried. In law court basilicas a semi-circular apse was added with a raised dais and seats and throne (tribunal) for the presiding judge and altar at the front; sometimes there were two apses, often separated from the main body of the hall by a screen of columns or a balustrade. Entrances were usually at the side or opposite end from the apse. A simple timber roof of low pitch, sometimes open along the sides, finished off the outside of the building which was very plain compared with the interior.

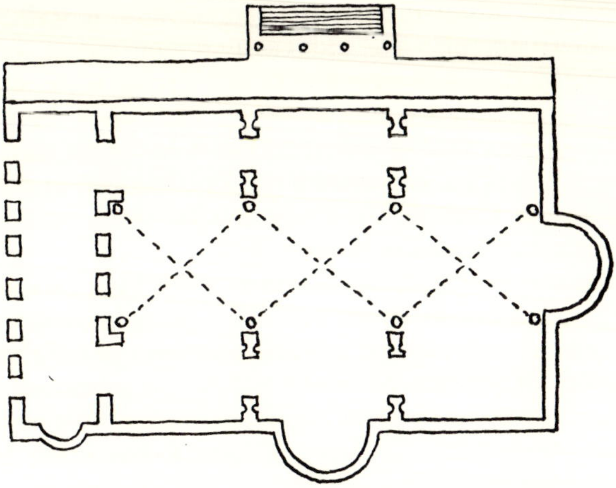

BASILICA OF MAXENTIUS, ROME

The oldest remaining basilica is that at Pompeii (*c.* 100 B.C.) with its 28 large columns but the oldest on record dated from less than a century earlier. Rome, as would be expected, had many of the largest basilicas. Trajan's Basilica (A.D. 98) by Apollodorus of Damascus, already mentioned, had double aisles with columns of red granite from Egypt with Corinthian capitals of white Pentelic marble, and apses at both ends. The main entrance was at the side through a portico from Trajan's Forum. On the far side were a pair of libraries (Greek and Latin) separated by a small court at the centre of which Trajan's column was erected.

The Basilica Nova of Maxentius (*c.* A.D. 300) by the Forum Romanum, often called Constantine's, is different from the earlier one in that the nave and aisles of the compact plan are not separated by continuous colonnades but are divided into compartments or bays which were then not timber roofed but vaulted with great daring. The nave was roofed by three great cross vaults, while the corresponding aisle bays on both sides were covered by great barrel vaults set at right angles to the main axis of the building, thus buttressing the nave vaults. Already the Romanesque and Gothic systems are being anticipated by this structural system and articulation of interior space. The vault surfaces were deeply coffered and there are two apses, this time one at the side, opposite the entrance.

The Romans admired grandeur and bigness of scale and they had, as their use of arch and vault demonstrates, a practical engineering skill greater than that of the Greeks who outdid their conquerors in intellectual and aesthetic achievement. Nowhere can this be better seen than in the great thermae. There were, during the Republic, simpler and smaller public baths but in the days of Imperial Rome thermae were constructed on a scale of great magnificence and luxuriously appointed.

The thermae combined the functions of bathing establishments giving the pleasures of steam and water bathing, and social and sports centres, with cultural amenities thrown in – lecture halls, libraries, etc. They tell us much about the particular kind of materialism which the Romans practised. They usually consisted of three main parts: a main building, a surrounding open space (the xystus, planted with trees, fountains, and statues and laid out

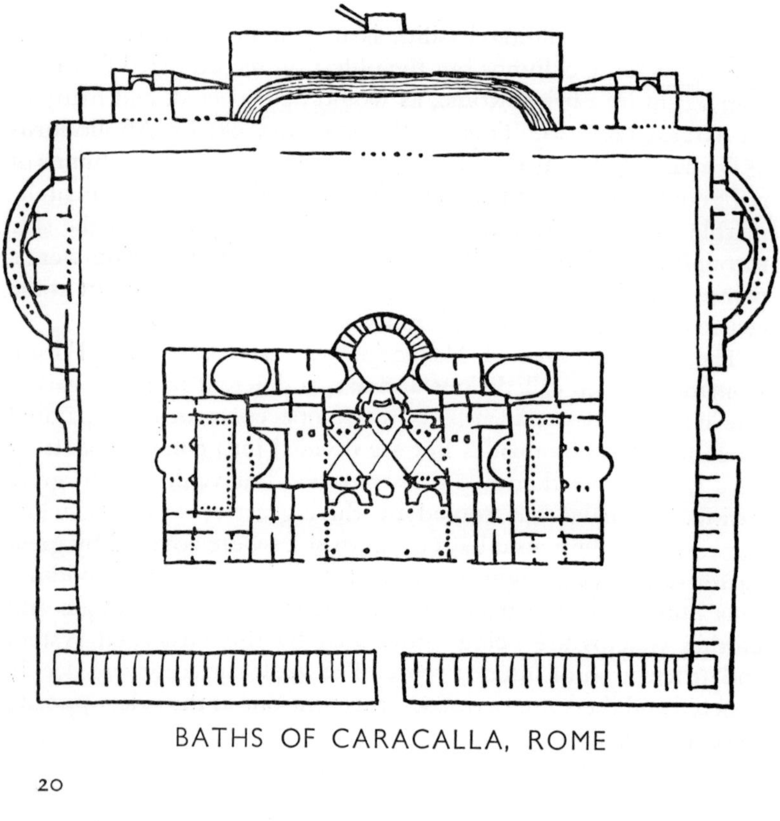

BATHS OF CARACALLA, ROME

with a stadium for athletic activities) and an outer frame of colonnaded ancillary buildings such as lecture rooms, libraries, exedrae, shops, and slaves' quarters.

The main central structure was raised on a basement containing service rooms, furnaces, hypocausts and ducts below. Above were the dressing rooms, lounge, sweating room, oiling rooms, and of course hot and cold water baths, which received water piped in lead and earthenware pipes from a large reservoir with furnaces to heat it, located in the perimeter and fed from an aqueduct. The interior heating was obtained from the hypocausts underneath the floors of the main building, the hot air passing through hollow tiles in the floors and flues in the walls. Sometimes there would be a games room, a library, or even a small theatre too.

This, broadly, is the layout of the great Thermae of Caracalla (*c.* A.D. 215) whose impressive ruins give a good idea of the original complex which could accommodate 1,600 bathers. The main building is symmetrically planned to give vistas through its huge halls and internal courts, the immenseness of the scale being pointed by the screens of columns and exedrae. In the centre was the large tepidarium, a moderately warm chamber, with the other apartments grouped round it. It was roofed by three enormous concrete cross vaults supported on eight massive piers with attached granite columns 40 ft high and roofed from clerestory windows under the side vaults, since it stood up above the surrounding halls. On one side it opened into the frigidarium or cold-water bath, probably open to the sky, and on the other side, through an anteroom, to the circular calidarium or hot room with hot bath, which was probably domed. Flat roofs were also used in thermae besides the vaults described.

Of all Roman buildings the thermae were the most elaborate and splendid and the interior of the Baths of Caracalla must have been sumptuously decorated. Indeed, compared with the refinement of Greek, Roman decoration is florid and ostentatious to a degree. Mouldings, for example, do not rely on contour for effect but on bold, often coarse ornament. The lower parts of the wall were sheathed in marble with painted and ornamental stucco above. Vaults were coffered, as we have already seen, but were sometimes decorated with mosaic. Walls were relieved and ennobled by superimposed aedicular niches, and sculpture and fresco painting, much of it Greek or modelled on Greek exemplars, was much in evidence. Floors were brick or tessellated with ornamental marbles or covered with mosaic patterns, either geometric or depicting figures. By contrast brick and stucco exteriors were relatively plain.

Similar in plan to the Thermae of Caracalla were those of Diocletian (A.D. 300), the calidarium of which was converted by Michelangelo in 1563 into the church of S. Maria degli Angeli, but the accommodation was twice as large. Again there was a huge tepidarium at the heart of the complex roofed with cross vaults, but this time carried on 50-ft composite columns supporting a bold entablature. No Roman remains are more extensive than these great baths and most of the remains of others are also to be found in Rome.

A very interesting building once attached to the Baths of Gallienus which also testifies to the quality of Roman civilization is the Minerva Medica, Rome (A.D. 260), a nymphaeum or building designed to provide a sort of cool retreat from the summer heat of the city, a great conservatory of plants and running water decorated with sculptures. It was a centrally planned building with entrance and nine semi-circular apses and it is of interest structurally as being the first example of a device later adopted in Byzantine architecture, the use of pendentives to support the dome over the central space as at S. Vitale, Ravenna, the dome of which is also concrete ribbed with tiles. There is top-lighting from large windows below the dome with buttresses between, another innovation which enabled a thinner wall to be used than in, say, the Pantheon which has no such abutment.

Decadent as it was in many ways, late Roman society clearly made architecture one of its greatest creative achievements, energetic, resourceful in spatial composition, and with a fine instinct for sculptural modelling and the use of mosaic and marble.

1*a*. Greek sensibility: Doric temple of Poseidon, Paestum. Smooth stucco once coated the roughly-textured travertine, and the figure sculpture from the pediment has long since gone.

1*b*. Roman vigour: a great engineering work carrying water across the Campagna. Compare the arcuated Roman system in the aqueduct with the trabeated of the Greek shown in the temple above.

2. Interior of S. Vitale, Ravenna (*c.* 530). A magnificent example of Byzantine architecture in Italy. Its spatial sophistication and richly decorated surfaces create a strongly emotive atmosphere.

CHAPTER THREE

Roman II

OF THE great palaces of Rome, the first was the Domus Augustiana (A.D. 3) on the Palatine Hill and here are extensive ruins of a whole group of imperial palaces.

Enormous structures on the immense foundations which can be seen today they must have been of very great magnificence, glorious settings for displays of unequalled power and indulgence that contrasted starkly with the widespread squalor of the many urban poor of a city with a population approaching one million. They were built by Tiberius, Livia, Nero, and Septimius Severus. Later additions were cleverly adjusted to existing ones and there were many vistas along the main axes. Among the principal apartments were the tablinum (throne room), symbolically placed between the temple and the basilica, the open peristylium, centre of the court life, and the triclinium (banqueting hall). Unlike the Greeks, the Romans did not confine themselves to buildings of one storey.

There are few remains of ordinary urban domestic architecture except for the ruins at Pompeii but it must be remembered too that here the style of life was subject to Greek influence. Of early Roman times there is much less evidence but it must have been a good deal simpler and more primitive. Late Roman art is heir to the Hellenistic or late Greek style of the first century B.C. Besides the remains of a sixth-century Doric temple, miraculously brought to life by excavations and mostly dating from between the earthquake of A.D. 63 and the volcanic eruption of A.D. 79 which destroyed them, are the buildings of the Graeco-Roman town of Pompeii. Elliptical in plan it was laid out in rectangular plots with streets 14 to 24 ft wide, paved with lava blocks and with fountains at the main intersections. There were two large fora surrounded by peristyles, a basilica, open and covered theatres, two thermae (baths), a store and many shops.

Domestic architecture of many types shows a preference for planning round an internal court for coolness and security and the

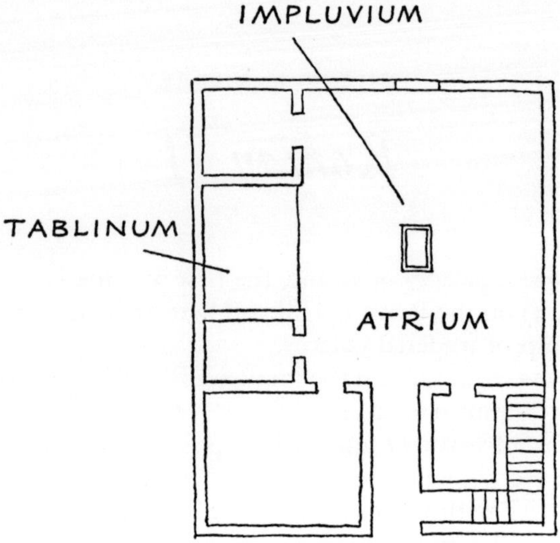

SMALLER HOUSE, POMPEII

best rooms of the best houses were richly decorated. In Rome the commonest type of dwelling appears to have been a kind of apartment house block (insula) the height of which was limited to 75 ft by Augustus, an early example of a building regulation of which there were several in Roman times.

Such multi-storey housing was for poorer people. There were shops on the brick-built ground floor, opening on to the street, and flats on the timber-framed upper floors which were sometimes overhanging. The latter were reached by staircases next to the shop. As in medieval Edinburgh, the shortage of land led to building upwards and much of the development took place on sloping hill sites. Ostia, however, once the port of Rome, has several restored examples of this type. Slaves, of whom there were very large numbers, were commonly housed in prison-like barrack buildings of similar design.

Below the church of SS. Giovanni e Paolo in Rome, the only one of its kind to survive in that city, are the remains of a three-storeyed house of palatial proportions. A prothyrum or vestibule led into an atrium or 'common room' and on to the tablinum or open apartment for the master. Beyond, another garden-like court was surrounded by the private rooms of the family and there were

INSULA (RECONSTRUCTED), OSTIA

baths, slaves' apartments and store rooms. This was a Christian house of the third century. Pompeii, that unequalled source of information about Roman town life in the later period, has several examples of richer town houses of the courtyard type, sometimes two-storey but more often of one. The usual material was brick, cored with whitewashed stucco, and the roof was of timber covered with terracotta or tiles. The 'domus' was probably derived from Etruscan and Greek types. It presented a plain windowless front or front with few windows, placed high up to the narrow street, with sometimes shops let out on either side of the entrance. At the House of Pansa this led to the atrium with its altar and family statues. This was an open court with roofs all round sloping down towards the centre, where runoff was collected in a sunken cistern (impluvium). This is where visitors were received and round it they and the house servants were lodged in small chambers either walled or half-walled off. There were store rooms also. Straight forward was the tablinum, and beyond lay the peristyle or colonnaded court round which were grouped the private apartments – triclinia (dining rooms), aecus (reception room), cubicila (bedrooms) and alae (conversation recesses). Smaller houses dispensed with some of the apartments round the peristyle but here there were also kitchen and pantry attached, farthest from the entrance but conveniently near the street. Beyond the peristyle was the xystus or walled garden.

The splendid Vettii house is another well-preserved variation and gives a good idea of the way richer patrician houses were appointed within. Walls were plastered to form a ground for frescoes of mythological or everyday scenes with architectural features, sometimes even in perspective, or painted to resemble marble or enriched with mosaics, composed into geometrical patterns or illustrating some scene, made by setting small pieces of stone or glass tesserae in cement. The latter was a refinement which, like more rarely used glass, was not confined to the most luxurious houses. Floors were laid of marble slabs or composed of mosaics of coloured marble or black and white patterns. Heating in winter was by brazier and in larger houses by underfloor hypocausts. Very restricted daylighting came from small shuttered windows opening on internal courts and artificial lighting was by

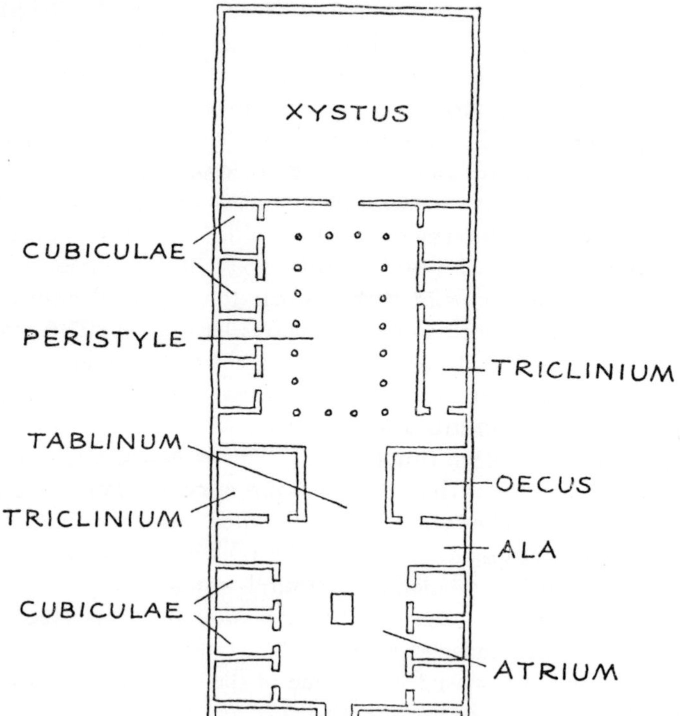

GENERALIZED PLAN OF LARGE ROMAN TOWN HOUSE

oil lamps and candelabra. Other modern-seeming amenities were the drainage, private baths, lead plumbing and taps, and the rising mains which brought water to upper floors. Mortise locks were used.

Other interesting examples are the house of Seraphis, Pompeii, and in Rome, the house of the Vestals. There was no segregation into residential and commercial districts as there had been in early Greek cities.

In the countryside poorer homesteads consisted of a single room with rammed earth floor and a roof of double pitch, thatched or shingled, open at the centre to admit light and allow smoke to escape. The large country houses which were the centres of estates were the villas and were of different designs, although like those in the province of Britain the grandest were of the courtyard type with first-class decorations and amenities for their day, such as baths and hypocausts.

The sophisticated Villa of Hadrian, Tivoli (A.D. 124), is really misleading if it suggests one of these since it was a large if rather diffuse complex, the size of a small town. But as a conspectus of Imperial Roman architecture it is excellent.

Roman theatres were based on Greek examples and consisted of a semi-circular auditorium with tiers of seats but the type was modified by making the 'orchestra' part of the auditorium and enlarging the stage. Examples in a ruined state may be seen at Ostia and Pompeii but the finest is the Theatre of Marcellus, Rome (11 B.C.) which shows how, because of their superior engineering skill, the Romans were not dependent like the Greeks on excavating a slope but could build up the auditorium on concrete vaulting supported by radiating walls. It is, incidentally, in its engaged columns an example of the Doric order, infrequently used by the Romans. This same system of construction can be seen on an even greater scale in the Flavian Amphitheatre or Colosseum, as it is more often called.

The Colosseum, Rome (A.D. 70), is a complete oval, a type of building peculiar to the Romans and without Greek precedent. It was used for gladiatorial contests and animal fights and its descendent is the Spanish bull ring.

The central space enclosed by a 15-ft wall was the arena where the policy of 'bread and circuses' reached its hideous conclusion, and around it in rising tiers of marble seats sat the audience of

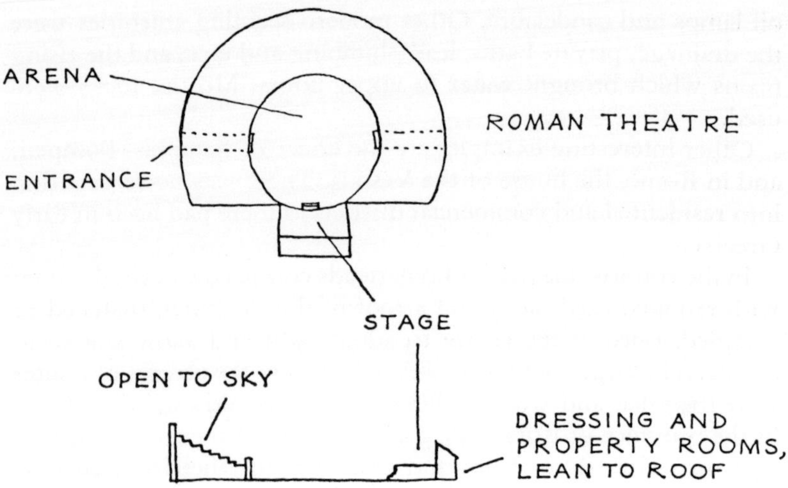

ROMAN THEATRE

50,000 sheltered from the sun by an enormous canvas awning (velarium). These seats were reached by stairs at intervals rising from vaulted circular corridors below. Directly above the arena wall were the boxes for emperor and consul.

All tiers of seats in the vast auditorium are supported by a hidden structure below. From a series of massive piers arranged in radiating lines spring great vaults inclined towards the centre, carrying on their backs the great superstructure. Beneath the vaults and adjacent to the arena at ground level were the dens and

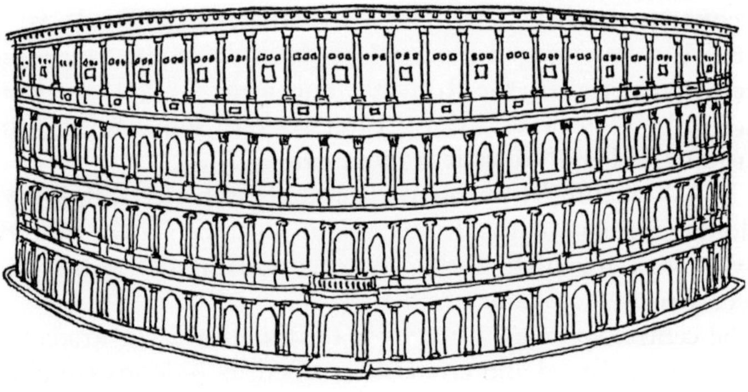

COLOSSEUM, ROME

cells where beasts, victims, and gladiators awaited their fate, whilst tunnelled passages led to the interior from outside entrances. Though the cross and tunnel vaults are not employed so boldly and on such a scale as in the later great thermae, the Colosseum is a truly remarkable piece of, largely concealed, complex engineering in stone and concrete, evincing an adroit use of materials of which one example is the use of pumice stone in the vaulting to reduce its weight.

Externally this huge elliptical building (620 × 500 ft) can be seen to be a pier and arch structure. Archivolt mouldings follow the lines of the arches and rest upon impost mouldings at the springing of the arches. It is divided into three storeys, the final storey being an addition some 200 years later. To the façade are applied encircling orders of Doric, Ionic and Corinthian, half columns reaching from the ground floor up, and composite pilasters on the top, unarcaded storey, pierced by rectangular openings. What is singular about this is that the Romans have taken their own pier and arch system and applied to it the trabeated system of the Greeks in an entirely non-functional way. This development was inevitable for, once away from temple designs, it is obvious that the load-bearing column and stone lintel are not strong enough to carry the great weight of large buildings. Yet it is not pure decoration since non-functional and functional are usually so integrated in Roman buildings as to conform to the same basic grammar of design which is strictly disciplined and interdependent.

Other well-preserved amphitheatres are to be inspected at Pompeii and Pozzuoli near Naples; and a later example at Verona (A.D. 290) in north Italy.

The grandest of the stadia or circuses where horse and chariot races took place was the once magnificently embellished Circus Maximus (200 × 650 ft) accommodating a quarter of a million spectators on tiered seating. Now all is gone though there are slight remains of the Circus of Maxentius (A.D. 311) at one end of which was the main processional entrance and stalls for the competitors and at the other the Porta Triumphalis.

The triumphs of the Roman emperors and generals were celebrated by the building of massive archways: either a single great opening or triple openings, a large central one flanked by two lesser ones, for pedestrian traffic. The arches spring from piers

ARCH OF CONSTANTINE

which are fronted by engaged or detached columns, frequently of Composite order, 'supporting' an entablature above which was an attic decorated with a dedicatory inscription, bas-reliefs, and statues, and formerly a bronze quadriga or chariot drawn by four horses.

The Arch of Titus (A.D. 81) is a simple archway with the earliest example of the use of the Composite order. Two triple arches in Rome, larger and more complex in design, are the white marble, coffered, Arch of Septimius Severus (A.D. 204) and the Arch of Constantine (A.D. 312). The columns here rise from pedestals and are detached, Composite in the former and Corinthian in the latter. Outside Rome there is the Arch of Trajan, Ancona (A.D. 113). Once again one sees applied orders cleverly integrated with what is basically an arcuated structure so that the outcome is a unified design.

Scarcely buildings, these great archways together with the Colosseum and the thermae, were destined to provide the men of the Renaissance with the vocabulary of Roman architecture which they were then to bend to their own purposes and needs.

Trajan's columns (A.D. 112), already referred to, is another type of triumphal monument, a pillar of victory which consists of a Roman Doric column on a pedestal covered with spiral sculptural reliefs, commemorating the campaigns, and surmounted by a statue. It is large enough (115 ft high) to contain a tomb chamber and a spiral stair to the top. A similar design is the Column of

Marcus Aurelius (A.D. 174). Their progeny were legion in the commemorative columns of Europe.

Another characteristic feature of ancient Rome which set a tradition that has lasted continuously to the present day, especially in that city, was the many fountains. Tombs were also numerous. The Christian catacombs derived from Roman cemetaria or underground vaults, for the mausolea, deriving from Greek examples, were great square or circular architectural tombs (containing a richly carved sarcophagus) rising from a podium and capped with a pyramidal roof. Such were the vast Mausoleum of Hadrian (A.D. 135), now the Castel Sant' Angelo, and the Mausoleum of Augustus. The first of these, though 220 ft in diameter and a fortress since the third century B.C., is only a stump of the original mausoleum. It was crowned with a pyramidal roof topped by a huge fir cone. But designs were numerous. Thus there was the concrete pyramid of Caestius (12 B.C.) and the temple tombs of the Via Appia and Pompeii.

But it is time to conclude this brief account of Roman building by referring to some of the greatest engineering achievements of the ancient world, the aqueducts, straightforward expressions of structural form, the finest examples ever built until the works of the nineteenth century which were themselves directly inspired by them. Dramatically their great arched piers built of stone or concrete faced with brick stride across intervening alleys carrying fresh water from the hills in cement-lined channels and winding where necessary to maintain a steady fall to the thirsty cities. Rome had no less than nine focused on it in the days of Augustus, some of them tiered, such as the Aqua Marcia (144 B.C.) one of the oldest Roman structures in Italy with triple channels superimposed. The finest was the Aqua Claudia (38 B.C.), part solid, part arched, it reached 100 ft high over its 45-mile length.

Drainage was equally a concern of the Romans who laid out systems for towns, the main sewer of Rome being the vaulted Cloaca Maxima.

Of stone bridges the Pons Mulvius (Ponte Molle) (109 B.C.) still stands, if restored, reaching acoss the Tiber with its massive piers (with cutwaters and flood water apertures) and wide spanning arches. Also in Rome is the two-arched Pons Fabricius; but much the finest example extant is the five-arched Bridge of Augustus (14 B.C.) over the Marecchia at Rimini.

The final word should be devoted to the designers and originators of these great works. It is obvious from their scale and efficiency that the profession of architect and engineer had become firmly established in Roman society at a high level. That the wonderful account in Vitruvius of what it took to make a good architect, not only a high degree of skill but adherence to a code of professional and ethical conduct and a solid background of learning and general culture, was not just an ideal but a real instance of one of the best elements in Roman civilization.

CHAPTER FOUR

Early Christian

THE Early Christian period of architecture begins in the reign of the Emperor Constantine with the Edict of Milan in 313 which granted the once persecuted Christians freedom of worship and thereby laid the way open for them to build their own churches. As Rome was then the hub and greatest city of the Empire, so most Early Christian architecture was built and is still to be seen there.

Until Christianity became the official religion of the Roman state it was only one of several religions of oriental origin appealing to the mythical instincts of man and it is among the meeting places and temples of these sects that we must look for the immediate progenitor of the Christian church as a building type. Thus there is the little first-century so-styled Basilica of Porta Maggiore, Rome, and the mid-second-century temple of Mithras, London, both with nave and apse, aisles and piers, and obviously owing a good deal to the Roman secular basilicas already described. Pagan temples could offer no suitable precedent. They were essentially shrines, their interior arrangements unsuited to the accommodation of a big congregation who worshipped in common whereas the basilica was not only capable of being used as a large hall for public assembly and already associated with secular authority but was also adaptable to the symbolism and ritual of the church.

Thus the earliest Christian churches modelled on the Roman basilicas were to establish the essential arrangements of most Christian churches from that time onwards. Some of the fourth- and fifth-century churches, compared with the Basilica of Porta Maggiore, were very large and impressive buildings, constructed from materials obtained from Roman temples and ruins; their appearance was both grave and dignified, representing a monumental architecture.

Typically, though in no sense standardized, they consisted of a large rectangle divided into a nave flanked by two or four lower,

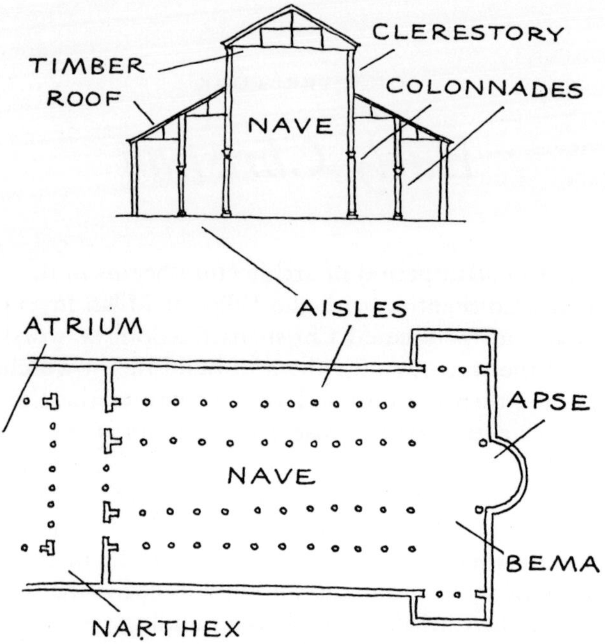

EARLY CHRISTIAN BASILICAN CHURCH

narrower aisles separated from one another by colonnades, though these did not, as in secular basilica, run across the building too. The colonnades, moving forwards irresistibly and without interruption, supported the walls of clerestories rising above the aisle roofs, producing the characteristic staggered section of the basilica. To one end was added a tribune or semi-circular apse to form a sanctuary where the high altar was placed under a ciborium, or canopy, and seating for the priests was arranged round the outer wall. This was the architectural and emotional climax of the horizontal progression and the entrance to the tribune was a kind of triumphal arch, a symbolically important feature.

At the opposite end was usually a narthex or arcaded porch or wide vestibule and sometimes this was approached through an atrium or rectangular colonnaded, cloistered forecourt of a type similar to that already noted in larger Roman houses and the ancestor of the cloister of the medieval monastery. Occasionally there was only the atrium.

Walls were constructed of concrete or rubble faced with stone. brick or stucco and the columns of the nave were either closely spaced and carrying an entablature or with a wider intercolumniation supporting an arcade of semi-circular arches. Sometimes these rose directly from the capitals of the columns, the entablature being omitted. Windows were round-headed and the nave was lit from ranges of them in the clerestory; otherwise it would have been very dark because of the distance between it and the outside walls. Windows were small and instead of being glazed were fitted with sheets of translucent marble, alabaster or plaster.

Sometimes narrow side aisles were vaulted but there was no attempt, perhaps out of humility, to emulate the great vaulting achievements of Imperial Rome and the usual main covering of the basilica was a simple open truss roof of timber, low pitched and flat, often provided with a coffered ceiling at the time of the Renaissance. The relatively low timber roof and perspective effect of the long repetitive colonnades make Early Christian basilicas seem even longer than they are, while magnificent marble columns of varied styles, and carved capitals, mostly Corinthian, frescoes and rich glass mosaic decorations create colourful and opulent interiors. If there was nothing structurally new about basilicas they did have a new oriental colour and atmosphere through their Christian connection, glass mosaic in particular having an insubstantial quality which helps dissolve in appearance the wall's solidity. But carving and mouldings resemble Roman work, though they are a little coarser than the best, and floors were paved with marble and porphyry, again quarried from Roman remains.

The tribune or apse was not always at the east end (for orientation was not practised at this time, as it is not found at St Peter's, Rome today) and entered from the nave under the tribune arch already referred to. The latter was the forerunner of the chancel arch of the medieval church, the 'cancelli' being originally the barriers between tribune and nave. The apse was vaulted with a semi-dome in the Roman manner and beneath the sanctuary was frequently a crypt containing the relics of a saint or martyr.

Important interior features were the ambones or reading desks, one for the gospel to the right of the chancel, the other for the epistle to the left of it. Segregation of women was usual; in some basilicas special galleries above the aisles overlooking the sanctuary were provided for them, in others they were accommodated in a screened-off part of the nave.

Externally, Early Christian basilicas were plain with bare walls and without domes or bell-towers (campanili) or other prominent features except for a pair of towers on either side of the narthex in some later examples built under Byzantine influence.

At one time Rome had no less than thirty-one Early Christian churches and, fortunately, despite subsequent restorations, there are still important examples surviving from this period, even though they cannot be said to have survived unaltered.

Old St Peter's, S. Pietro in Vaticano, on the site of St Peter's burial and Nero's Circus by Vatican Hill, was founded by Constantine in 324. Though it no longer exists its importance as the direct spiritual ancestor of the present St Peter's, and as the most influential (being the principal) church of Early Christendom, demands that it be briefly described first.

It was a great brick basilica with double aisles approached through a colonnaded atrium and narthex. Between the main body of the basilica and the apse ran a transverse bema, a feature which had first appeared in some Roman basilicas and which was the ancestor of the transepts of later cruciform churches, though it was not a common feature of Early Christian basilicas. Low walls (cancelli) enclosed the chancel and there was a crypt below where the bishops of Rome (the popes) were buried.

This great church, the centre of a whole complex of buildings, was replaced by the present Basilica of St Peter's (not of course technically a basilica) of the sixteenth and seventeenth centuries but not before it had exerted the immense force of its example on the design of Early Christian Churches. Its destruction and replacement by Pope Julius II with an entirely new church was at once an act of incredible vandalism and at the same time a gesture of Renaissance self-confidence and certainty in the continuity of faith.

Six years after Old St Peter's was founded the cathedral of Rome, S. Giovanni in Laterano, where the coronation of the Popes took place. This is a spacious double-aisled basilica with a wide transept beyond which rises a great tribune splendid with mosaics; but the seventeenth-century Borromini sculptures and eighteenth-century façade have so much altered its Early Christian character that we may soon pass on to consider S. Maria Maggiore

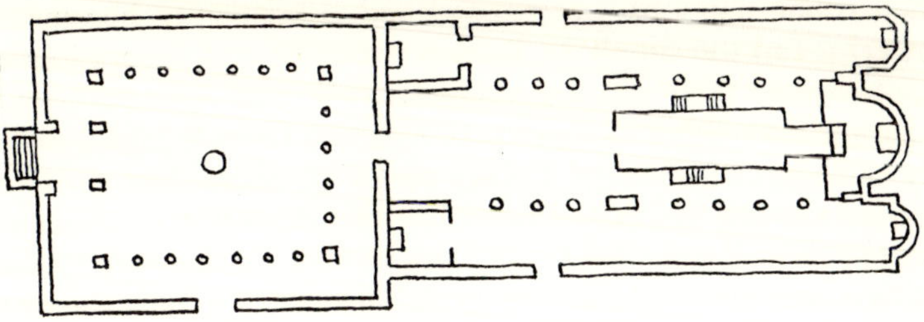

S. CLEMENTE, ROME

(432) on the Esquiline Hill the interior of which gives a much more accurate idea of a great Early Christian basilica.

It is in fact the oldest and most splendid in Rome, originally a classical secular basilica adapted for Christian worship and having the large spaciousness and clarity that one comes to associate with typical Italian architecture. Like Old St Peter's it had a bema, a feature which remained a rare one and one confined to larger churches of the period.

The colonnades are those of the original design consisting of forty-two Ionic columns of marble from Mount Hymettos in Greece and carry a fine entablature. There is much splendid decoration from fourth-century mosaics, the most beautiful and mysterious in Rome, to a sixteenth-century gilded ceiling. The outside shows the basilica to have been remodelled in the Late Renaissance of the seventeenth and eighteenth centuries but the campanile is medieval. Bells were first used to summon the faithful to worship in the early seventh century and the earliest campanili which were the prototypes of the later bell towers must have dated from this period.

Among the several smaller examples of Early Christian basilicas is S. Clemente, founded in 385 but rebuilt in 1084. It has arcades of semi-circular arches and no bema but perhaps its most interesting feature is the stuccoed chamber preserved under the apse which seems to have been a place of Christian assembly as far back as the first century.

S. Sabina (425) is rather bare internally as well as externally giving it abstract qualities of lucidity and plainness which make a powerful appeal. Its impressive Corinthian colonnades have been constructed from the materials of Roman temples. After 380, when other religions were proscribed, Christianity became all-powerful and the supply of Roman materials and decoration was supplemented from disused temples.

Larger than either of these is S. Lorenzo fuori le Mura, originally outside the walls of Rome, hence its name, but now in a modern suburb. An early Constantinian foundation of about 330, another church was added to it, back to back, in the sixth century, the two being thrown into one great church in the early thirteenth century, from which time much of it now dates. It has an attractive narthex and an interesting two-storeyed aisle, i.e. with smaller gallery columns above the main colonnade.

Other special features of this exceptional church with its rich and colourful interior are the nave pavement of opus Alexandrinum (geometrical patterns of coloured marble), the thirteenth-century wagon roof over the nave, the Early Renaissance coffered roof over the chancel, rich with purple and gilt, and two beautiful thirteenth-century ambones.

S. Paolo fuori le Mura, containing the tomb of St Paul, was founded in 380 and rebuilt in 1823 but with such faithfulness to the Early Christian conception that its grand interior with its eighty columns, fine arcades, and coffered ceiling gives a very good impression of the style. It has double aisles and a double bema and being the largest basilica after Old St Peter's it is now the largest

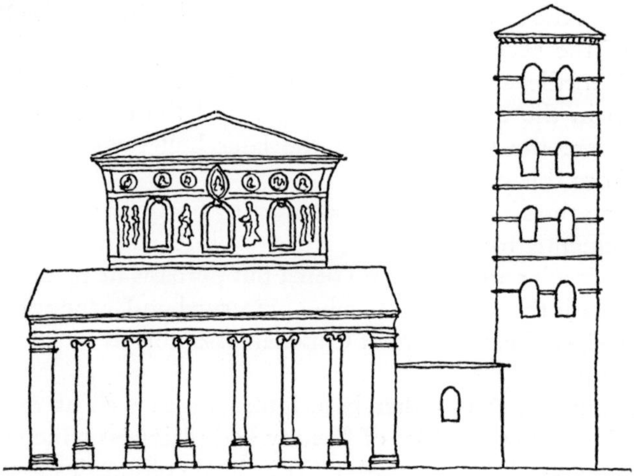

S. LORENZO FUORI LE MURA, ROME

3*a*. S. Giovanni in Laterano, Rome. The Cosmatesque cloisters of this large double-aisled basilica are thirteenth-century masterpieces of Petrus Vassallettus.

3*b*. S. Ambrogio, Milan. Brick-built and arcaded in the Lombardic Romanesque manner. The atrium through which the west front is approached is the only one extant.

4*a*. S. Antonio, Padua (1232). An Italian Gothic domed church with obviously Lombardic and Byzantine characteristics. To the left is Donatello's equestrian monument, Gattamelata (1445).

4*b*. The Certosa, Pavia (1396), Bernardo da Venezia's church of the Carthusian monastery. The elaborate brick and terra cotta architecture of Lombardy has some German features, Gothic pinnacles, and a later central tower. The west front is not shown.

surviving one. Its atrium and campanile are rather disappointing but inside is a splendid sculptured Paschal candelabrum by the Cosmati artists of the thirteenth century whose work will be referred to later, in the chapter dealing with Italian Romanesque architecture.

Lying below the level of the modern street is S. Agnese fuori le Mura (324), rebuilt three hundred years later but still preserving its galleried aisles; and another fourth-century church, S. Pudentia, which, if spoiled by restorers, has in its apse some of the finest Early Christian mosaics, a pagan technique being put to the service of Christian art.

Most Early Christian buildings are of the basilican type but there were a few centrally planned ones seemingly developed from circular buildings such as the Minerva Medica and Roman temples and mausolea already described; though they were less heavy and sculptural than their prototypes and introduced a surrounding aisle or ambulatory. They took a variety of forms. One of the most important, S. Constanza (320), began in fact as a mausoleum for two daughters of the Emperor Constantine and only became a church in the thirteenth century. It consists of a well-lit rotunda, its walls of concrete faced with brick, surrounded by a lower, darker, barrel-vaulted ambulatory from which it is separated by a ring or 'screen' of complex Composite columns from which spring arches. The dome-shaped roof of the rotunda was originally a cupola and there was once an outer circular colonnade surrounding the building. The rather oddly shaped narthex, however, remains.

Such circular plans were admirably adapted to emphasizing the special location of a hallowed place, and were symbolic of the world, the internal dome providing an image of heaven.

On the Coelian Hill is S. Stephano Rotonda (468) another early example of a centrally planned church; though reduced in size in the fifteenth century it is still the largest circular church in existence. Here two surrounding ambulatories are separated by circular colonnades which support both the aisle roof and the high central drum of the rotunda.

The baptistry too was a type of building the function of which suggested a central plan. Probably the oldest is S. Giovanni in Fonte adjacent to S. Giovanni in Laterano, an octagonal building surrounded by an ambulatory with a two-storeyed porphyry

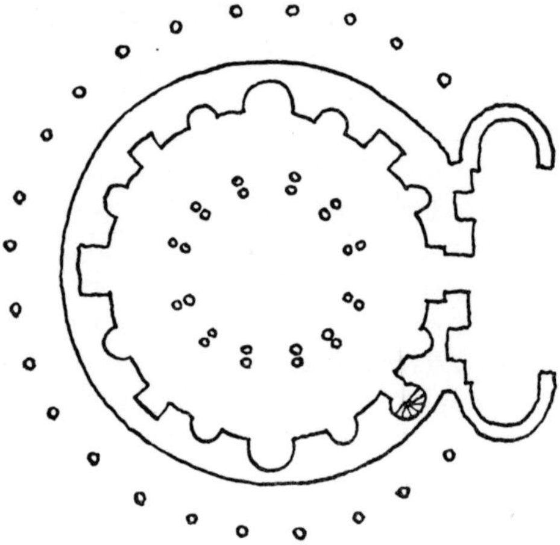

S. CONSTANZA, ROME

colonnade and a great Roman bath of green basalt for the font at the centre.

The Baptistry at Nocera (350) is circular with what seems to be the earliest example of an internal dome covered with an external timber roof, a notably un-Roman practice. Octangular or circular, this was the pattern generally followed from now on by Italian baptistries, made large enough to accommodate big numbers and usually attached to the atrium of the largest church. The Baptistry at Ravenna (449) is an octagon with no ambulatory, a dome of hollow tiles, and its upper internal wall arcaded with triplets of arches under the main arches, the earliest example of what was to become a common Romanesque feature. Both basilicas and these rotundas eloquently express the nature and liturgical needs of the early Christian church and their designs affected nearly all Christian architecture to come.

If Rome was the centre of the first phase of Early Christian architecture, Ravenna on the Adriatic coast of the peninsula was undoubtedly the centre of the second. One of the most important acts of the Emperor Constantine was to make the old Greek colony of Byzantium (Constantinople) his capital, soon to become capital of the Eastern Empire while Rome remained the capital of the Western. But when Rome began to wane in strength as the barbarians made their inroads from the north (it was sacked in 410), Ravenna was made the new administrative centre of the Western Empire and thus gained a special importance. When Italy fell to the Ostrogoths in 476 their King Theodoric made it his capital and there followed a period of stability and prosperity during which was received the fertilizing influence of the art of Byzantium reaching out from what was now the principal city of the Christian world.

From now on most Early Christian churches are found in this Adriatic region of north-east Italy and they all display to a greater or lesser extent the features of Byzantine architecture which had been developing in the Eastern Empire. Some are basilicas such as the most impressive S. Apollinare Nuovo (493), built by Theodoric himself and finished by Justinian, and S. Apollinare in Classe (534), in and near Ravenna.

The Byzantines made skilful use of salvaged columns and carvings from antique ruins and this is evident from these churches.

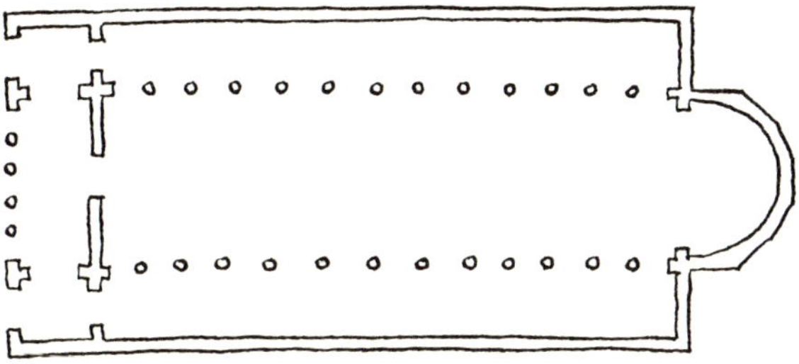

S. APOLLINARE NUOVO, RAVENNA

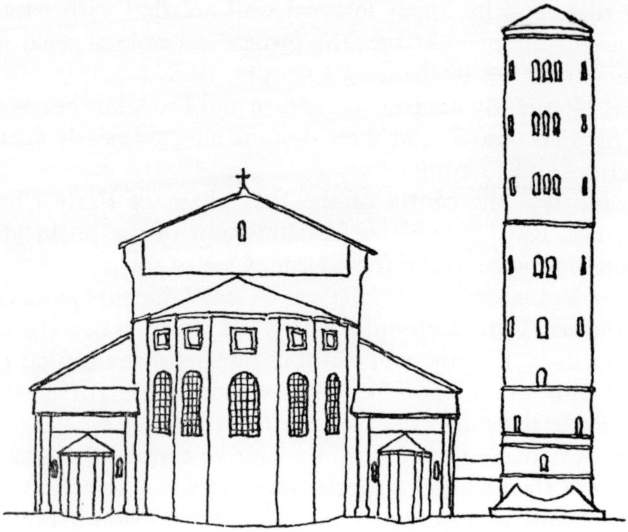

S. APOLLINARE IN CLASSE, RAVENNA

Another Byzantine feature is the way the arches do not spring directly from the capitals but from pulvins or dosseret blocks which sit upon the capitals. These too are Byzantine in type with 'wind blown' acanthus leaf carving or elaborate perforated lace-like effects. Great interest lies in their magnificent mosaics which give a spiritual dimension to the architectural composition most appropriate to its function. The main surfaces where they were placed, their deep full colours glowing richly on a glimmering gold background and contributing to the mystery and solemnity of the interior, are the apse and along the clerestory walls where rows of hieratic figures in the formalized Byzantine convention look down upon the nave. There was no place for the idealized figure sculpture of classical antiquity in such a setting. An interesting architectural feature of the mosaics of S. Apollinare Nuovo, which show episodes from the Bible and processions of martyrs, is the illustration of the once splendid palace of Theodoric where he held court in imitation of the Roman emperors and of which there are few remains. The principal apse of S. Apollinare in Classe is polygonal externally, reflecting a Byzantine preference, and apses also terminate the aisles. Its elegantly arcaded exterior

MAUSOLEUM OF GALLA PLACIDA

anticipates Lombardic yet exteriors of such churches perhaps are predominantly plain and lucid, with perhaps tower-like structures to the right and left of the narthex. Both these basilicas were later provided with round campanili.

Of centrally planned structures at Ravenna the mausoleum of Galla Placida (*c.* 450), the sister of the Emperor Honorius who first moved his court from Rome to Ravenna, is one of the earliest. It is the earliest known cruciform building in fact, a simple type of the detached Greek cross with four arms of equal length, a

TOMB OF THEODORIC

plan which became standard for Byzantine churches down to the fourteenth century.

But its exterior plainness gives no inkling of the interior. Beneath its timber roof are barrel vaults and pendentive dome, united into one continuously curved surface covered with glowing mosaics, and revetments of coloured marble; and in each of the four arms is a sarcophagus.

Near by is the contemporaneous Baptistry of the Orthodox, octagonal, domed, with another beautiful and colourful interior where surface decoration dissolves architectural forms.

The two-storeyed Tomb of Theodoric (526) has a solid lid-like roof scooped out below to form a sort of very shallow dome. Of a single huge piece weighing over 450 tons its positioning represents a remarkable technical achievement for that age.

The culmination of these experiments in central planning was reached under the Emperor Justinian whose despotic ambitions were so favourable to the arts in the sixth century. It was he who

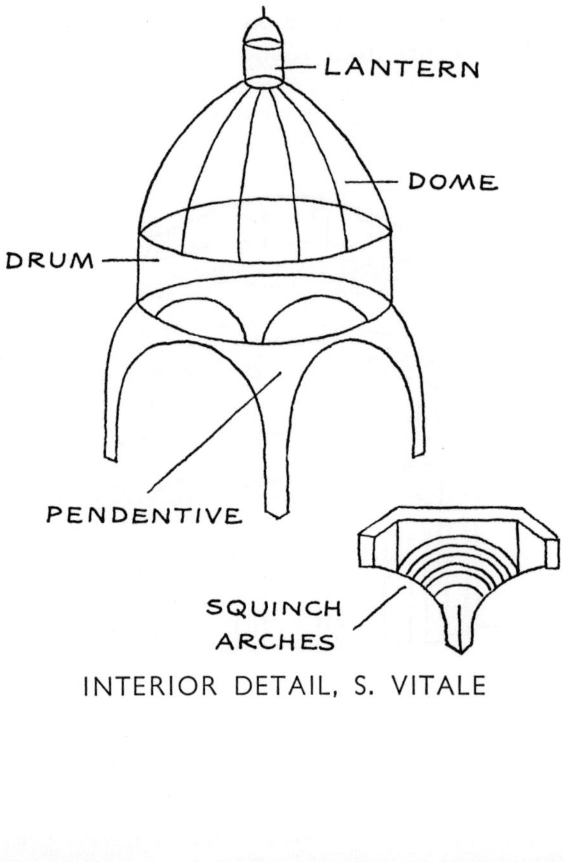

INTERIOR DETAIL, S. VITALE

built on the Greek cross plan inscribed in a square the churches of Hagia Sophia (532, architect: Anthemius) and SS. Sergius and Bacchus, Constantinople. In these the typical Byzantine solution to raise a round dome from square walls, a problem not faced by the Romans, is the use of spherical triangles called 'pendentives', a better alternative to the clumsier eastern method of using 'squinch' arches, a form of corbelling.

If Constantine had abandoned vaulting Justinian reintroduced it with unequalled boldness. But Byzantine architecture was much more than structural innovation. The basic motif of the domed centralized pavilion, often multiplied, and to which were added the apses and narthexes already noted in Early Christian architecture, became a sumptuously decorated envelope for the flux of space within, symbolic of the faith and adapted to the needs of its liturgy.

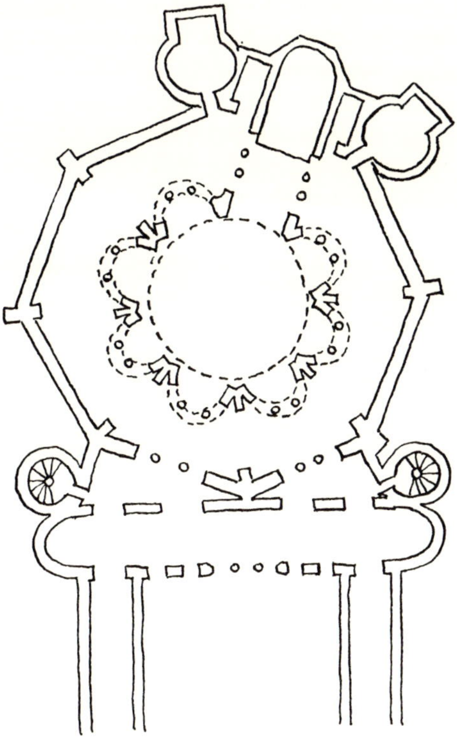

S. VITALE, RAVENNA

These developments were to have their effect in Italy when Theodoric died and, soon after, Ravenna fell to Justinian (540) who made it the seat of the Exarch and colonial capital of the Byzantine Eastern Empire. Thus a quite outstanding church there, built by Justinian himself, is S. Vitale (*c.* 530), his chief building in the west. Though it owes something to the Minerva Medica, Rome, its design is unique in Italy, being a domed octagon with a galleried ambulatory and narthex and apse projecting from opposite sides, the latter having a chancel and being flanked by a circular vestry and prothesis. The dome is carried on pendentives between the eight arches and is constructed, unusually but with great virtuosity, by interlocking earthenware pots to form a structure which is both strong and, because of its hollowness, light enough for its purpose. It is covered by a timber roof in the manner already noted at the Nocera Baptistry.

A fascinating spatial effect is the way the central domed octagon expands, and here we come to the most singular feature of the church's planning, between the piers on two storeys into three-arched open 'exedrae' or 'niches' so that there is no clear separation between the central space and the circular ambulatory but through the screen an intermingling of the two that is both aesthetically pleasing and as redolent of the mysteries of the Christian faith as its glowing mosaics. S. Vitale represents the architectural peak of its time in terms of spatial sophistication and the richness of its internal decoration.

Of particular note is the intricate lace-like carving of the capitals, carrying dosserets, where the dark background creates the same sort of mysterious effect as the gloom of the ambulatory seen through the arcade. Oriental as this decoration seems to be, it appears to have prototypes at Hadrian's Villa, Tivoli, and S. Lorenzo, Milan (*c.* 450).

In describing the spatial and decorative qualities of the interior of this wonderful organic design we must not neglect the brick exterior of prismatic geometrical forms piled upwards to the central octagon, the opposite of the unbroken flow of space within.

Other interesting churches of the period outside Ravenna are the sixth-century churches of Parenzo and Grado, near Trieste. The former is a large basilica with atrium, narthex, and its original ritual arrangements; and there is also a baptistry. At Aquileia the

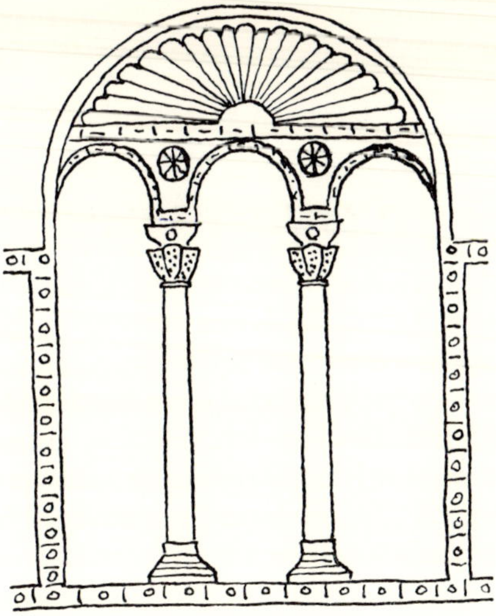

INTERIOR DETAIL, S. VITALE

Early Christian basilica has been so altered that it is much less interesting than the others just mentioned. The abbey at Monte Cassino, rebuilt since the famous battle, was a very much later building on the site of St Benedict's original foundation in 529, the progenitor of houses of the Benedictine rule everywhere.

Some twenty years after S. Vitale was finished Italy was conquered by the Lombards from across the Alps, and though basilican churches continued to be put up in Rome until much later the great period of Early Christian architecture had come to an end. Architecture in Italy now lay in a trough for some two hundred years until the Romanesque period began in the mid-eighth century, about the time much of the northern and central parts of the country became absorbed into the Holy Roman Empire. The Frank Charles the Great was crowned Emperor in Rome in the year 800.

CHAPTER FIVE

Romanesque

ROMANESQUE is really the name of a group of styles, the constructional forms of which descend from the last phase of Roman architecture, adopted throughout Western Europe during the long period between Early Christian times and the introduction of the Gothic system in the late twelfth century. There were many regional variants therefore but all were related in their employment of Roman-derived forms and motifs such as columns, round arches and cross and barrel vaults. But there was no systematic use of orders and vaulting was infrequent at first, the techniques developed by the Romans being largely neglected in the preceding Early Christian architecture.

In 568 the Lombards, a barbarian people from Hungary, entered northern Italy from across the Alps and ruled it for the next two hundred years, until in 774 it became part of Charlemagne's Holy Roman Empire. There is little evidence that the Lombards themselves possessed much knowledge of architecture and it is possible that most of the building work executed in their time was done by the Comacini guilds of master masons who, originating in Como, were already established in Italy. Certain it is that during this period the Lombards took over the Early Christian tradition of basilica building and initiated the first phase of Romanesque.

Not much in fact remains from this period which is really one of artistic decline. There are however S. Salvatore, Brescia (753), S. Maria in Cosmedin, Rome (772) and the nave and eastern parts of S. Pietro, Toscanella, not far away. S. Maria in Cosmedin was an earlier church on the foundations of a temple in the Greek quarter of the city and was restored again later, thus showing the long continuity of some of these religious sites. The second remodelling is ninth- and tenth-century and the slender campanile early medieval. So are the mosaic pavement, the ciborium over the high altar and the ambones, fine examples of the work of Cosmati artists and decorators.

Ninth-century churches include three Roman churches – S. Maria in Domnica, with fine mosaic work on the tribune arch, S. Prassede, with the earliest extant cloister, a beautiful campanile and more mosaics of the period showing Byzantine influence, and S. Giorgio in Velabro, a small complete basilica with narthex and Cosmatesque campanile and decoration in its appealingly austere interior. S. Maria in Trastevere began as a fourth-century basilica and was enlarged in the ninth, though what we see of this fine church today is largely Romanesque of the early twelfth-century rebuilding. Outside Rome are the small aisled church of S. Maria della Valle at Cividale, with a tunnel-vaulted nave, S. Pietro at Angliate, near Monza, and perhaps the campanile of S. Satiro, Milan. S. Pietro, with its apsed sanctuary raised over a groin vaulted crypt (875) and twelfth-century campanile, shows clearly how 'First Romanesque' evolved into later, mature Romanesque.

It will be realized however that in the long centuries which have elapsed since their foundation these early Lombard churches have undergone many restorations and modifications so that it is hardly possible to discover examples that are stylistically pure.

Novara Cathedral is a tenth-century basilica, vaulted a century later, with atrium to which is connected a round baptistry showing

CHEVET OF S. PIETRO, ANGLIATE

the circular centralized plan which was continued from the Early Christian period.

It was only in the eleventh and twelfth centuries that the full potentialities of Romanesque developed and it is at this point therefore, before embarking on individual descriptions of the chief works of these centuries, that it seems most appropriate to attempt a summary of the general characteristics of Romanesque architecture in Italy.

As we have said Roman constructional techniques were largely followed but in Italy, closer to the source of Roman tradition, Romanesque was generally lighter and more graceful in its use of forms than other variations of the style. Walls are of rubble construction with brick and stone increasingly used for facing, though there are notable exceptions in the brick construction of the plain of Lombardy where building stone was scarce, and the use of marble in central Italy where supplies were available.

Churches are basilicas, mostly with triple apses, i.e. with apses terminating the aisles as well as the nave. Nave and side aisles (often tunnel-vaulted) are separated by arcades; some aisles are two-storeyed with thick walls between side chapels thus giving abutment to the high vaults when they were constructed in the later period without the need to reduce the width of the nave. Unlike those of other countries Italian Romanesque plans are generally without transepts or do not express them externally. Where there are transepts they are wider than before and there is a tendency to extend the chancel. North Italy eventually developed hefty compound piers which were to facilitate the construction of high vault systems but central Italy continued to re-use Antique columns as it had done in Early Christian churches. Capitals are variations of Corinthian and Ionic with, later, cushion or cubiform types. Arcades are round arched and set in the thickness of the walls are round-headed windows, sometimes divided into two lights by a colonnette. Both windows and doors are rather small, for climatic reasons, the latter with jambs and doorheads set in receding orders with side or 'nook' shafts, a distinctly un-Roman arrangement, later developed in Gothic architecture. Glass became fairly widely used from the ninth century but stained glass was rare.

Towards the end of the Romanesque period interior space, instead of being as in Early Christian churches a long uninterrupted flow towards the altar, began to be articulated by being marked out into separate bay units, an effect increased of course when the normal brightly-coloured open timber roofs were replaced by the development of rib vaulting, over naves as well as aisles, following trans-Alpine influence. This practice seems to begin first in Germany, e.g. St Michael's Hildesheim, Saxony (*c.* 1000) but as there were both political and cultural connections between Germany and Italy it was soon taken up by the Lombard masons, though in a less complicated way.

The cultural connections between the Rhineland and north Italy present a confused picture however, and by the twelfth century there is evidence of Lombards working in Germany indicating a feedback of ideas and technique.

Just as Romanesque interiors differ from Early Christian ones, so do exteriors to the extent that added towers and turrets made them more impressive and imaginatively varied compositions, though Italy did not go in for very elaborate effects in this respect. Octagonal lanterns over the crossing were favoured features, however, and roofs were low pitched. Here again a debt is owed to Germany. Originally a Carolingian development from the Rhineland the evolution of towers later spread all over Western Europe – St Michael's, Hildesheim, is again a key design – reaching Italy in the eleventh century. The Rhenish motif of a two-tower façade was not however popular in Italy.

Italian west fronts usually take the form of a 'screen' placed across and hiding the typical basilican section. North Italian versions are often rather flat and plain but with a large arched central, sometimes two-storeyed, porch projecting, its two columns borne on the backs of lions which symbolize David as the Lion of Judah, or even perhaps go back to a pagan origin. Above is commonly a large rose or wheel window and an obtuse gable ornamented with raking or horizontal open arcading which first evolved as arcading under the eaves of round apses.

The latter type of 'dwarf gallery' is another motif common to both Italy and the Rhineland. Arcading used in this way is one of the most characteristic features of Italian Romanesque architecture. Exterior walls have as a rule only pilaster strip buttresses to articulate the bay division outside, but these are often connected at the top by a horizontal band or moulding and a row of small

S. ABBONDIO, COMO

round arches springing from corbels, as at S. Abbondio, Como, where the pairing of the eastern campanili is an interesting fusion of German and Lombardic motifs. In addition to the eaves arcading, larger attached arcading, though not full size, is sometimes used on gables superimposed in galleries to emphasize proportions and obtain elaborate ornamental effects of light and shade. Pisa is the best known example of this practice of using a series of scaled-down semi-circular arcades to decorate a façade, sometimes with great elegance. Other decorative effects are obtained with ornamental carving in the decoration of capitals. Unlike Norman with its preference for the abstract, Italian Romanesque keeps to natural, foliate forms.

The campanile is a distinctive feature of Romanesque churches in Italy, now made an integral part of the church group, though it is still detached or connected only by cloisters. Tall, square, unbuttressed, brick-built towers, often more than just belfreys and also symbols of civic pride, they are divided into stages by horizontal bands of marble and arcading with eaves arcading.

They usually have just a few staircase windows but upper stages commonly have windows made up of several lights separated by shafts or there may be a loggia at the level of the belfrey. A pyramidal roof is the usual termination. Pomposa (1063) is a fine early example of five stages.

S. Miniato al Monte, Florence (1013), is one of the most important Romanesque churches in Italy. It is a basilican design with a chancel approached by steps because it is at a higher level than the nave being built over a crypt. This is an occasional feature of such churches, the relics of a saint or martyr being entombed in the crypt.

A new development is the division of the interior into three compartments, one of which is the chancel just described, by the use of piers. This is the breakaway from the basilican tradition and a step forward in the articulation of space, soon to be confirmed by new departures in vaulting, already referred to in our general account of Romanesque characteristics.

Another feature of the lively interior, covered with a timber roof, open and coloured as was the fashion, is the lavish use of black and white marble in bands and panelling; and to pick out architectural membering. This is eminently characteristic of Italian Romanesque but it is not of Roman origin. It is probably derived from Byzantine practice as we shall see later in this chapter. It was destined to have a long life in Italian architecture which greatly indulged it, even in the Gothic period.

The Corinthian columns and arches of the main front, which also employs marble in the way just described, though slenderer and more delicate, have departed little from the classical convention and there is a triangular pediment which obviously derives from the pagan temple. In short there is displayed in S. Miniato a classical feeling compounded of grace and reason that is not to be found so early anywhere else, a remarkable Tuscan anticipation of Renaissance aims.

It may have had some influence on the design of a fine group of churches in Emilia: Modena Cathedral (1099), the early twelfth-century Cathedrals of Piacenza and Parma and the churches of Borgo S. Donnino. S. Antonino, Piacenza (1104), has a good tall polygonal tower and a great Gothic west porch added later.

The capital of Lombardy at this time was Pavia and the cathedral

S. MINIATO, FLORENCE

of S. Michele is one of the finest churches of the period. Dating from 1117 it is a large cruciform building with an apse. Like S. Miniato it has a choir raised over a vaulted crypt.

Marking an advance on S. Miniato, however, its nave is not only divided into square bays by clustered piers but also these bays are rib-vaulted in the northern manner. The aisles are two-storeyed and vaulted in square bays, two to each bay of the nave. S. Michele also has prominent transepts of the German type, another foreign influence from the north. The wide entrance façade has three portals, not common in Italy, tall, pilaster strips, and open stepped or raking arcades. It is rather a flat design in terms of surface relief and is thus typical of northern Italian compared with central Italian Romanesque façades. The octagonal dome over the crossing is carried on squinch arches below four of its sides; we shall have more to say of the dome in Romanesque architecture later.

Deriving from Cologne churches in plan, and therefore illustrating the intercourse between Lombardy and Germany, is S. Fidele, Como, with its centralized east end and identical apses tacked on to transepts and chancel. The ultimate inspiration was probably Byzantine but again this is something that will be better appreciated when we come to consider the Byzantine-Romanesque style of north-east Italy.

S. Zeno Maggiore, Verona (1117), is rather similar to S. Michele, Pavia. The somewhat severe entrace facade has a fine two-storeyed porch of about the same date and an especially fine rose window above it. Long narrow pilaster strips are connected by tiny arcades under the gable slopes.

S. ZENO MAGGIORE, VERONA

The choir, with a fourteenth-century vault, is raised above the nave level in the manner already noted and the nave arcade is carried on alternating massive compound piers and more slender columns. These massive piers and columns supporting round arches are characteristic of developments in north Italian Romanesque where vaulting was becoming commoner by the eleventh century, especially over aisles, semi-circular or stilted arches being used, with transverse arches to separate the bay compartments. Ribs were unmoulded until the end of the eleventh century.

The plain square unbuttressed campanile is built of alternate courses of brick and marble, has open arcades to the belfrey, and forked battlements known as Ghibelline battlements.

The Guelfs and Ghibellines were opposing parties who supported the popes and the emperors respectively in their wrangles over Italy. They had a complicated history with varying aims and continued their conflicts into the Gothic period. As a sign of their partisanship in the civil strife they each adopted characteristic battlements – forked, as we have seen, for the Ghibellines and a more orthodox rectangular outline for the Guelfs.

S. Lorenzo, Verona, is also twelfth-century, showing very interesting brickwork construction.

Another very impressive church in Lombardy is S. Ambrogio, Milan, a ninth-century basilica with triple apse, crypt, and timber roof replaced by vaulting in the early twelfth century, when its low wide nave was shortened and its aisles raised to abut the high rib vault supported on large compound piers. With its broad prototype ribs this is one of the earliest rib vaults in Europe. There is a triforium and over the 'crossing' of this simple, impressive, sombre interior, is an octagon. Like Modena Cathedral it has no transepts and an austere entrance façade. Altogether, with its wide cross vaults, galleried aisles, and pylogonal dome, S. Ambrogio sets a pattern for many Lombard churches to follow. Campanili stand to the north and south of the narthex, and an atrium to the west, the only one extant in Lombard churches, makes a rather complicated approach.

Designed without structural innovation, despite its elaborate exterior, by a master mason named Buschetto, Pisa Cathedral dates from 1093. It is a basilica with double aisles and transepts, with apses to the transepts in addition to the main apse, thus

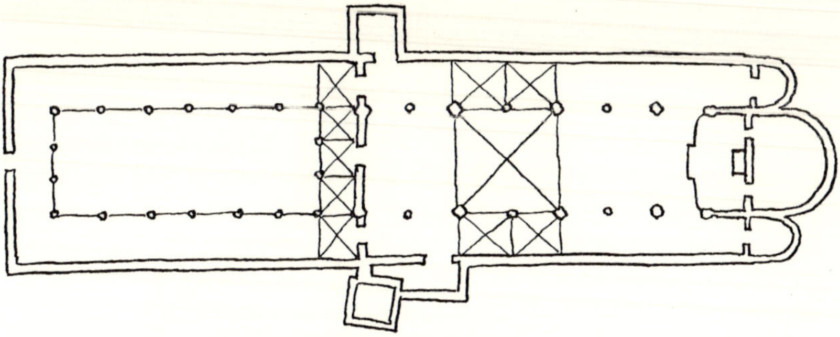

S. AMBROGIO, MILAN

showing a characteristic plan development. An elliptical dome of later date covers the crossing.

Externally, especially on the entrance façade, there is an abundant use of alternate bands of marble of contrasting tone and a great deal of elegant arcading applied in superimposed galleries in the manner favoured by central Italy in particular. The proportions of the columns and arches, despite their reduced size, are quite classical in feeling and the general effect is one of lively but refined ornament. The practice of applying arcades in this way may owe something to the Pisan contact with the Arabs of the south in the eleventh century or to Byzantine influence. Compared with the very Tuscan qualities of S. Miniato there is something somewhat oriental about this design, despite its classical lucidity and restraint.

Near by is the circular Baptistry by Dioti Salvi begun nearly a hundred years later and continued to the Gothic period as the thirteenth-century gallery and decoration of its upper part clearly testifies. Nicola Pisano's celebrated pulpit (1260) shows a similar blend of classical forms and feeling with new Gothic elements. It may be compared with that by his son Giovanni in the Duomo some fifty years later. The conical dome over the central nave is of structural interest rising as it does through the outer dome.

The famous campanile, the 'leaning tower', built on piles on account of its unstable site is late twelfth- and thirteenth-century. Its eight stages are again marked by a profusion of open arcading. Modern engineering skill has been greatly tested recently in an effort to halt its slow decline. Together, Cathedral, Baptistry and

PISA CATHEDRAL

campanile form one of the most striking groups in European architecture of that period.

The Cathedral of Pistoia (1150) with its arcaded main front, rather spindly at ground floor level, in black and white marble is in some measure a reflection of Pisa, and in its turn exerted a strong local influence. S. Martino, S. Frediano, and S. Michele, Lucca are other notable twelfth-century churches in central Italy and again the so-called ornate Pisan style with its tiers of arcaded galleries is evidence of the political and artistic influence of the greater city.

Arezzo, an Etruscan town lying south-east of Florence, though better known for its fourteenth-century church of S. Francesco where Piero in the quattrocento marvellously depicted the Story of the True Cross has the interesting twelfth-century Romanesque S. Maria della Pieve with its galleried façade and many-windowed, five-storey campanile.

In addition to the circular Baptistry of Pisa quite large octagonal ones may be seen at Cremona (1167), Asti (1050), and Parma (1196), the last two based on Constantine's in Rome. The first of the three, however, is the best design with a typical Lombardic

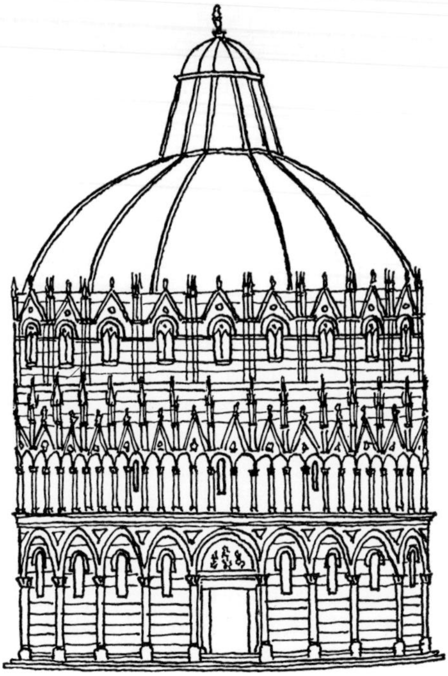

BAPTISTRY, PISA

porch, being north Italian, and open arcading, but the Gothic sculpture at Parma is of outstanding interest.

Other interesting structures at this time are the tall towers characteristic of later Romanesque and continuing into the succeeding Gothic period. The city of Bologna has two notable specimens, the Torre Garisenda and the Torre Asinelli, but the fortified hilltop town of San Gimignano near Florence once had seventy. The height of these Guelf and Ghibelline tower dwellings, for this is what they really were, was controlled by the Commune and thus afforded an example of early building regulation.

One of the features of the late Romanesque was the impetus it gave to the development of craft skills not only in the sympathetic handling of materials but also in the high standard of art work used to embellish churches. This is perhaps best illustrated by the twelfth- and thirteenth-century work of the Cosmati. Many examples of their work could be quoted such as the porch of the

Cathedral of Civita Castelland and the early arcaded cloister with coupled columns by Paulus, the first of the *Marmorari romani,* at SS. Quattro Coronati, Rome. But their masterpiece is perhaps the thirteenth-century cloisters at S. Giovanni in Laterano by Petrus Vassallettus. Here the arcades have delicate coupled columns, many twisted and like the architraves inlaid with glass mosaic. The capitals and arches are beautifully carved and the cornice has sculptured heads. Despite the richness of effect they are executed with remarkable feeling and sense of style. Similar work may be seen in the cloisters of another Early Christian church, S. Paolo fuori le Mura. Arcades were left unglazed because, unlike that of northern Europe, the climate of Italy did not require it.

Cosmato work, with its characteristic decorative forms in marble and mosaic and abundance of Christian symbolism, is very original; but the tendency in central Italy where the influence was strongest was to keep closest to classical precedents in mouldings and ornament, if not actually to re-use Antique fragments as in an earlier period. This classicism is noticeable too when, with the return of the plastic sense in the twelfth century, figure sculpture came back. It had always been an important element in the decorative schemes of the Romans. In north Italy, nearer to different traditions, features of the ornamental carving were genre scenes and grotesques of human figures and beasts, besides strings or flat moulded bands.

Just as Early Christian architecture was modified at Ravenna in the north-east as it came into contact with Byzantine culture, so when what is known as the Romanesque style reached the same region it too suffered a partial transformation. The political connection of old might be broken but trading contacts between Venice, which had succeeded Ravenna as the chief city of the Adriatic, and Constantinople, her rival in the eastern Mediterranean until defeated in the Fourth Crusade (1204), were sufficient to strengthen what had already become a regional tradition so that what we find in the north-east during this period is a mode best referred to as Byzantine-Romanesque.

If Lombardic architecture followed Early Christian in adopting a basilican church plan, the most characteristic in the north-east is a type already noticed in the reign of Justinian at S. Vitale, the centralized plan, square or polygonal, with a dome lifted above the central space by the skilful manipulation of arches, penden-

APSE, S. M. E DONATO, MURANO

tives, and semi-domes as abutment. This kind of system was made possible by adopting the arcuate system of the Romans, also inherited by the Byzantine Greeks, and marrying it to, first, the dome, so prominently expressed in the external design of buildings in the eastern tradition and not just internally as in the Roman; and, second, sensuous decorative ideas of oriental provenance. In this last respect it is noticeable that as western influence declined in Byzantium so its art became increasingly modified by oriental elements making it more distinctive.

The basis of the structural system was loadbearing walls and massive piers, columns being cast into a subordinate role supporting arcades and galleries. Generally the walls were of thin brickwork in the Roman manner, often with a concrete core. If they were not left plain they were relieved by brickwork patterns or bands of stone and marble, coloured varieties of which were also used to face internal walls. Domes and vaults were constructed of brick or concrete.

In ornament incised decoration and the perforated, cushion or cubiform capitals are hallmarks of the Byzantine-Romanesque style while the love of deep-coloured glass mosaic gleaming richly on a unifying gold ground on the curved surfaces of domes and vaults are equally characteristic and carry forward a long tradition. Mouldings, once so prominent in Roman architecture, are used very rarely and are often replaced by bands of mosaic. Gone is the clear articulation of the Roman interior; all is now merged in an exotic emotional atmosphere that dissolves and blends individual

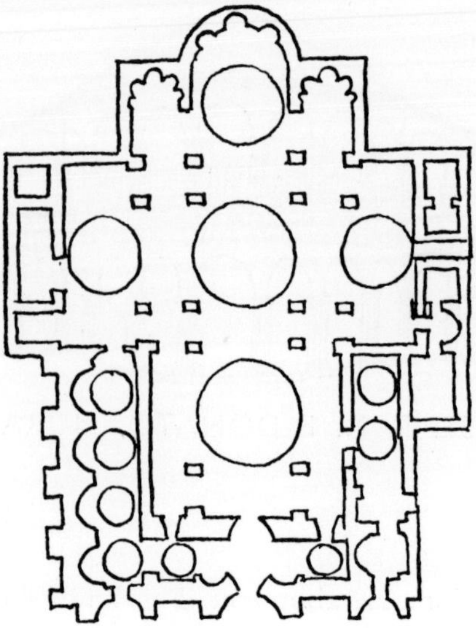

ST MARK'S, VENICE

forms. Campanili, so typical of Romanesque churches elsewhere in Italy, are not a notable feature of Byzantine churches.

On the island of Torcello, near Venice, the Cathedral (with campanile, however) and S. Fosca were remodelled in the early eleventh century and are typically Byzantine. The Cathedral has a remarkable lightness and freshness about it, without an excess of decoration; while S. Fosca, though dreary internally by contrast, has a centralized octagonal plan. At Murano, better known for its glass factories, is the Basilica di Santa Maria e Donato with rich decoration and a most unusual and attractive apse.

But the greatest monument of the Byzantine-Romanesque style is of course the Cathedral of S. Marco in Venice itself, a tenth-century church rebuilt in 1063 by Greeks from Byzantium and Lombard masons so that it has, as one would expect, something of both traditions even if the principal impression is a Byzantine one.

The plan is a Greek cross with eastern apse and follows a Byzantine precedent, the fourth-century Church of the Apostles, Constantinople (demolished 1463), rather than the better-known Hagia Sophia. It was later extended by throwing an aisle round the three sides of the western arm of the cross. Five domes cover the

ST MARK'S, VENICE

building, one large one over the centre space and four smaller ones over the four arms of the cross. This arrangement again goes back to earlier Byzantine churches and appears in some Roman designs too. There are internal arcades through which space flows out from the centre as at S. Vitale.

The entrance façade has five arched portals and a most elaborate decorative scheme of columns, trophies, and mosaic panels integrated by a series of arches which repeat those of the portals on a lesser scale. One would hardly suspect the original simple brick-built structure which lies behind this magnificently encrusted front.

The gilded domes which can be seen rising above are in effect thirteenth-century outer domes on timber frames but they too echo the arch motifs of the main front, and at the same time provide by their static calm the necessary foil to its restless complexity, increased in the fourteenth and fifteenth centuries by the additional encrustation of Gothic crockets, pinnacles, and canopied niches.

The interior of S. Marco, very dark after the bright sunshine of the Piazza, consists essentially of two intersecting volumes dominated by the five low hemispherical surfaces of the original inner domes carried on arches and pendentives. But here again the

CAMPANILI: VENICE AND FLORENCE

formal simplicity is submerged by the wealth of decoration applied over the two hundred years following its construction – splendid pictorial mosaics on walls, vaults, domes, and apse, and ornamental marbles from a great variety of sources such as towns like Aquileia devastated by the barbarians. The whole Roman world was in fact ransacked for materials in this way. The famous bronze horses over the entrance came originally from Rome, were taken to Byzantium, and from thence reached Venice in 1205. Such is the artistic richness of S. Marco that the architectural values are very much obscured by an overburden of decoration which can only be read item by item. Yet the overwhelming impression of an exotic oriental atmosphere does give the interior a certain unity.

The 300-ft campanile actually predates the present church having

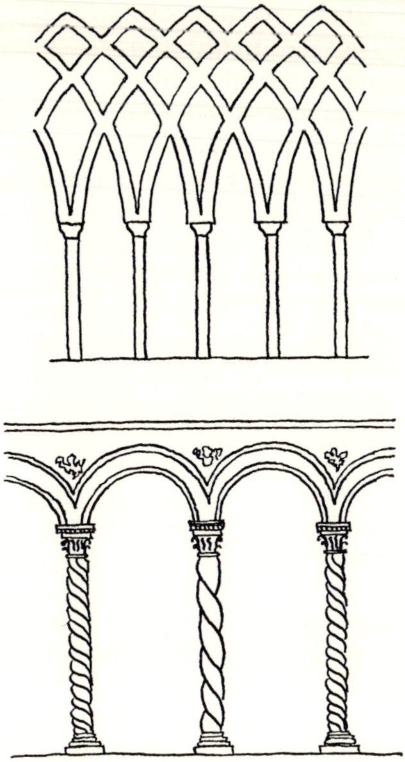

CLOISTERS: ISLAMIC (AMALFI) AND COSMATESQUE (ROME)

been begun in 888, but it has since been rebuilt on two occasions, the last time after its collapse in 1902. Among rare examples of twelfth-century secular architecture a number are to be seen in Venice, notably the Palazzo Loredan and the Palazzo Forsetti (now housing the Municipio), with their arcades of stilted arches springing from cubiform capitals in the Byzantine manner, and the Fondaco dei Turchi, a most elegant piece of commercial architecture. Even though it has since been rebuilt this beautiful warehouse is an eloquent reminder of the basis of Venetian prosperity which, like wool in medieval England, paid for all.

South along the Adriatic coast Ancona is an interesting transitional district where Byzantine-Romanesque, Norman and Islamic influences may be studied in the medieval architecture of S. Maria di Portonuovo and the cathedral.

In the provinces of Calabria and Apulia, occupied by the Byzantines for five centuries, their influence produced a number of small but remarkable churches such as the eleventh-century La Cattolica at Stilo in Calabria, an original variation of the five-domed scheme with five little tower-drums topped by saucer roofs. But their influence may also be detected in much larger churches including the Saracenic and Norman Romanesque architecture of southern Italy and Sicily. These regions had also followed the lead of Rome in building basilicas during the Early Christian period but their architectural tradition was to be modified by a succession of influences reflecting political control and variously felt over a thousand years.

The centrally planned and domed church of La Martorana, Palermo, illustrates Byzantine ideas but with the spread of the moslem world these southern parts of Italy came under the domination of the Arabs with their Islamic architecture during the ninth and tenth centuries.

A feature taken over and given prominence was the pointed arch used structurally, not to be seen in the rest of Europe until the end of the twelfth century when the Crusaders brought it from the Middle East to become one of the essential elements of

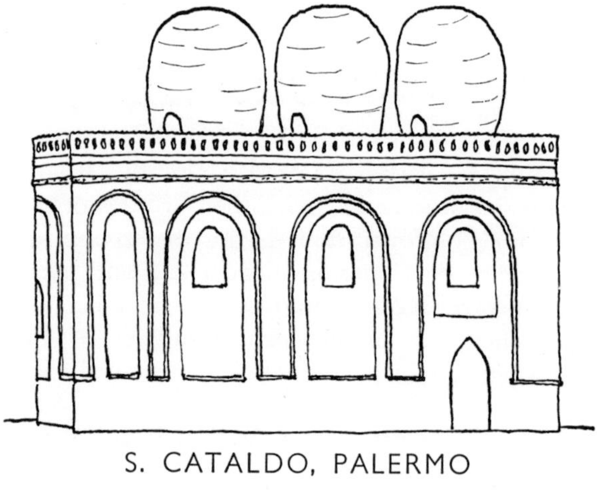

S. CATALDO, PALERMO

the Gothic style. But the Sicilians acquired it more directly long before this, which accounts for the time lag between its occurrence in France and its use in southern Italy.

It was mainly in decorative techniques and motifs, however, that Islamic influence can be observed – in the way mosaics and coloured marbles were used, often in strips externally, and in abstract patterning, since the Koran forbade the portrayal of living forms. Timber roofs too are sometimes given richly moulded and coloured 'stalactite' ceilings.

Thus Sicilian Romanesque churches, small by standards further north, are either basilican with a domed apse, timber roof (they are seldom vaulted) and perhaps a low lantern over the crossing; or they are centrally domical in the Byzantine fashion; or they are a combination of these two types. Some have crypts and entrance façades with projecting porches on columns supported by lions,

CEFALÙ CATHEDRAL

and rose windows above, all of which are features associated with Romanesque churches of north Italy.

But even when dating from after the Norman conquest of the south from 1061 they still exhibit domes on pendentives, a great variety of column types, and Islamic features such as stilted and pointed arches, crested parapets, transennae (pierced window slabs), and interlace and stalactite ornament together with Romanesque pilaster strips on walls connected by small corbelled arcades and rose windows so the general appearance is hybrid and eclectic but distinctly orientalized.

Palermo and district has a number of such churches including the tiny eleventh-century S. Giovanni dei Leprosi and the twelfth-century domed churches of S. Giovanni degli Eremiti, an exotic Norman church with five tall orange tinted domes, the Capella Palatina in the Royal Palace, La Martorana, S. Cataldo with three domes, and the Cathedral (1123), later modified. All are extensively decorated inside, the execution being of a remarkably refined character, and show an interesting mixture of Byzantine and 'Saracenic' features including mosaics in abstract designs, graceful mouldings, intricate carving, stalactite ceilings and elaborate bronze doors similar to those found in southern Italy.

Other cathedrals of the period are Cefalù (1129) – a very handsome design with minaret-like western towers – and Monreale

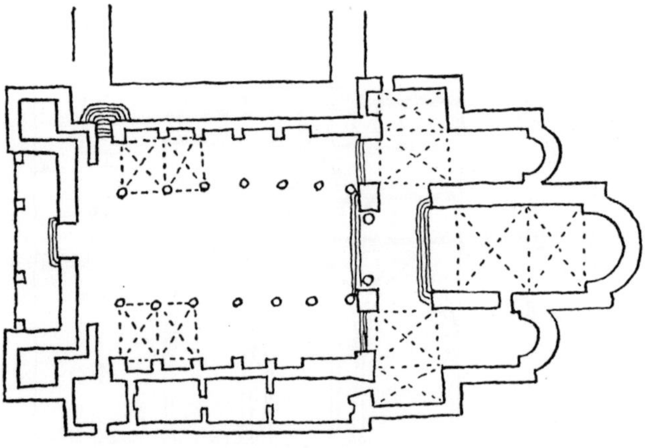

CEFALÙ CATHEDRAL

(1174). The latter appears to be modelled on the Capella Palatina. Its plan is a combination of basilican and Byzantine with eastern apses, a choir above the level of the nave, and a low lantern over the crossing.

The arcades have columns with Byzantine capitals and dosserets from which spring stilted pointed arches while the aisle windows are also pointed. There is lavish use of mosaic, marble, and porphyry to embellish the interior, bronze doors, and an intricate open timber roof highly coloured in the 'Saracenic' manner; all of which produce an effect of considerable richness that contrasts with the severity of the basic forms which have a massive Norman character. The cloisters, remaining from the former monastery,

TRANI CATHEDRAL

with their coupled columns, carved capitals, and pointed arches, also show the same mixture of Byzantine, Islamic, and Norman elements that go to make up Sicilian architecture of the eleventh and twelfth centuries. The splendid contemporary mosaics in the apse, in particular, are by Byzantine craftsmen.

It must be said that the importance of the Norman contribution to southern Romanesque architecture is still a matter of debate. However, on the mainland of Italy the Norman town of Aversa (1029), near Naples, has a fine cathedral with a complete French chevet east end, i.e. with radiating chapels, and there are cathedrals with Norman work at Bari (S. Nicola (1097) the first great Norman church in Apulia), Trani (the Duomo), Siponto (S. Leonardo), and Otranto (with a many columned crypt) all dating from the period of the occupation; and there is SS. Niccolo and Cataldo, Lecce (1180), with its exquisitely enriched Norman doorway. Molfetta Cathedral, like the Normano-Italian Trani, has Lombardic features; but has three domes in octagonal towers as well as twinned eastern campanile. Its date is late twelfth-century.

Notable twelfth-century secular examples in Palermo are the Palazzo La Cuba, and La Zisa (1154), a rectangular Norman keep-like building with crenellations and 'Saracenic' features such as stalactite vaulting and coloured tiles, a blend that effectively reflects the fusion of Norman feudalism and an Islamic life style that took place here on this southern fringe of Europe.

CHAPTER SIX

Gothic

Any date given to mark the beginning of the Gothic style in Italy must be a qualified one, for Romanesque gave place to Gothic only slowly and at different times in different places. It came as a French fashion somewhere about 1200 and when it did so found itself up against a classical tradition that had never really died out in Italy. Early Christian was in a sense the last phase of Roman architecture but much of the same spirit passed into Romanesque and even persisted into the Gothic period when elsewhere it was almost totally absent.

CHIARAVALLE ABBEY

This vitality of the classical tradition may be seen in Italian Gothic in the continued emphasis given to horizontality by means of string courses, cornices, and roofs of very low pitch (instead of the verticality of northern Gothic which never appealed in Italy despite the great height of some of its large churches) but also more fundamentally it is apparent from the fact that the Gothic system of concentrating vault loads and thrusts along a framework of ribs, piers, and buttresses was never wholly adopted; the structural logicality of true Gothic is lacking. The solid flat wall never lost its dominance over openings, piers were massive and widely spaced, and buttresses were little used. The exterior without flying buttresses, pinnacles, and western towers and spires of Gothic type had less variety than was usual in France and the typical interior, instead of giving the impression of great height and a dynamic equilibrium, has a feeling of breadth and static repose.

As for the pointed arch, rightly regarded in Northern Europe as one of the key elements in Gothic, not only did it fail to oust the round arch (to be found, with round-headed windows throughout the period) but also it could not claim to be a specifically Gothic innovation, as it did in trans-Alpine countries, for it had already appeared in Sicily owing to its connection with Arab North Africa. Nevertheless, the dissemination of the pointed arch and rib vault is very much connected with the rapid spread of the reformed order of Cistercians all over Western Europe in the twelfth century and there are examples of their particular version of French

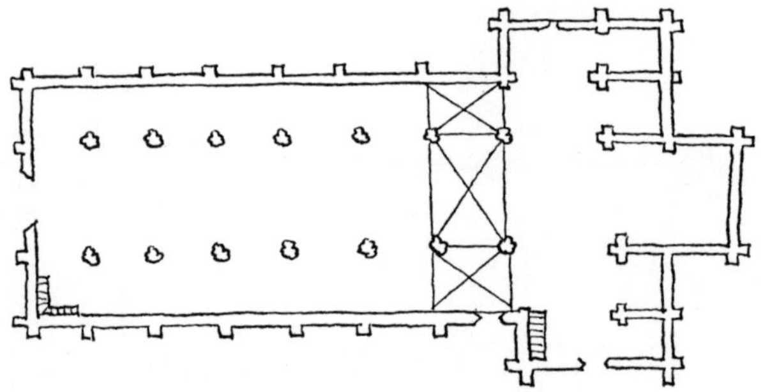

FOSSANOVA ABBEY CHURCH

Gothic to be seen at Chiaravalle near Milan (1135), with its exuberant fourteenth-century crossing tower, and the early thirteenth-century abbey churches of Fossanova and Casamari, south of Rome.

Together with pointed arches, high stone vaults, and a French emphasis on verticality in bay design, we can see here typical Cistercian planning in the eastern parts, modified in the direction of what was to become one of the distinctive features of Italian Gothic architecture – a preference for squarish nave bays and rectangular aisle bays, instead of the other way round which was usual in French Gothic. The same may be observed at the ruined church of San Galgano near Siena, also dating from the early thirteenth century.

In contrast with these 'French' examples, what strikes one about the Italian Gothic church plan is, as we have already remarked, a breadth of space and proportions that owe a good deal to the persistence of classical feeling. This is partly achieved by the tall wide arcades which allow a continuous flow of space from aisle to nave and help to unify them. The arcade supports are either columns in the classical tradition or piers. The latter are sometimes composed of four pilasters arranged in a square and are curiously primitive and unsophisticated compared with examples of northern compound piers, the developed response to the demands of vaulting.

The articulation of interior space, already observed in the bay division of S. Miniato and S. Ambrogio in the Romanesque period, is now carried to its conclusion in the fully vaulted church. Usually the nave is divided for this purpose into square vaulting compartments and the aisles into rectangular ones. This is a striking reversal of the system followed in northern Europe, as we have seen. The vaults are usually quadripartite and their thrust is taken by the solid unbuttressed wall; but tie beams, often of iron, are sometimes used to prevent spreading of both vaults and arcades.

Triforia and clerestories are much less important elements in bay design than was usual in Gothic; the former were often omitted altogether and the latter reduced to small circular windows. Windows generally are small with little tracery, often divided into two lights by a centre shaft supporting two round arches in the Romanesque manner. Pointed arches are sometimes placed in a square frame, and moulded keystones are often a feature.

Elaborate stained glass was not fitted but its place in the decorative scheme was taken by mosaic work and magnificent fresco paintings on walls.

Italian Gothic west fronts carried on much of the classical tradition observed in those of the Romanesque period, modified by the use of such features as steep gablets and pointed arches. They differ from those of northern Gothic in a number of ways and obviously owe more to the earlier façades in Italy.

Thus they are similarly wide independent composition, screening the basilican three-fold division into central nave flanked by lower aisles, and they often have projecting porches with columns supported by recumbent lions, instead of the deep portals of the north. Doorways themselves continue a Romanesque development and are sometimes flanked by small half-columns in recessed orders and are elaborately moulded. Above the porch is commonly a traceried rose window but there is a notable absence of towers, other than the traditional campanile, flying buttresses and pinnacles.

When a single gable covers the entire front it is like an echo of the pediment of a classical temple but in elaborate compositions sometimes a group of three sharply-pointed gables rise screen-like above the flat roof in a way which is closer to the spirit of Gothic. But domes are occasional features and central towers of diminishing stages rise from Romanesque lanterns; and there are the campanili, still resembling Romanesque examples, without spires but often embellished with surface ornament.

The Italian taste for polychromatic effects comes out again in the use of coloured marbles, often applied in alternate bands of contrasting tone – again the horizontal emphasis – to face essentially brick structures. The practice, so different from the grey monotone of northern Gothic stonework, goes back to Romanesque once again, as does the occasional use of coloured marbles disposed in framed panels, and derives ultimately, as we have seen, from the Byzantines' frequent use of stone and brick in alternate layers.

Gothic architecture is noted for the variety of mouldings which were developed in each phase but Italian Gothic was less inventive and they have not the same importance, sometimes being replaced by strips of marble. Mouldings found in the brick and terracotta churches of Lombardy still resemble classical mouldings and in doorways are the same in arch and jamb. In this medium some ornamental detailing is very fine, in both senses of the word. Carved capitals and sculpture in marble are often of a very high standard too, as in the new interpretations of the old Corinthian theme, less foliate and much closer to classical types than northern Gothic carving. In the thirteenth century the Cosmati were still very active and their style persists.

These then are the general characteristics of Italian Gothic architecture. It was not, however, associated with a period of political unity; it was the great age of the communes, the city states. On the one hand feudalism had never really struck deep roots in Italy and not a large number of medieval churches were built; on the other hand the permanent state of rivalry between the communes ensured considerable support for large prestige works and fostered individual differences, so that instead of the chronological changes discernible in, say, English Gothic architecture there are stylistic differences due to regionalism.

In the brief review which follows it is therefore convenient to deal with the principal buildings of the period in three sections, North, Central and Southern Italy with Sicily, pointing out their regional characteristics at appropriate points.

The greatest Gothic monument in the whole of Italy is Milan Cathedral (1386) in the north, but as both French and German master masons are known to have worked on it it is not typically

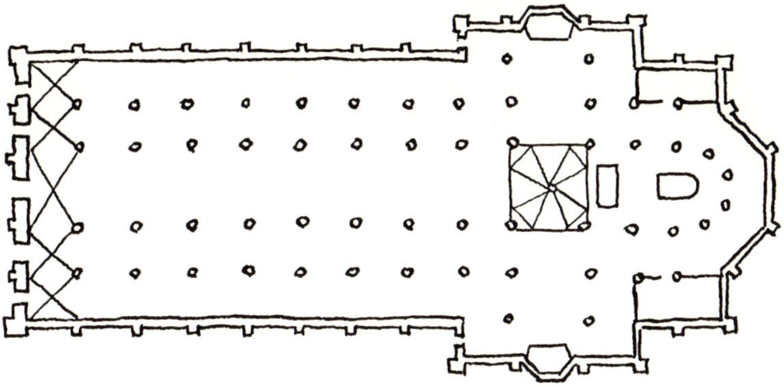

MILAN CATHEDRAL

Italian. We therefore begin with a building whose features are in many respects at variance with the general characteristics just described.

Milan is one of the largest medieval cathedrals having a cruciform plan, very broad, with double aisles, broad shallow transepts, and a polygonal east end of the German type enclosing a French ambulatory. Enormous compound piers of the nave arcade have tabernacle capitals and support the high vault above which is the low pitched marble-slabbed roof. There is no triforium (the inner aisles are very high) and there is only a small clerestory.

The large traceried windows, especially the three very large ones of the apse, are not typically Italian even though north Italy went in for larger windows than other regions did. For obvious climatic reasons central Italy and the south favoured smaller openings and more shady arcades than the cooler north. The latter were usually composed of slightly pointed arches, often with iron ties to counteract their spread, supported by slim columns with Corinthianesque capitals.

MILAN CATHEDRAL

Returning to the Duomo at Milan, in contrast to the gloom of the interior the outside gleams with crystalline marble and has an attenuated spiky outline which is unusual for Italian Gothic. The complication of wall and flying buttresses is French and there are over a hundred and thirty tall, delicately wrought pinnacles and statues which with tracery and other features are associated with that elaborative phase of the late Gothic style known as Flamboyant.

A polygonal lantern with a domical vault over the crossing was topped with a high flèche in the middle of the eighteenth century. Even the Gothic parts of the cathedral, however, were not finished until 1485 so that building extended well into the period of the Early Renaissance by which time Florence had many buildings in the new revived classical style. The west front was partly finished in the later sixteenth century, but not completed until the early nineteenth. It is a rare example of late Gothic in Italy.

The Certosa, Pavia (1396), an important Carthusian monastery, is constructed in a different material – the brick and terracotta favoured in Lombardy because of the absence of good building

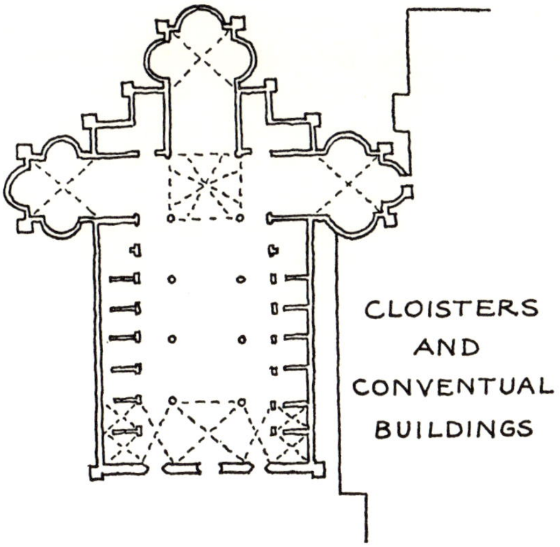

LA CERTOSA, PAVIA

stone, though no doubt its colour and fine detailing compared with the bolder modelling of central Italy were appreciated for their own sake – as in S. Marie del Carmine (1370), in the same city, which continues Lombard Romanesque with subtle Gothic modifications. The Certosa too shows some foreign influence: the cruciform plan of the church has square nave bays and rectangular aisle bays in the Italian fashion but the triapsal choir and transepts are German, like some of the external features. The arcaded cloisters have much fine terracotta ornament.

The internal dome, external central tower, and façade are late fifteenth century and are in a later style that in its turn had a great influence on French architecture of the early sixteenth century, the style of the Loire châteaux. The façade with its golden marble and rich assembly of Early Renaissance features and fine sculpture, is said to be by Borgognone; but another architect associated with the Certosa is Giovanni Antonio Amadeo who did the very elaborate Colleone chapel at Bergamo (c. 1470), Renaissance building. Also at Bergamo is S. Agostino with its large fifteenth-century windows whilst at Ferrara Cathedral there are elaborate porches.

At Bologna, S. Petronio (1390) by Antonio di Vincenzo, the nave arcade is widely spaced as in the Duomo, Florence; whereas the effect of the aisles diminishing in height from the central nave is similar to that at Milan. This arrangement is clearly expressed in the entrance front which has a magnificent doorway by the sculptor Della Quercia. The east end of a French chevet type was never built. S. Francesco (1236), on the other hand, has a radiating east end that is distinctly northern Gothic and for a mendicant church is untypical. Its local influence, however, was considerable.

S. Antonio, Padua (1232), is a church of obviously Byzantine inspiration with its seven domes on pendentives (placed over the square nave bays, the transepts, and the choir) and its attenuated turrets. The chevet east end is, however, again French Gothic while the exterior preserves Romanesque features such as the open arcade of the entrance façade and dwarf arcading at the eaves.

The mention of Byzantine influence is one which inevitably in Italy suggests the architecture of Venice whose highly individual version of Gothic so enraptured Ruskin. Like the Republic itself it was compounded of many influences, not just Byzantine,

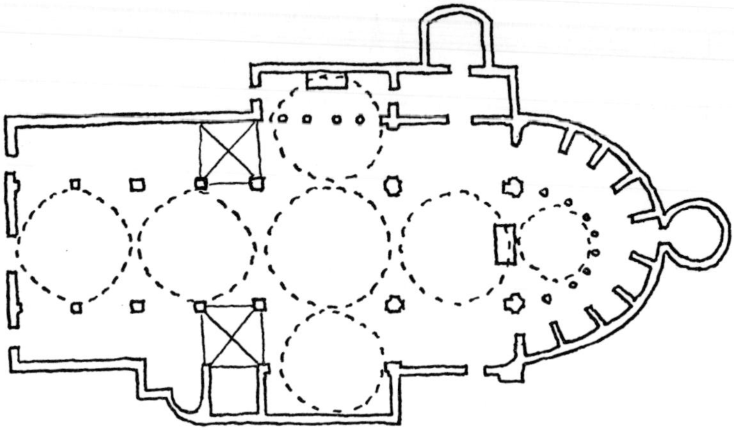

S. ANTONIO, PADUA

but classical and oriental. With its warm tones, quick movements of light and shade and general picturesqueness it is well suited to the reflective waters of that most beautiful and colourful of cities.

Venice of course was a great trading power, holding 'the gorgeous east in fee', whose wealth and material concerns found as much expression in the palazzi or large town houses of its merchant-nobility as in its churches. The greatest of these in a sense is the Palazzo Ducale, the Doge's palace, which is certainly the largest of Venetian palaces and perhaps the best example of Venetian Gothic architecture, though there is much internally of a later date.

Enjoying a stable government, the security which comes from economic strength, and a relatively isolated position, Venice had no need for palaces to be formidably solid and severe like those of Florence, and this can be seen in the open arcaded façades of the Palazzo Ducale, the seafront façade (*c.* 1345) and the Piazzetta front (1423) by G. and B. Bon. The lowest storey is all open, the one above with light open tracery, making a transition to the solid wall later added higher up. The upper arcade is composed of smaller pointed arches of the ogee type moving in a quicker rhythm and the marble capitals from which the pointed arches spring are carved with great delicacy. The total effect is one of

PALAZZO DUCALE, VENICE

great splendour and richness, a fitting symbol of the Republic at the height of its power.

The arrangement of the arcades of the Doge's palace with wider arches below and narrow ones above in contrasting rhythm can also be seen in later palace designs in Venice such as the Palazzo Pisani and the Ca' d'Oro. The latter was built in 1421 for the Contarini family by the same architects responsible for the Palazzo Ducale. Its title comes from the liberally gilded (but unfinished) façade, the windows of which are grouped centrally, lighting the

CA' D'ORO, VENICE

principal apartments on the first floor, and are set off in the Venetian manner by areas of plain flanking wall. The two upper storeys have characteristic lace-like tracery and, at the side, balconies, features abounding in Venice. The crested parapet is in the 'Saracenic' manner, an example of orientalism in Venetian architecture. Such effusions are not typical of other parts of Italy and may thus owe as much to eastern influences as to decorated Gothic and certainly the taste for them did.

Another highly ornamental if tiny work is the Palazzetto (1487), probably by Pietro Lombardo. A work of the jeweller's art almost, its polychromatic marbles and mosaics are here carried to a degree that anywhere but Venice would be regarded as excessive.

The typical Venetian palazzo, being open, does not need the internal cortile found elsewhere in Italy. Other 'blocks' with similar features to the Ca' d'Oro, such as the characteristic Venetian tracery which is geometrical in type, finishing in a horizontal line which makes it adaptable to the flat ceilings of buildings other than churches, are the fifteenth-century palazzi of the Contarini-Fansan and the Cavalli on the Grand Canal. They seem to derive a good deal of their effect from the reflection and movement of the water below, so much so that it is impossible not to think that their architects took this into consideration as a design factor. The transition from the Gothic to the Renaissance styles may be studied in the Palazzo Vendramin-Calergi (*c.* 1500) by Pietro Lombardo as well as in the cortile of the Palazzo Ducale (1490) already referred to.

Though the Vendramin-Calergi Palace is an essentially classical composition, balanced and symmetrical with revived orders, it still has mullioned and traceried windows.

The Piazza San Marco and the Piazzetta, though most of their surrounding buildings are of a post-medieval date, are nevertheless good instances of the spacious squares which sometimes formed the hearts of great medieval cities, and were early examples of urban design.

Turning again from secular to ecclesiastical architecture we begin by considering two Venetian churches built for the new orders of the twelfth century, the Franciscans and the Dominicans, and since the character of these new orders bore importantly on the buildings erected for their use it will be necessary first to explain briefly this relationship in order to understand better the individual designs.

Earlier medieval orders had been French in origin and character. St Francis's protest was against the growing materialism of the merchant cities and their world-wide commerce and Franciscans were vowed to poverty. Like them the Dominicans were evangelist friars who moved among the people had no need of the monastic communities of earlier orders who had removed themselves from the world. They required instead preaching halls where large congregations could gather to hear them. Thus the typical friars' church was a big, often aisleless, building, without the large choir required by a monastic church, from which most of the earlier ecclesiastical mystery and gloom had been banished.

The church of S. Maria Gloriosa dei Frari, the Frari, is typically north Italian in its fine use of brick and terracotta and has a magnificent interior, its massive piers bridged by timber tie beams to counter the thrust of the brick vaulting. The plan is cruciform with a splendid polygonal apse with two tiers of traceried win-

THE FRARI, VENICE

dows and six transeptal chapels. The pointed aisle windows are longer than usual, in the north Italian fashion, and there is Romanesque eave arcading all round the church, the tripartite west front of which is pierced by four circular windows and finished off with three pinnacled canopies. The ascription of the Frari (1250) is doubtful; Vasari has it by Nicola Pisano, the sculptor, yet there is the magnificent tomb erected to Fra Scipione Bon. The campanile is finished with an octagonal lantern.

Built for the new Franciscan order this church shows one of the answers to the need of the friars for large preaching churches. Another solution may be seen in the Dominican church of SS. Giovanni e Paolo (1234) in the same city for there was nothing here comparable to the standardization of the Cistercians. Another fine brick exterior crowned by a later dome presents inside a large vaulted space, cruciform with a polygonal apsed choir and transeptal chapels. Here the Doges of Venice lie buried. Of the same family as these two friars' churches is S. Nicolò, Treviso (1303).

Verona, not far from Venice has two attractive thirteenth-

LOGGIA DE MILITI, CREMONA

century churches: S. Andrea Vercelli and S. Anastasia with a campanile resembling St Mark's, while other medieval structures are the Palazzo del Comune of the same century, the late twelfth-century Torre del Comune, later finished with a tall fourteenth-century octagonal lantern, a graceful symbol of civic pride (though the mid-thirteenth-century Torazzo at Cremona – where there is the fine Loggia de Militi – is the tallest in Italy) and a fourteenth-century bridge over the River Adige, fortified with towered piers and Ghibelline battlements. With this the high single-arched bridge across the Serchio near Lucca may be compared, a Romanesque structure dating from about 1000.

Other medieval secular buildings in north Italy, civic and commercial, are the Palazzo della Regione, Padua (1306) – with its great boat-like wooden ceiling – the largest medieval town hall in Italy, and the Palazzo Pubblico, Piacenza (1281), which, like the Loggia dei Mercanti, Bologna (1382), by Vicenzo again, the architect of S. Petronio, has a ground storey of open arcades with traceried windows, a projecting 'ringhiera' or balcony from which the citizens could be addressed, and Ghibelline battlements above. In Mantua is the battlemented Palazzo Bonacolsi.

LOGGIA DEI MERCANTI, BOLOGNA

In central Italy we find that just as brickwork and terracotta were characteristic of Lombardy so here the Italian taste for polychromatic effects comes out in the use of coloured marbles often applied in alternate bands of contrasting tone to face essentially brick structures. The practice is well exemplified in the cathedrals of Siena and Orvieto.

Siena (1226), spacious and sophisticated, is cruciform in plan with shallow transepts and a wide choir built over the Baptistry crypt of S. Giovanni and set against the slope of the site, the south-western parts of the church being raised on a stepped platform. The interior shows lavish use of marble stripes on piers and walls and beautiful marble paving. The unusually shaped hexagonal crossing is covered with a dome on squinch arches. The cathedral was to be a monument to civic pride as well as a house of God so that all the artists of Siena contributed to its embellishment. There is an ornately sculptured entrance façade (1370), better related to nave and aisles than is customary, with black and white marble strips, mosaic decoration, and three portals topped by gablets and a rose window, the portal being echoed by the

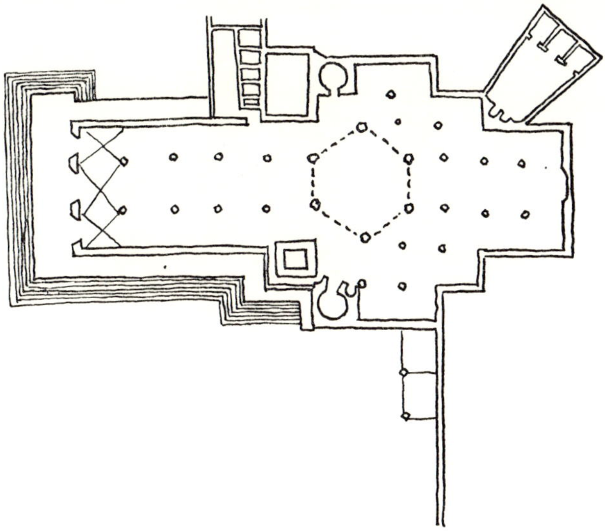

SIENA CATHEDRAL

three gables above. Pinnacled turrets here and on the high campanile and a lantern on the dome provide vertical Gothic accents.

Here is another pulpit by Nicola Pisano. It is interesting to see sculpture undergoing something of the same transformation towards the Gothic style that architecture was undergoing. The two equally famous pulpits by his son Giovanni, especially that in Sant' Andrea, Pistoia, are even more Gothic and dramatically intense.

The façade of Siena Cathedral is the work of Giovanni Pisano, pupil of his father, Nicola; both were architects as well as sculptors. The thirteenth-century work at Pisa has already been referred to in the chapter on Romanesque but the cloisters of Giovanni di Simone's Campo Santo, Pisa (1278) are a notable work in the Gothic style, tall, elegant, round-arched arcades with open tracery. These too are by Giovanni Pisano who also built the oratory of S. Maria della Spina (1323) which, with its crocketed gables and canopy

S. M. DELLA SPINA, PISA

pinnacles, seems to owe something to the jeweller's architecture of shrines. Generally the fourteenth century in Italy was not a period propitious for church building owing to the unsettled state of the church, the Babylonian captivity being followed by the Great Schism. But Siena has two of the most important Gothic churches of central Italy apart from the Duomo. Brick-built and striped internally like the latter, both S. Domenico and S. Francesco date from the early fourteenth century.

The Palazzo della Signoria (Pubblico) in Siena (1288) is one of the largest medieval town halls in Italy, so representative of the flourishing civic and commercial life of the city states (Italy was largely unhampered by feudalism) with their growing institutions. Like the Palazzo Ducale in Venice it shows that economic power can find expression in magnificent buildings of considerable aesthetic merit and need not be symbolized by utilitarian structures

PALAZZO PUBBLICO, SIENA

on the one hand or vulgar display on the other, which have so often been the alternatives in modern industrial society.

The façade of the Palazzo della Signoria is composed of three tiers of pointed windows and has a high centre and battlemented parapet. With its large porch and its exceedingly tall crenellated and machicolated watch tower, from which the tocsin could be rung, it is perhaps the best and most elaborate of these town halls. Certainly it is the most effective design. Inside are the impressive allegories of Good and Bad Government by the Sienese painter Ambrogio Lorenzetti.

Other interesting examples of thirteenth-century town halls may be seen at Perugia, and Volterra (both Palazzo dei Priori), and at Montepulciano; rather stern and thick-set fortress-like buildings with battlements and centrally placed parapeted watch towers. The Palazzo Comunale, Piacenza (1280), is a more elaborate and sophisticated design while Viterbo has in addition a fine medieval papal palace (1266) and remains of its town walls and medieval streets. Of about the same date are the crenellated walls, pentagonal towers, and fine gatehouse of Montagnana; and on a smaller scale the walled town of Villafranca di Verona.

So far no reference has been made to the castellated architecture of Italy. In the north are the interesting thirteenth-century keep-and-curtain wall Castello Scaligero with its fortified harbour and Ghibelline battlements overlooking Lake Garda and, not far away, the late medieval Castello di S. Giorgio, Mantua, with its Mantegna frescoes lodged within its formidable walls. Both Mantua and the Castello Estense at Ferrara (1385) show the later medieval preference for a compact plan with four angle towers and greater ease and comfort internally.

Another fourteenth-century example is the castle of Gradara, near Rimini, a stronghold of the powerful Malatesta family which was soon to patronize the new art of the Renaissance. It shows how the old static keep-and-curtain wall system was replaced by a more dynamic complex with opportunities to outflank an attacker by means of mural and corner towers. Fenis in the Val D'Aosta shows the even later shift already referred to, towards more spacious accommodation coupled with greater compactness and concentration; but its mass is irregular and diversified by a variety of picturesque towers. The great castle of the Visconti at

FENIS CASTLE, VAL D'AOSTA

Pavia (1360) is both castle and palace with large windows and open 'cloistered' interior elevations.

The castle at Volterra (1343), not far from Siena, is a remarkably impressive example of European fortification though it is now a prison. It has a high central keep and squat round bastion towers at the angles of the curtain wall. All have beautifully proportioned deep machicolations which carry forward the parapets above the wall faces and their aesthetic qualities show clearly that, while military needs were uppermost, this aspect was not overlooked by their designers.

Orvieto Cathedral (1290) – to return once more to ecclesiastical architecture – is a basilican church with a screen front of the type just described at Siena. The narrow nave is flanked by tall columns carrying round arches with pointed clerestory windows above.

The whole interior, roofed in the basilican manner with an open timber roof, is everywhere striped with black and white marbles. Outside, the walls are also ornamented by horizontal stripes of contrasting marble.

Both the cathedrals of Orvieto and Asti (1348), 20 miles east of Turin, have been attributed to Arnolfo di Cambio, another pupil of Nicola Pisano and sculptor of the ciborium in S. Paolo

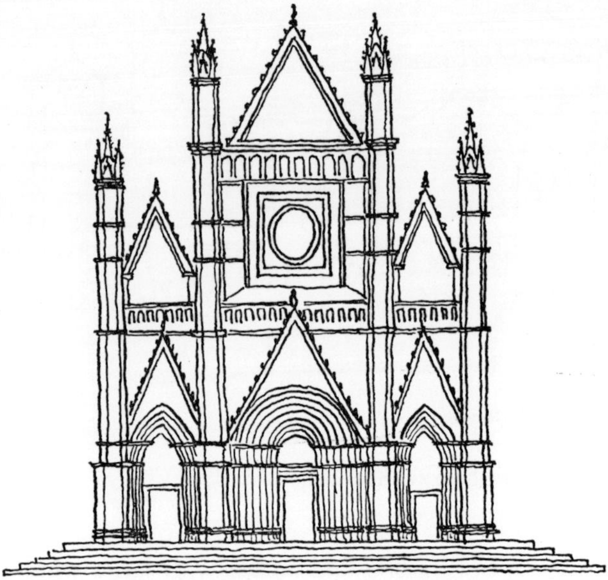

ORVIETO CATHEDRAL

fuori le Mura, Rome (1285); but a far more famous Florentine church is the Cathedral of S. Maria della Fiore begun by Arnolfo in 1294.

Like Siena Cathedral the Duomo at Florence was built as an expression of civic pride, a great corporate enterprise intended to rival Siena and Pisa; and was added to over the next 150 years by several architects – Taddeo Gaddi, Audrea da Firenze, and Francesco Talenti who modified Arnolfo's plan (1351). Its present plan is a Latin cross with centralized eastern parts; an octagon to which are added three tribunes (the transepts and choir) terminating in polygonal apses with radiating chapels.

The breadth of the nave and wide spacing of the arcade (there are only four rectangular bays) are Italian characteristics creating an interior that by the standards of northern Gothic is very clear, static, and spacious. The massive piers have attached pilasters and though they support an arcade of pointed arches without mouldings their heavy bases and capitals and the breadth of the arches counteract any Gothic verticality of emphasis. So does the

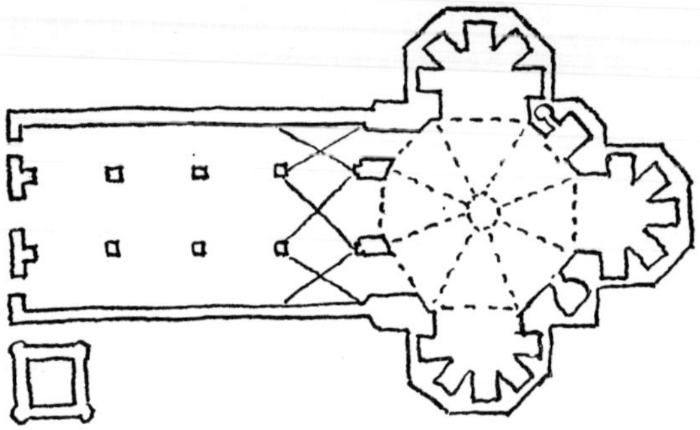

THE DUOMO, FLORENCE

horizontal string course or cornice. There is no triforium and the clerestory windows are round. Domical cross vaults emphasize the bay division and therefore help to clarify the interior space, whilst further articulation is produced by the picking out of various members in a darker tone than the white background.

The exterior walls have small traceried windows and much coloured marble panelling as surface decoration but there are no buttresses or pinnacles. The west front was never finished and what is there now is a respectable Gothic revival by Emilio de Fabria dating from 1866. By the time Brunelleschi began his dome over the great central octagon in 1420 the Early Renaissance was under way and further discussion of this interesting church, in which we can study the transformation from Gothic to Renaissance styles taking place, is therefore deferred until the next chapter.

The fourteenth-century campanile, with larger Gothic windows than most and more coloured marble panelling, is by Giotto, better known as the painter of the frescoes in the Arena Chapel, Padua, where some of the first stirrings of the Renaissance may be seen. The third of this great group is the large octagonal Baptistry, perhaps going back to the eighth century. The walls are decorated with black and white marble inlay in the Romanesque manner and over the shallow internal dome is a low roof and lantern. Its bronze doors (1402) by Lorenzo Ghiberti are among the most famous sculptural works transitional to the Early Renaissance.

Arnolfo also worked on the Abbey Church of the Badia (1284) completed in the Early Renaissance style by Brunelleschi, and on S. Croce, Florence (1294). Friar's churches have already been briefly discussed. S. Croce, one of the largest churches ever, was built for the Franciscans as a great Gothic basilica with a wide open timber roof (commoner than vaulting in Italy) requiring the support of only slender piers. The nave and aisle bays are both rectangular, yet the feeling of the interior is one of openness, of classical breadth and calm. The façade, like that of the Duomo, is as recent as the last century.

One of the special features of S. Croce is the large number of chapels it contains, such as the Bardi with Giotto's famous 'Death of St Francis'. In this, as in its clarity, spaciousness, and horizontality it compares with S. Maria Novella (1246), a church for the new Dominican order, reputedly by two Dominicans, Frati Sisto and Ristoro. Again we have an aisled church, with square nave bays, rectangular aisle bays, round clerestory windows, and internal tonal contrasts, all Italian Gothic features, where the aisles are so high and shallow and the arcades so wide as to give the impression of a large hall. This is typical of the architecture of the medicant orders and was a development towards that spatial unity which was to become characteristic of Late Gothic against Early Gothic, where nave and aisles were kept much more as separate entities. The frescoes are Ghirlandaio's finest.

S. Maria Novella is a vaulted cruciform church with adjoining cloisters. Like S. Croce it too has a later façade but this time

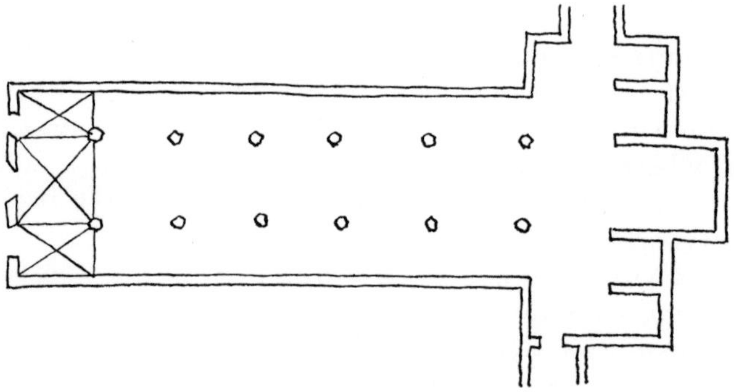

S. M. NOVELLA, FLORENCE

only a little later. It is an interesting work by the Renaissance architect Alberti and as such it is described in the following chapter.

The two Dominicans who built S. Maria Novella are also credited with S. Maria sopra Minerva, Rome (1280), greatly restored in the nineteenth century. At that time Rome still had a great many Early Christian churches so that hardly any were built there during the Middle Ages and S. Maria sopra Minerva, so-called because it stands on the ruins of a Temple of Minerva, has the distinction of being the only Gothic church in Rome. It has like S. Maria Novella classical-looking columns and bears a close resemblance to that church; if it is less beautiful it has a marked 'Florentine' character.

A fourth Gothic church in Florence of special interest is Or San Michele (1336) by Arnolfo or Taddeo Gaddi. Here again the ground storey hints at the Renaissance with the traceried windows so set as to suggest the ghost of a Roman pier and arch system. Other significant features are the elaborate window tracery and especially the sculptured Renaissance figures by Ghiberti and Donatello in canopied niches.

Like the other great trading cities of Europe in the Middle Ages Florence built its complement of civic buildings including the Palazzo del Podesta (Bargello), 1255, which was the headquarters of the chief magistrate and served as court and prison and the Palazzo Vecchio (della Signoria), 1298, the town hall, attributed to Arnolfo once again. A quadrangular building with inner cortile, its main elevation is divided into storeys by horizontal string courses and pierced with windows (small and high up on the ground floor for security) of pointed arches separated by a shaft in the Romanesque manner. Both the Bargello and the Palazzo Vecchio are somewhat severe in aspect and have the usual high towers.

There is also the Loggia dei Lanzi (1376), a setting for civic ceremony, whose huge vaulted semi-circular arcade on compound piers was intended to be part of an ambitious design for the whole Piazza della Signoria, and another fourteenth-century arcade is the Bigallo or foundling shelter. The famous Ponte Vecchio over the River Arno has elegantly curved arches, massive piers, and a street of shops in the fashion of large medieval bridges.

As with the Cistercian abbeys and the Cathedral of Milan, at the pilgrimage church of S. Francesco, Assisi, there is evidence of a foreign hand in a design that differs from the usual versions of the Gothic style found in Italy. There are really two churches, a lower dating from 1228 and an upper built over it twenty-five years later, standing at the centre of a great complex of rose-coloured conventual buildings, splendidly sited on the southern slopes of Mount Subasio.

Both churches are aisleless and vaulted. The lower one has a vaulted transept resembling work done in Anjou at this time and a polygonal apse. The upper church is loftier and has widely spaced engaged piers carrying the vault with relatively small windows set between so as to allow plenty of room for the frescoes by Cimabue and Giotto which are such a feature at Assisi. The building and decorating of S. Francesco gave the first great impulse to the development of Italian painting.

The main exterior features are the arcades of the substructure and cloisters, the buttresses of the upper church, like round stair towers with flying buttresses assisting, and the campanile of a Lombard Romanesque type. S. Fortunato, Todi (1292) is another Franciscan church with Poitevin antecedents, a fine thirteenth-century design like S. Francesco, Gubbio; and the cathedral at Arezzo (1277) has the compactness and breadth characteristic of both Central Italian Romanesque and friars' churches. Gubbio, often overlooked, has other fine Gothic buildings in the cathedral and in the civic architecture associated with Angelo da Orvieto, all from the fourteenth century.

Lastly we come to the architecture of the Gothic period in southern Italy. In this peripheral part of Europe, where highly individual characteristics had been developed as a result of previous influences, the Gothic style made little impact; though Naples has two or three from the fourteenth century – executed under Angevin influence – notably S. Chiara, which contains the tomb of Robert of Anjou, and in Messina is S. Francesco (1254), a new variant of the hall-church of the mendicant orders.

The great cathedral of Palermo, basilican like that of Messina, was altered towards the end of the fifteenth century however. It was given a large porch with tall elegant stilted arches, which like the west façade is 'Saracenic' in style, and horizontal crenellations resembling those of the Palazzo Ducale in Venice. Tall towers provide strong vertical accents, for the dome, of course, is a Renaissance addition. The exterior walls are decorated with stone of two colours, the best features being the polychrome interlaced blind arcading of the apses.

The Palazzo Arcivescovile has sophisticated fifteenth-century flamboyant tracery which must owe something to Islamic inspiration and the Palazzo Duca S. Stefano, Taormina (1396) has other variations of Gothic windows and a striking cornice.

It is well known that the experience of the Crusades modified European castle design and that the thirteenth century saw the introduction of the concentric castle, a system of curtain walls punctuated by mural towers, sometimes one inside the other, the inner wall of course higher and therefore commanding the outer one.

The crusaders took the type from the Saracens, who in turn had taken it from Byzantium, and they added a unity and symmetry in planning that introduced an aesthetic element into the design, over and above its efficacy as fortification. The Emperor Frederick II who came near to uniting medieval Italy built several in south Italy and Sicily at Lucera, Catania (Castel Ursino), Siracusa (Castel Maniaco) and near Andria in Apulia (Castel del Monte, *c.* 1240), the finest of all. This is a bold unusual octagon with polygonal towers at the angles. The octagon is a range of

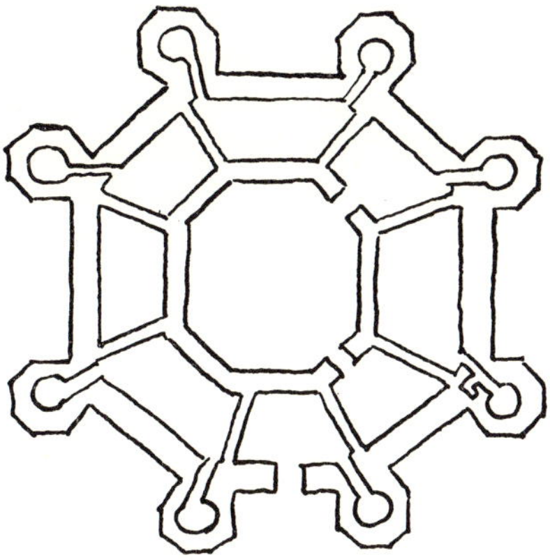

CASTEL DEL MONTE, ANDRIA

buildings in depth, the inner wall surrounding a small courtyard. There is something Roman about the conception as well as Burgundian Gothic, which is not surprising perhaps when one recalls the Roman motifs of the same emperor's gate at Capua and the use of pediments with rib vaults in other buildings put up at his direction. Truly the classical style in Italy was never totally submerged.

At Naples the Castel Nuovo (1279) is a tall rectangular fortification with machicolated curtain walls, now pierced with windows of Renaissance design, and round towers. There is a splendid sculptured gateway (1453) of massive proportions, astonishingly antique in feeling.

No account of the Gothic style of Italy, however brief, can conclude without some reference to the superb sculptures and paintings which enhance and in some instances surpass, the architecture which they adorn. The Arena Chapel, for example, would be little without Giotto's frescoes (1305), the forerunner of so many magnificent series to follow in the quattrocento some of which have been mentioned in connection with the buildings where they are to be found.

The Pisano pulpits have also been mentioned and there is the early Fontana Maggiore at Perugia by Nicola; but these are only exceptional examples of a vast wealth of carving and sculpture – altars, reredoses, aumbries and canopy tombs, like those of the Scaglier at Verona – that despite the use of motifs such as crocketed gables often employ distinctly classical forms and when compared with northern Gothic are seen to be infused with a distinctly classical feeling, especially in the figure sculpture.

For this reason the Gothic style was destined to be shorter lived in Italy than in any other country; the indigenous classical tradition was too strong. Moreoever the Renaissance began here earlier than anywhere for a variety of reasons and though there is no doubt that the influx of Byzantine Greek scholars, following the fall of Constantinople to the Turks in 1453, has been very much overstressed as a contributory cause, there can be equally no doubt that a cultural influence from this direction much before this date did tend to limit considerably the ability of Gothic to take a firm hold in Italy.

Be that as it may, Italy was already well advanced with her new Early Renaissance style in the fifteenth century when the other countries of Europe were still evolving their variants of Late Gothic. It is a measure of the difference between them that St George's Chapel, Windsor, in all its Perpendicular rich elaboration, was only begun in 1481, a generation after Brunelleschi had finished his elegant Foundling Hospital in Florence, a building in the van of the Renaissance, and raised in a totally different spirit.

CHAPTER SEVEN

Early Renaissance, c. 1420 - c. 1500

THAT great cultural movement the Renaissance – the rebirth of classical art and learning and, in its wider sense, liberation of the human spirit and intellect – which with its origins in the thirteenth century swept in the fifteenth like a great tidal wave over Italy and immersed Europe for the next two hundred years, began in the city-states of Tuscany, in particular in the republic of Florence.

Architecture was affected by the new spirit rather than literature and the visual arts, but already in Florence the new cathedral of S. Maria del Fiore and the churches of S. Maria Novella and S. Croce, though Gothic buildings, displayed a clarity and spaciousness that were conspicuous qualities of classical architecture. In this way it seems the Florentines especially had prepared a fertile seed bed for the ideas and forms of Renaissance architecture to strike root in.

What were these ideas and forms? Briefly, for we shall still examine them in greater detail and show them in practice as soon as we come to describe actual examples of Renaissance buildings, they involved a rejection of medieval asymmetry and variety for a classical sense of balance and regularity, an emphasis upon the horizontal rather than the Gothic vertical, or at any rate an equilibrium of columns and pilasters, with their entablatures, pediments, mouldings and ornament, applied with more restraint, regularity, and careful positioning than decoration was applied in medieval architecture. Naves of churches have fewer bays and there is a reversion to semi-circular cross vaults. Doorways are square-headed or pedimented. Finally, there is the achievement of harmony throughout a design by employing mathematical proportions in all the parts, related to the basic plan, the adoption of a modular system. Clearly the emphasis is on design, for most problems of a stone and brick technology had been solved by the end of the Middle Ages; 'composition' meant much more to Renaissance architects than 'structural expression', and for this they have sometimes been criticized.

More than this, however, goes to the make-up of Renaissance architecture. So much would imply mere copyism. Despite similarities between the ideologies and values of the Ancient World and Renaissance Italy, antiquity has now to be infused with the nobility of the Christian ideal; new types of buildings, churches and palaces, have to be designed, and, unconsciously perhaps at first, a new ethos and a new sense of independence and individuality have to find expression in fresh variations upon classical themes.

The leading figure among the architects and artists of Florence at this time was Filipo Brunelleschi whose work was to initiate a new age in architecture as Masaccio's frescoes in S. Maria del Carmine did at this time in painting. Though Brunelleschi had been trained as a goldsmith his main interest was architecture and it became his avowed purpose to revive the study and practice of the architecture of Ancient Rome. To this end with his friend Donatello, the first great sculptor in the Renaissance style, he visited Rome, where he stayed for some time studying and drawing the Roman remains of that city. Many more survived there than exist today and there is no doubt that they had begun to haunt the imagination of the pioneers of a new age.

Brunelleschi's first job in Florence after winning the competition for it was to provide a dome over the spacious crossing of the new cathedral (1420). Spanning such a large area was a great technical achievement. He did it without using centering and making use of his practical study of Roman ruins, for he was the first Renaissance architect to understand their constructional principles and to adapt them to new ends.

The dome is octagonal, the first use of the double shell, and for lightness is a ribbed structure with bricks in the upper parts rather than stone, as in the lower. It is this ribbed construction, reminiscent of the Gothic vault, and its slightly pointed profile which has earned it the epithet 'Gothic'. It is however one of the first great monuments of the Renaissance, a work of genius, and a source of considerable influence on the domed structures which were to follow in such large numbers. Unlike earlier shallow, partly obscured domes, such as those of the Pantheon or the Byzantine church of Hagia Sophia in Constantinople, it was intended to

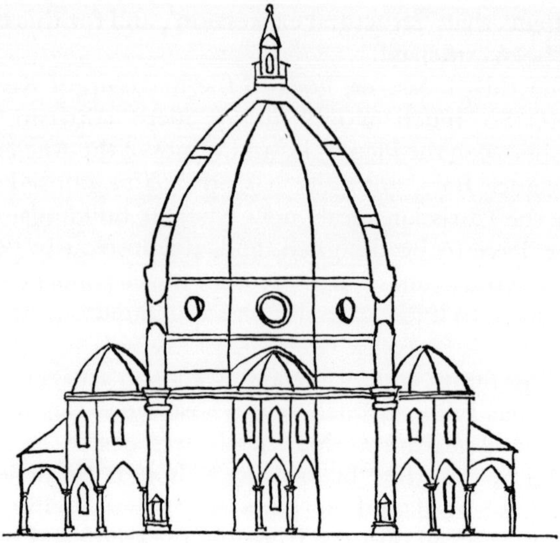

THE DUOMO, FLORENCE

dominate the exterior mass of the great church in a new way. Thus it is raised up on an octagonal drum pierced with circular windows to light the crossing. The fact that the drum has an external abutment is a constructional reason for pointing the dome.

Unfortunately the interior effect is partly mitigated by the presence of the nave and it may have been the realization that a centralized plan would have served it better that encouraged later architects to explore the possibilities of Greek cross and square plans for Renaissance domed churches. Nevertheless it is a design of much grandeur, the father of all Renaissance domes, and a magnificent symbol of the Christian humanism of its day for the Renaissance had introduced a scale of values and state of mind different from those of the Middle Ages. There was a new confidence in human powers and aspirations – 'Men can do all things', as Alberti put it – and from this the personality of the artist gains a new stature and he emerges as an individual creator.

Brunelleschi's first entirely Renaissance building is the Ospedale degli Innocenti (the Foundling Hospital), Florence, begun in 1419. It is in fact the first Renaissance building in Europe and illustrates well Brunelleschi's practice of using classical elements

FOUNDLING HOSPITAL, FLORENCE

(columns, pilasters, cornices, etc.) not to imitate ancient buildings but employing them freely in original designs that were without Roman precedent in a strict sense.

Thus the ground floor loggia, vaulted in bays by small domes, has slender Corinthian columns recalling those of Tuscan Romanesque, supporting wide, graceful round-headed arches which spring not directly from the capitals but from Byzantine dosserets above them. Above are a horizontal entablature and an upper storey pierced with widely but regularly spaced pedimented windows.

But the feeling is distinctly un-Roman. It is too graceful and elegant, much closer to certain Tuscan work of the eleventh and twelfth centuries which has already been described, notably the west front of S. Miniato al Monte. The slender columns, wide arches, and general air of refinement are seen in the Ospedale and they are qualities which became hallmarks of Brunelleschi's style. The fine blue and white terracotta medallions in the spandrels of the arches are by Lucca della Robbia.

The Capella Pazzi in S. Croce was built by Brunelleschi about 1430 as the chapter house of the convent. Its plan, based on a prostyle Roman temple, recalls the Old Sacristy of S. Lorenzo, to be described next, but with a vestibule added. Roofing takes the form of a larger ribbed dome and barrel vaults over the main space, with smaller domes over the choir and centre of the vestibule. Inside, the atmosphere of clarity and lucidity is increased by an original device, the use of colour contrast between structural and decorative members, e.g. pilasters, and their pale background. Despite the grace and refinement, however, the columns for example are heavier than in Brunelleschi's earlier

CAPELLA PAZZI, FLORENCE

work and indicate a stylistic change towards a later more Roman manner.

Brunelleschi built two large churches in Florence: S. Lorenzo (1425) and S. Spirito (1436). The first of these was similar to S. Croce in plan, except that by making the eastern parts into four squares (choir, crossing, and two transepts) he made the eastern parts more regular and more centralized. In the outer angles of the transepts were inserted two domed sacristies, the later one by Michelangelo. Brunelleschi's sacristy contains the first use of the *pietra serena* technique to contrast structure members with the background as in the Pazzi chapel. The Roman columns of the nave have dosserets from which the arches spring and are widely spaced at the corners of rectangular bays. The nave itself is covered by a coffered timber ceiling (timber roofs are no longer left open) and the aisles have domical vaults.

The interior feeling of S. Lorenzo is characteristic of Early Renaissance work. It is spacious with clear-cut lines, well-defined forms, and a sense of freshness and refinement.

S. Spirito is a very big basilica of nave, with flat coffered timber roof, and two dome-vaulted aisles with its eastern parts so planned that the choir and transepts are identical projections from the

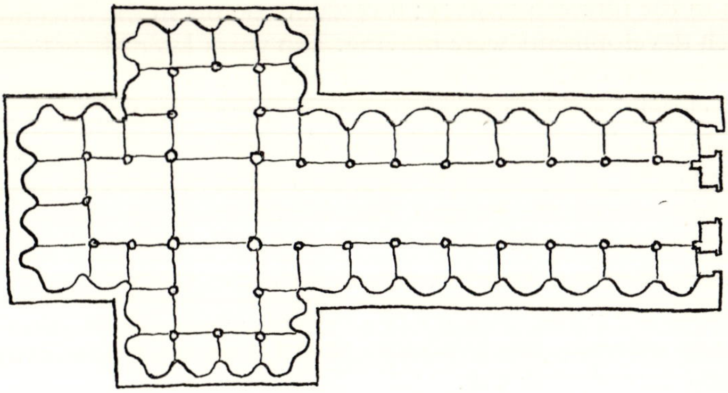

S. SPIRITO, FLORENCE

crossing over which rises a large low dome. So far this is very close to S. Lorenzo but the design is further unified by carrying the aisles right round the church, even, as originally intended, across the west end of the nave. The nave arcade is better proportioned, the detailing of the Corinthian colonnade has a new correctness, and the niches in the walls are a classical motif; on the other hand, as before, the arches do not rise from capitals directly but from dosserets in the Byzantine manner.

Here again is the same cool lucidity, the new Early Renaissance mathematical sense of space as something rationally worked out in the shape and size of internal divisions and the relationships of their parts. Thus, for example, the heights of both nave and aisle bays are double their widths. Architects, as well as painters like Uccello, were engaged in the search for a new kind of consistently ordered space and it was in fact Brunelleschi who had worked out the mathematics of linear perspective, made use of by the circle of painters with whom he was associated.

When it came to the abbey church, the Badia, at Fiesole, Brunelleschi accepted the Latin cross plan but we know that he projected a domed entirely symmetrical and centralized plan for S. Maria degli Angeli (1434), unfortunately never completed. A late work, like S. Spirito, it was a grander and more sculptural design than his earlier style, more massively and closely Roman.

A domed octagon surrounded by radial chapels, it was based on the Temple of Minerva Medica, Rome, the first use of the central plan in the fifteenth century; it certainly points in the direction in which developments were moving. Ten years later Michelozzo di Bartolommeo added a centralized east end to SS. Annunziata, very closely based on an actual Roman temple. It too has a polygonal central space surrounded by eight chapels. The Palazzo di Parte Guelfa, Florence, was designed by Brunelleschi about 1420 and his part of the Palazzo Pitti in the same city dates about ten years later.

Leone Battista Alberti was a quite outstanding figure of the quattrocento – patrician, lawyer, scholar, artist, athlete: in short an *uomo universale,* much more so than Leonardo, whose name is usually quoted, ever was.

He is a follower of Brunelleschi for, in no sense a mere copyist, he too wished to revive the Roman system of architecture and to apply it to the design of new types of buildings such as churches and town houses or palazzi. But there are differences between the two men. Whilst Alberti lagged behind Brunelleschi in his understanding of contructional principles, he went beyond him in his understanding of the grammar of design in classical architecture and in his grasp of the essential philosophy and feelings which lay behind it.

A new kind of scholar-architect, he was capable of writing his *Ten Books on Architecture* ('De re aedificatoria') modelled on the work of the Roman authority, Vitruvius, rediscovered in manuscript in the early fifteenth century and first printed in 1486. These important books contain the first theory of Orders since the time of Vitruvius and also a theory of beauty and ornament in architecture that is very characteristically based on a system of simple harmonic proportions by which the Ancients had related architecture to music. 'I shall define Beauty,' he says, 'to be a harmony of all the parts . . . fitted together with such proportion and connection, that nothing could be added, diminished or altered but for the worse. . . .' Moreover, mathematical ratios could express the divine order according to the Platonic ideal. Yet like Brunelleschi and unlike some later revivalists, Alberti still considered the social responsibility of the architect, and function, to be of the highest importance.

Whatever Alberti's work owes to Vitruvius it nevertheless expresses his own original ideas on classical architecture and was to have a tremendously important place in the theory of the subject.

From now on architectural treatises fall in quick succession from the presses since classical architecture being based in the first place on a 'received' grammar tended to encourage an academic approach. Even if architects were to break with its precedents, as they did in the later Renaissance, its canons must first be understood properly before they could be rejected.

Thus Alberti, though in some sense a dilettante, was a new type of architect capable of making architectural design a more scholarly art, its mathematical and aesthetic planning based on philosophical laws. The conception of the architect as a cultivated scholar, theoretician and artist is very different from that of the medieval master mason as a craftsman for whom, for the most part, anonymity was quite proper. It is a profoundly Renaissance one, expressed by Lorenzo Ghiberti, the sculptor of the bronze doors of the Baptistry, in his *Commentaries,* itself an important contribution to quattrocento culture, and once again it goes back to Vitruvius like the Orders themselves.

In 1446 Alberti remodelled the church of S. Francesco, Rimini, the so-called Tempio Malatestiano, since it was commissioned by the Renaissance gangster whose name is so arrogantly flourished in the inscription it bears. Its significance is that here we have the first Renaissance solution of the problem of what to do in classical terms with the west front of the church. Taking the triumphal arch motif from the Arch of Constantine and some of the detail from the local Arch of Augustus, Alberti proceeded to adapt the arrangement of triple openings framed by columns to the façade,

S. FRANCESCO, RIMINI

the high deep portal between Corinthian pilasters representing the centre arch. The adaptation made here for the first time was varied endlessly by later architects and is a good illustration of the way in which Roman motifs were re-used at the Renaissance. Such structures as the Arch of Constantine are full of rich suggestions and are among the major sources of Renaissance architecture.

The interior of S. Francesco is largely Gothic but the side, with its massive piers and arches, and sarcophogi lodged in the niches thus created, is very Roman, grave and rather austere, without the lightness and grace of early Brunelleschi. The plan is the more usual longitudinal type and therefore different from Alberti's design for S. Sebastiano, Mantua (1460), which, altered in restoration, was the first of a long sequence of Greek crosses. Ravenna, not far away, might have inspired this reversion, e.g. the Mausoleum of Galla Placida, but as we have seen it was also part of the current trend towards centralized plans. Here the front of the church is based on a classical temple motif. Thus Alberti has introduced a new note of Roman grandeur and gravity which he so admired in the originals and in these two solutions he provided the basic motifs to be used from now on in the composition of classical church façades.

Alberti's greatest church, executed by Fancelli, is also in Mantua, S. Andrea (1470). The Latin cross plan takes up the theme of Brunelleschi's S. Spirito in its attempt to combine a longitudinal nave and aisles, still necessary for liturgical reasons, with the

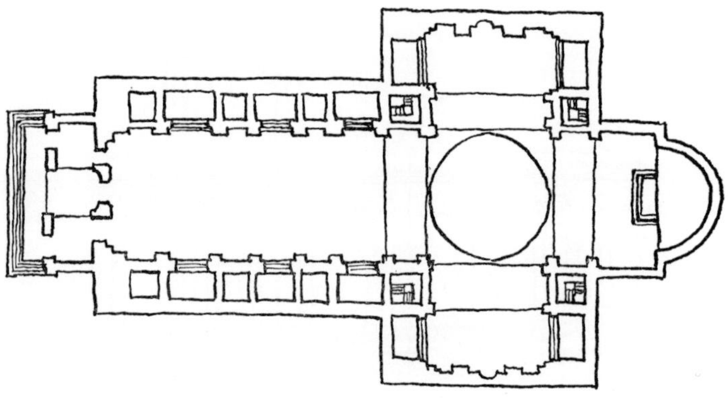

S. ANDREA, MANTUA

fashionable centralized plan. But though the nave is covered with a coffered barrel vault and therefore drives forward, Alberti unlike Brunelleschi adopts an original arrangement of side chapels at right angles facing inwards across the nave instead of the continuous aisles that were formerly found in medieval churches, though fifteenth-century Catalan churches had side chapels between internal buttresses. There was one in Rome in 1496.

This arrangement of aisles, superseded by open side chapels rhythmically alternating with openings in the vast piers faced with coupled Corinthian pilasters on pedestals, obviously owes something to the triumphal arch again, a framed larger opening between smaller ones, and to the interiors of Roman baths. The nave and side chapels are externalized in a west front which is a combination of triumphal arch and temple, with a pediment taking the place of an attic storey, repetition of motifs and rhythms, inside and out, being one of the ways in which order and harmony are achieved and the aesthetic success of the design assured. This is one of the first consistently classical churches, but the eastern parts and dome are early eighteenth-century.

Back in Florence, his own city, Alberti put up a new façade for

S. ANDREA, MANTUA

S. Maria Novella (1470). Perhaps because it was a Gothic church there are still some medieval touches to it and it recalls, if anything, S. Miniato; but its main divisions are squares, mathematically related in proportions 1:2 or 1:4 in the usual manner of Alberti and the first Renaissance use of harmonic proportion. (Alberti was aware, as a classical scholar, of the Pythagorean link between music and architecture.) Worthy too of special note is the way he uses scroll forms to cover the aisle roofs and make the difficult transition to the higher nave roof when a classical system of design was being used.

Products of the new secular spirit of the Renaissance are the palazzi, huge town houses or palaces built for the oligarchic families of the merchant cities, businessmen and international bankers who required a strong semi-fortified dwelling over their premises; as in Roman insulae, their prototypes, flats had been built over shops and warehouses. There was a great outburst of palace building in Florence in the second half of the fifteenth century, but before discussing Alberti's important Palazzo Rucellai (1446) it is desirable to mention one or two other early examples.

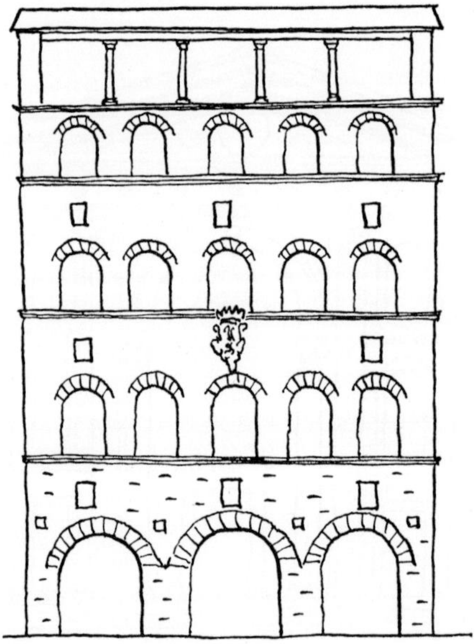

PALAZZO DAVANZATI, FLORENCE

PALAZZO MEDICI–RICCARDI, FLORENCE

An interesting late fourteenth-century design is the Palazzo Davanzati, Florence. It shows a number of features which were to become typical, notably a symmetrical façade with a rusticated ground floor to give an appearance of strength and power, and the principal living rooms on the first floor, the *piano nobile*; the attractive loggia on the fourth floor, however, is unusual. Rustication was originally a Roman technique and was revived at the Renaissance.

The Palazzo Medici–Riccardi was begun in 1444 by Michelozzo Michelozzi, capomaestro to the cathedral after Brunelleschi, who had remodelled the monastery of San Marco and evolved a style which closely resembled Brunelleschi. Though the functional arrangement is much the same as the earlier palace there is a greater regard here for symmetry and proportion.

This, Michelozzo's most famous work, has no specifically Roman precedent despite insulae and the fact that the cortile of the squarish quadrangular plan goes back ultimately to the Roman atrium. The lowest of the three storeys, flush with the street, is rusticated with large arches set in, pierced only with small windows for security. The first floor is, as before, the *piano nobile* with the main apartments; and both it and the top floor have larger, regularly spaced round-headed windows of a Romanesque type with two lights separated by colonnettes. The three storeys are divided by cornices and a further division between them is created by the grading of the masonry of the façade: rusticated on the ground floor, as we have seen, channelled at the second storey, and plain ashlar at the third. The whole dignified design is finished off with an enormous overhanging cornice to provide some shelter from the sun, instead of the earlier projecting eaves.

The turning inwards of the plan towards the internal courtyard is dictated by the desire for security and privacy while at the same time obtaining light and air. Compared with the more massive and forbidding external elevations those of the cortile are lighter and more graceful, with open arcades on the ground floor in the Brunelleschian manner. The dignified and spacious rooms of the *piano nobile* also open on to the cortile. The best contemporary interior decoration is exemplified by Benozzo Gozzoli's colourful frescoes in the private chapel.

Alberti's contribution to palace design in his Palazzo Rucellai, also in Florence, dating from about 1460 and built by Rossellino the sculptor, is the practice of using orders, in this case pilasters, freely interpreted to articulate the wall surface, and to introduce windows of a more classical pattern. This decorative use of Roman motifs is, as we have seen, a characteristic of Alberti's classicism.

On a wholly channelled wall surface, Alberti employs Tuscan,

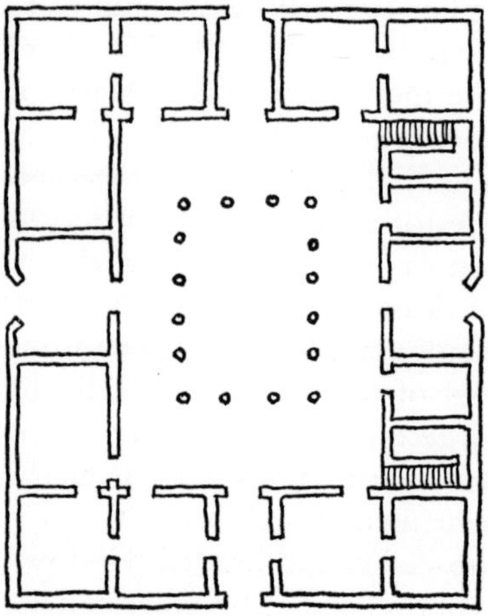

PALAZZO STROZZI, FLORENCE

PALAZZO STROZZI, FLORENCE

Doric, Composite, and Corinthian orders and their entablatures from the ground floor up, thus following the Roman convention, except that Composite replaces the more usual Ionic, as illustrated by the Colosseum, another great source of inspiration to Renaissance architects on the look out for authentic classical ideas. The Colosseum shows that the Romans themselves had used the orders in a non-functional way as Alberti was using them, since they are applied to what is basically a pier and arch structure and are not part of a post and lintel one.

The richly textured façade has much more variety than that of the Medici Palace and there are two entrance doorways, not one; but as in S. Andrea all the proportions and relationships between the various elements are carefully worked out according to Alberti's theories so that nothing could be removed or displaced without introducing a discord into the total harmony. Italian Renaissance staircases show a broader step and gentler rise than utilitarian medieval ones but no attempt is made to exploit their spatial effects. Alberti, for all his architectural sense, could still regard them as inconvenient space-wasters in a design.

Two Florentine palaces of a little later and closely following the Palazzo Medici are the Palazzo Strozzi (1489), usually ascribed to Benedetto de Maiano but built by an architect of the next generation, Giuliano da Sangallo, who also built the second, the Palazzo

Gondi (1490). Both make use of rounded rustication. An interesting contribution to the domestic architecture of the Early Renaissance is Giuliano da Sangallo's villa, a country house type discussed in a later chapter. The Villa Medici at Poggio a Caiano (1480), with its wide overhanging eaves, is one of the very earliest examples and its rather Etruscan-looking portico is the first of many to be used in villa design. It has a large barrel-vaulted central salone but the outside staircase dates from the seventeenth century. Giuliano da Sangallo's S. Maria delle Carceri (1485), Prato, is a development of Brunelleschi's Pazzi Chapel and the first Renaissance church on the plan of a Greek cross.

To return to the early palazzi, an interesting feature of many of these early palazzi was the way they used iron work with a fine architectural sense. Examples may be seen at the Strozzi and Guadagni palaces, Florence, with their link holders, angle lanterns, and grilles.

The Ducal Palace at Urbino (*c.* 1465), probably by Luciano Laurana and if so his one extant work, has one façade that is but a shadow of its original conception with unusually designed openings in a solid front and a façade, flanked by twin-turreted and machicolated Gothic round towers, at the centre of which rises a series of arched openings with free standing classical columns. But its most striking feature, apart from its beautiful quattrocento decoration, is the sensitively proportioned cortile. Still of the Florentine type, it is yet a considerable advance on them, for example, in the clever and effective way in which the difficulties created at the corners are dealt with.

It is probably the solution of Francesco di Giorgio who carried out Laurana's design. In his churches of the 1480s – S. Bernardino, near Urbino, and S. Maria del Calcinaio, near Cortona – Francesco shows the same tendency to appreciate the structural character of Classical architectural members as Giuliano, but uses them with more grace. Unlike Alberti's, his system of proportion attempted to relate the parts of a building to the parts of the human body, a conception typical of Renaissance humanism.

As part of Pius II's scheme for Pienza (1458) Bernardo Rossellino built a palace of the Rucellai type (the Palazzo Piccolomini) with a portico specially designed to take advantage of the view, and in Rome an early work of Albertian style is the cortile of the Palazzo Venezia (*c.* 1465) with its two-storey arcades, more severely Roman than most in its use of piers and attached columns, in the manner of the Colosseum already referred to. The use of L-shaped piers at the awkward corners of the cortile again offers a much better alternative to Brunelleschi as it enables them to be strengthened at these critically weak points of the design.

During the fifteenth century, Venice, that great entrepôt of Eastern trade was slower in accepting the Renaissance style than either Florence or Rome. Less susceptible to its influence it did not begin to put up buildings in the new mode, such as the Palazzo Dario and the Arsenal Gate, until the 1450s and when it did so it gave to them something of its almost oriental richness and festive colour. Undoubtedly there is a parallel here with Venetian painting like that of Giovanni Bellini which developed in a similarly colourful and sensuous way compared with the more restrained and intellectual art of the Florentines. Despite their hard-headed practicality in business the Venetians were encouraged to indulge their love of splendour and display in rich pageantry and gorgeous works of art.

This can be seen in the coloured marbles and delicate ornament of the Palazzo Dario, just mentioned, but there are also other special characteristics of Venetian palaces due to their siting and social environment. Their façades are straight, lined up with the waterfront, and there are no cortili. The relative isolation of Venice and greater political stability reduced the need for stern fortress-like façades which are in consequence much more opened up, and there is a tendency for them to be divided vertically into three with the Gran Salone occupying the centre of the *piano nobile*. Rustication is unusual at this time in Venice but balconies are prominent features.

As in the rest of Italy, for climatic reasons, roofs are very low-pitched but sometimes chimneys are more prominent, a reflection of local conditions. Later of course tiled roofs disappeared from view altogether out of deference to the Renaissance love of horizontality.

The Early Renaissance architecture of Venice is chiefly the work of the Lombardi school. Their Palazzo Corner–Spinelli (1481) has a rusticated lower storey and classical cornice but the symmetrically arranged round-headed windows still show the Gothic-like tracery which was so persistent in Venice.

Pietro Lombardo's Palazzo Vendramin–Calergi (*c.* 1500) is

PALAZZO CORNER—SPINELLI, VENICE

more classical but still old-fashioned by standards outside Venice. The balanced symmetrical façade is divided into three storeys by cornices and finished with a heavy top cornice. There is a contrast between the heavier ground floor and the lighter parts above and the façade is decorated with applied orders of attached columns.

It has windows, round-headed with two lights and a circle of tracery, still harking back to a pre-Renaissance style, which give it the characteristic Venetian openness and emphasis at the centre by placing there the largest of the groups of three windows corresponding to the Gran Salone.

Other fifteenth-century Venetian palaces were mentioned in the previous chapter, together with the Palazzo Ducale. There the cortile was begun by Antonio Rizzi in 1486, more classically than the exterior façades, continued by Pietro Lombardo, and completed in the sixteenth century so that the arcaded façades vary in character though sharing a common picturesqueness which is Venetian. The Scala dei Giganti (1470) is a feature of special interest. Of all the apartments so profusely enriched by the paint-

S. M. DEI MIRACOLI, VENICE

ings of the great Venetian masters, Tintoretto and Veronese, the most magnificent, taking up most of one façade, is the Scala del Maggior Consiglio where the patrician assembly met.

Among Early Renaissance churches in Venice there is Mauro Codussi's S. Micheli Isola (1469), plainer than most Venetian churches and in contrast to Pietro Lombardo's small but exquisitely decorated S. Maria dei Miracoli (1480) with its large, very distinctive semi-circular pedimented front and its ornate and marbled interior after the colourful Byzantine manner of St Mark's; but of course much less grand and simpler, lacking both aisles and transepts. S. Zaccaria, with its tall commanding façade which also makes use of segmental forms, is a Gothic church remodelled in the late fifteenth century by Mauro Codussi whereas the Scuola Grande di S. Rocco, famous for the stupendous series of paintings by Tintoretto, dates from 1516 and is the work of several hands, a magnificent synthesis of Venetian Renaissance. The Scuole were religious confraternities typical of Venice and therefore much influenced by local tradition. The Scuola di S. Marco rebuilt by Pietro Lombardo in 1488 is also a fine example with curious *trompe l'oeil* effects to make it look larger. The church of S. Rocco, originally by Bon, was remade in the middle of the eighteenth century in a style deliberately old-fashioned by then to relate it to the Scuola.

Another local tradition, a Byzantine one, is reflected in Giorgio Spavento's design for S. Salvatore (1507) which is created by overlapping three central plans of the St Mark's five-dome type and then adding an apse and transepts to make a Latin cross plan out of the whole. While Bramante is deciding on a purely central plan for St Peter's in Rome, Spavento is perfecting the combination of central planning with the indispensable nave. By now, however, the High Renaissance had already begun in Rome and before embarking upon this phase of Renaissance architecture we must first survey the work that was going on in the north-west in the quattrocento.

We have already noted the transition from Gothic to Early Renaissance in the façade of the Certosa, Pavia. This is carried a stage further in the cathedral at Como, the work of local architects to which Juvara added a high dome in the eighteenth century; but Milan was still building the cathedral in late Gothic flamboyant and did not early acquire Renaissance aspirations in architecture. Michelozzo designed a Brunelleschian cube with dome in the Portinari Chapel of Sant' Eustorgio (*c.* 1460) but gave it Lombardic turrets at the corners.

It is nevertheless an early centralized plan of a type which aroused much interest in Milan, notably in Antonio Filarete who designed many such plans, which though never realized had great influence on later architects through Leonardo da Vinci and Bramante (who were working in Milan at the end of the century) and on the design of new St Peter's. Their fascination was evidently both aesthetic and symbolic for their unity is an attribute both of works of art and of the Deity. As Palladio summed it up later, speaking of the circular plan: 'It is the only one . . . simple, uniform, equal, strong and capacious . . . it is exceedingly proper to demonstrate the Unity, the Infinite Essence, the Uniformity, and the Justice of God.' When Filarete designed a town, Sforzinda, in his *Trattato d'architettura,* that too was centralized, this time an early example of the star-shape within a circle.

Filarete was the sculptor of the bronze doors of Old St Peter's, later transferred to the new Basilica. His greatest work in Milan is the great Ospedale, for the one time condottiere Francesco Sforza, Duke of Milan, who dominated the city from the middle of the century and rebuilt the castle of the Visconti as the Castello Sforzesco. It is one of the earliest municipal hospitals, planned as a great rectangle with four cortili so that the centre, where the centrally planned church was placed, is the centre of a cross. Despite the classical planning, the cortili façades were modified in the direction of Gothic, being transitional with ornamental use of classical motifs in terracotta detail. In this they are typical of north Italy at the time which was only now becoming touched by the Renaissance spirit in architecture.

The north façade, however, is by Bramante and a little later. Both he and Leonardo da Vinci, who had also come to Milan to work for Francesco Sforza, became interested in centralized planning. Leonardo did a series of sketches of variations, many very complex, which together with his theoretical writings did much to influence sixteenth-century ideas through Bramante who was greatly impressed by them. Under Andrea Mantegna, Donato Bramante trained as a painter, like many other Renaissance

S. SATIRO, MILAN

architects, and was also influenced by the 'architectural' style of Piero della Francesco who painted the great series of frescoes in the church of S. Francesco at Arezzo. As an architect he did a good deal of work in north Italy in the early part of his career, before going to Rome; in general he followed in the footsteps of Alberti. Thus he built the fine church of S. Bernardino in his home town of Urbino in 1475 and two churches in Milan.

There Bramante saw the fifth-century Early Christian basilica, S. Lorenzo, before it was much altered in the sixteenth century, as one can appreciate when examining his reconstruction of the ninth-century church of S. Satiro. The plan is an Early Christian central one of the cross-in-circle type and Bramante follows this in his new sacristy (now baptistry) in the Florentine manner with a squat octagonal lantern above. In its turn, small as it is, it was to contribute to the evolution of the new St Peter's, Rome, and the centralized designs of the sixteenth and seventeenth centuries in the way already referred to. The choir of the main church of S. Maria presso S. Satiro on the Latin cross plan, creates an illusion of being longer than it is (the site is a cramped one) by the use of perspective. This is essentially *trompe l'oeil,* a painter's device and anticipates the illusionist effects of Baroque in the seventeenth century.

More early work by Bramante may be seen in the centralized domed eastern parts (1492) added to the longitudinal fifteenth-century abbey church of S. Maria delle Grazie, by Solari, which owe something to Alberti's S. Sebastiano perhaps, as well as the

S. M. DELLE GRAZIE, MILAN

5a. Siena Cathedral (1226): shows the screen-like entrance façade and Central Italian taste for the polychrome effect of marble stripes.

5b. Milan Cathedral (1386): a rare example of Italian late Gothic, elaborate, with French influence.

6a. Alberti's Palazzo Rucellai, Florence (*c.* 1460). This design of a palace façade shows the Early Renaissance revival of pilasters to articulate and decorate a wall surface: Doric, Composite, Corinthian from ground floor up. Note the channelled masonry.

6b. Palazzo Ducale, Urbino (*c.* 1465) by Luciano Laurana (?). Sensitively designed 'Florentine' cortile. Skilful treatment uniting the orders in the corners may be Francesco di Giorgio's.

centralized schemes of Filarete and Leonardo. The brick and terracotta exterior are transitional and the interior which is spatially impressive is decorated in a lighter and more delicate style than he was to adopt later on.

Bramante also did three cloisters for the Gothic church of S. Ambrogio, works that evoke the spirit of Brunelleschi, the colonnade outside S. Lorenzo, and in the best, the Doric cloister, the cortile of the Palace at Urbino. Here is the precision and restraint of his later style but not the *gravitas*, weight, and drama.

CHAPTER EIGHT

High Renaissance, c. 1500–c. 1530

FROM the time of Pope Nicholas V in the middle of the quattrocento the popes had done all they could to restore the prestige of the Papacy which had suffered as a result of the disrepute and discord of the Babylonian Captivity and the Great Schism and by the early sixteenth century Rome was becoming the first city of Italy.

The period of the High Renaissance is that in which Rome took over the architectural lead from Florence. For the sake of convenience the date 1500 is used to mark its beginning which coincides with the arrival of Bramante in Rome after Milan had fallen to the French King Louis XII in 1499.

But before dealing with Bramante's Roman period, which was to be the climax of his work, it is interesting to go back a little to consider the first important Renaissance building in Rome itself, the Palazzo della Cancellaria (1486), the huge Papal Chancellery, planned on an irregular site in conjunction with S. Lorenzo in Damaso. It is in some ways a transitional building between the earlier Florentine palaces and the sixteenth-century Roman ones.

The façade is very long with a highly rusticated ground floor and pilasters applied to the first and second storeys in the manner of Alberti's Rucellai palace and varied with the windows in wide

THE CANCELLARIA, ROME

and narrow bays in accordance with the new rhythmical ideas noted in his work at S. Andrea. But there is a further advance on Alberti in that some of the proportions of this more complex design are based on the Golden Section and not on the simpler 1:1, 1:2, 1:3 mathematical ratios favoured by the Early Renaissance.

Other advances are the logical way windows are given separate sills instead of being placed directly on the cornice below, and the way the end bays of the façade project to strengthen and close the composition. There is a fine Early Renaissance cortile within.

At one time the Cancellaria was thought to have been by Bramante but this is doubtful since he did not arrive in Rome until the turn of the century. But it certainly forms a link there between the work of the Early Renaissance and his mature Roman style.

In the progression from Brunelleschi through Alberti to Bramante one finds an increasing understanding of the Roman system of building and its grammar of design. Bramante, the greatest architect of his generation, was the first to understand and apply them to the full; though, once again, this is not to say that he wished to make imitations of Roman buildings but only to conceive new ones correctly in the language of antique architecture and to endow them with the spirit and feeling of the Antique.

The period when it was possible to do this was necessarily short since it represents a classic moment, a point of balance between forces moving towards it and forces moving away from it, and Bramante is its most representative figure in architecture for there was, of course, a corresponding High Renaissance style in painting. Moreover, it is in his work that the regional elements in Early Renaissance architecture became absorbed in the creation of a universal style.

Coming to Rome and being able to study for himelf the ruins of Imperial grandeur Bramante proceeded to modify his style to obtain similar impressive effects of weight and *gravitas*. It appears in the two-storey arcaded cloister he did for Baccio Pontelli's S. Maria della Pace (1500), notable for the increased number of openings in the upper storey, but even more in his Tempietto (1502) on the site of St Peter's crucifixion in the courtyard of S. Pietro in Montorio on the Janiculum. Here the transformation is quite complete.

THE TEMPIETTO, ROME

This small circular building (it is only 15 ft across internally) is based on classical models such as the circular Temple of Vesta, Tivoli. We have seen how Bramante had already made use of central plans and come into contact with those of Filarete and Leonardo in Milan so that when he came to Rome to design both the tiny Tempietto and the vast new St Peter's his mind was already much disposed to choose centralized schemes; and in any case there was already a tradition of centrally planned martyria or memorial churches from Early Christian times. As always in the Renaissance preferences are not nearly as purely pagan as they often appear to be; Renaissance humanism was not what is understood by humanism today.

Rising from steps a peristyle of plain Tuscan Doric antique columns encircles the inner cylinder and supports its proper entablature. It is the first correct use of this particular order. Above the top cornice a balustrade gives a contrasting lighter rhythm. Within rises the drum, pierced alternately with shell-headed niche and windows, carrying as the dominant feature of the design a fine hemispherical (inside and out) Renaissance dome finished with a lantern.

Originally the Tempietto was to have been surrounded by a centrally-planned cloister in the same order. Altogether the excellent simplicity of its proportions and the very restricted Doric ornament succeeded in endowing it with a monumental dignity, an effect of grandeur which is remarkable in a building of such small size.

The same authentic Roman feeling may be seen in his design of about ten years later for the Palazzo Caprini, or so-called House of Raphael as it was bought by the painter to live in himself. Though later pulled down this building had an important influence on palace design of the sixteenth century and we shall have to refer to it later on more than one occasion. Its façade of rusticated ground floor with shops and *piano nobile* above with Doric columns and pedimented windows repeats its elements with a new regularity and symmetry. It made a fit residence for one of the new princes of art who were the creators of, and at the same time were themselves created by, the Renaissance.

At this point, before referring to the next works of Bramante, it is convenient to refer to the Palace of the Vatican where Raphael himself was to execute his finest work. Not a single architectural essay, it is really the accumulation of five hundred years of building, a somewhat amorphous complex of palaces, courts, chapels, and galleries linked together by staircases and corridors. But it contains some of the most splendid interiors in the world, including the Apartamento Borgia, Michelangelo's Sistine Chapel (with its stupendous crowded ceiling) and the Stanze of Raphael. Compared with all this magnificence, however, the Oratory of Pope Nicholas v with its charming frescoes by Fra Angelico is a refreshing fragment of the Early Renaissance. The bulk of the Renaissance part of the Vatican Palace is by Domenico Fontana who also did the Lateran Palace. Better known as a distinguished engineer rather than a great architect his style is rather dull and somewhat arid by contrast with that of Bramante.

The High Renaissance was a period when the greatest patrons of the time were connected with the Papacy, concerned to use the best art available to strengthen and glorify both it and themselves. The greatest of them was Pope Julius II and it was natural therefore that Bramante should undertake for him work of great importance.

His remodelling of the Vatican Palace includes the buildings of the Cortile di S. Damaso, since glazed so that the original light and shade effects are now lost, and the great long Cortile del Belvedere which, starting originally with a museum and theatre, leads uphill in three levels to the small villa, the Belvedere itself, at the top. Again the Roman manner may be detected in the elevations which remind one of the schemes for the interior of S. Andrea by Alberti. Despite their subsequent modification (they are now cut into by the Library and the Museum) these were very influential designs. The whole parallel with the Imperial palaces on Palatine Hill would not have been missed by contemporaries.

At the Vatican Bramante, besides the fine spiral ramp in the tower of the Belvedere, employed a traditional square newel staircase round an open well; and also a new L-plan type, which was a more dynamic design described by Francesco di Giorgio in his book, outside in the Cortile del Belvedere.

But the most important commission Julius II could give Bramante was that to prepare a plan for the new church of St Peter's which was to replace the Early Christian basilica dating from the

S. M. DELLA CONSOLAZIONE, TODI

time of Constantine. Already, as we have seen, Bramante was thinking in terms of centralized plans. S. Maria della Consolazione, Todi (1508), is a Greek cross with apsidal arms roofed by semi domes supporting the high drum and central dome, a splendid spacious Bramantesque design by Cola da Caprarola. (Other possible influences on Caprarola's design are those of Leonardo and Peruzzi.) Bramante had also influenced Raphael's Sant' Eligio degli Orefici (1509), a Greek cross, with an exquisite dome and he himself designed (for Sangallo the Elder to build) the wonderful but incomplete S. Biagio, Montepulciano (1518) which combines Latin cross and central plans: so that he seems to have gradually felt his way to his final centralized scheme for St Peter's, all the time at the back of his mind remembering the work he had seen and carried out during his period in Milan.

Bramante's final choice was a perfectly symmetrical Greek cross to each arm of which he added an apse. The corners of the cross were to be filled in with smaller square chapels with apses to their two outer sides, and beyond them again were to be four corner turrets. Over the great centre space, round which ran a square ambulatory through the corners, was to be a great hemispherical dome, and over each corner space lesser domes to make a great five-domed scheme.

This magnificent central plan was, however, later modified by the addition of a nave for liturgical reasons. After Bramante's death he was followed at St Peter's by his pupils, Raphael and Peruzzi, and it seems that the addition of a nave was the task of the former. Even Sangallo the Younger took a turn after the interlude caused by the Sack of Rome in 1527 before Michelangelo was appointed to complete it. Just how we shall consider later in describing Michelangelo's architectural work.

The High Renaissance character of the new Basilica of St Peter's is not just in the plan; it lies also in the massive sculptural treatment of the elevations. This kind of modelling on a massive scale is a feature of late Roman work and it can be seen in the huge piers where part of Bramante's original work survives amid so much which is later. St Peter's was never finished as Bramante intended it, partly because the building funds gave out, and it is well known that the scandalous sale of indulgences to pay for it was one of the things that prodded Luther into action and thus sparked off the Reformation.

One of Bramante's successors at St Peter's was, as we have said, his pupil Raphael, who died so tragically young at thirty-seven, but with achievements in painting enough to immortalize his name. As in his painting his characteristics in architecture are rich harmonies of seemingly effortless perfection coupled with, when compared with Bramante, a certain gentleness of touch not usually found as an accompaniment of such masterly power.

His Palazzo Vidoni–Caffarelli (1515) is very like Bramante's House of Raphael, though now much altered and extended. There is the same boldly modelled surface and the Tuscan Doric columns replacing the earlier pilasters. There is too a marked horizontal emphasis in the heavy rustication and window architraves. This is a grandeur and strength very different from the refinement and grace of the Early Renaissance.

The desire to escape from time to time from the summer heat and pressures of the city has a long history in Italy, going back to Virgil's praise of rural life and the country retreats the Ancient Romans built for themselves at Frascati and Tivoli. The men of the Renaissance too, with their town-centred civilization, found themselves impelled, when they could, to imitate the buildings described in Pliny and to build villas that were not farms but suburban houses, near enough to their town houses not to need bedrooms, to which they could retire for a rest and a change.

One of the earliest villas in imitation of the Roman *villa suburbana* is Raphael's Villa Madama (1516) with its terraced garden near Rome. A circular court was planned but never finished, but the most impressive feature is the great loggia where Raphael, the Pope's superintendent of antiquities and student of Vitruvius, recaptured the richness and magnificence of Roman baths. Apses, niches and sumptuous Late Roman decorative motifs are all here.

The Palazzo Pandolfini, Florence, is a posthumous work. Its plain ashlar façade in contrast to the rustication, exploited at this time even more than in the Early Renaissance for rich textural effects, is strengthened at the corners by quoins, another variation of the almost indispensable rustication, and its windows have alternating triangular and segmental pediments in the manner of the complex façade of his lost Palazzo Branconio dell' Aquila whose somewhat capriciously applied decoration hints at the Mannerism to come and discussed in the next chapter.

PALAZZO FARNESE

The Sack of Rome in 1527 by an abominable mixed force of Germans, Spaniards, and Italians was the worst in its history and wrought enormous damage, creating further opportunities for the extensive patronage by papal families such as the Medici and the Farnese. We come now to the Palazzo Farnese (1534) by Antonio da Sangallo the Younger, a protégé of Raphael. Today the French Embassy, it is the apotheosis of the High Renaissance palace type, the largest and grandest of them all.

As in his earlier Palazzo Baldassini, Rome (1520) – the boldly modelled Palazzo Tarugi, Montepulciano (1530) is by the Elder – Sangallo shows his liking for massive effects. The plan is quadrangular round a central courtyard reached through a splendid colonnaded tunnel-vaulted entrance in the middle of the main façade. This also dispenses with rustication except for quoins, which strengthen the corners, and the rustication of the entrance flanked by antique columns. The windows, no longer flush with the wall, stand out from its plain surface in three ranges and have straight cornices on the ground floor and alternating triangular and segmental pediments on the *piano nobile*. This alternating of pediments was sometimes a feature of Roman designs and may be seen in the Pantheon. The top storey windows, with their columns curiously supported on brackets, and the great overhanging cornice, are later additions by Michelangelo.

The centrally-placed entrance carries a balcony and above it is a Michelangelesque window of 'negative emphasis' over which are the arms of the Farnese family.

The courtyard elevations combine the arch and lintel systems and show the influence of the theatre of Marcellus and the Colosseum, but rather unsystematically applied. There are Tuscan Doric arcades on the lowest storey and an Ionic order above with pedimented windows between. The top floor is again the work of Michelangelo.

The interiors, expressing the wealth and worldly grandeur of the age, were sumptuously and even grandiosely decorated. But staircases were still of a relatively simple type, a dog-leg between solid walls. Behind the palace, reached through a loggia, were the gardens.

The essence of the High Renaissance style, the Palazzo Farnese was to extend its influence far into the future where it showed that it could still be used with vitality and meaning in the Italianate Classicism of Victorian banks and clubs. In that sense it was a truly universal style.

Though older than Bramante, Baldassare Peruzzi was his chief assistant. A scholarly architect, he built S. Sebastiano in Valle Piatta and the Casa Pollini in his home town of Siena, a number of palazzi in Rome, and the early Villa Farnesina (1509), a small example of the type, with central block and wings, its loggia now glazed in to protect the frescoes of Raphael whose Villa Madama it antedates. The odd little windows set in the frieze, later used by Sansovino in the Library of St Mark's, are a reminder of the imminent breakdown of the conventions of the High Renaissance while his illusionist painting in the Sala della Prospettive shows that Peruzzi was also a stage designer.

The Orsini, Lante, and Ossoli Palazzi in Rome are ascribed to him and in the 1520s he did some work in Bologna, notably the Palazzo Albergati and the church of S. Michele in Bosco but his best-known work, and certainly the most successful, is his Palazzo Massimi alle Colonne (1532). But this is not a work of the High Renaissance; it is Early Mannerist and might therefore equally well be dealt with in the next chapter. It is, however, impossible to draw a neat dividing line between phases of Italian or any other architecture. Already Mannerism is there in its fully developed form in the Palazzo del Tè, Mantua, by Giulio Romano, the most consistent of the Mannerists, if that is not too paradoxical a description of him; and as discussion of his work is postponed until the chapter on Mannerism perhaps we may for convenience round off Peruzzi's work by describing here the Massimi palace which illustrates his sensitive personal qualities.

Like Sir Christopher Wren he had the knack of adapting designs to cramped and irregular sites, only in his case they were for town houses, not city churches. The plan of the Palazzo Massimi with its gently curving façade conforming to the street line clearly shows this. The design of the main façade is in marked contrast to the High Renaissance works we have been considering. First, instead of a solid basement we have a shadowy entrance loggia; then, instead of boldly modelled windows, there are smaller more reticent openings, undifferentiated on the second and third storeys. In the attic windows can be seen a new type of strapwork surround, a motif to be developed by his pupil Serlio from whom it spread into northern Europe and which was still going strong in the seventeenth century, albeit under Flemish inspiration.

The general feeling is one of almost Greek refinement rather than heavier Roman qualities of the High Renaissance style and there is an intentional avoidance of its correctness and decorum.

The more Roman main court (there are really two palaces here, for two brothers) is notable for the ingenious insertion of openings above the ground-floor loggia to achieve a balance with the taller second-storey loggia.

The classical art of town planning had lain neglected throughout the medieval period except for a few market squares and bastide

PALAZZO MASSIMI ALLE COLONNE, ROME

towns and it was left to the Renaissance to revive it along with so much else that belonged to the Ancient World.

Antonio Filarete, architect to Francesco Sforza, whose work at Milan has already been mentioned, was one of the first to show an interest in complete schemes of town design. As a writer on architecture he described in the 1460s, as we have seen, his conception of Sforzinda, the first entirely symmetrical town on a centralized plan with streets radiating from a central piazza where stood the cathedral and the palace.

At about the same time Pope Pius II rebuilt his birthplace, naming it Pienza after himself. The plan, an important step in the evolution of town-planning, was the work of Bernardo Rossellino and it also centred on a piazzo round which are grouped the cathedral, palaces for the bishop and Pius himself, and a town hall. It is the first regular scheme of the Renaissance. The development of the Piazza and Piazzetta in Venice are early examples of civic design which are freer, continuing the medieval use of squares.

Leonardo da Vinci, with his usual curiosity and interest in new ideas, also gave some attention to the theoretical aspects of town planning; but it was in Rome in the last quarter of the fifteenth century where the possibilities of the revived art were to receive their greatest opportunities.

Pope Paul III began a process which ended by changing the whole face of Rome by having the Corso straightened, later ending in Vignola's Porta del Popolo (1561). Sixtus IV had a plan prepared for the redesigning of the whole city and his successors followed it up despite the terrible setback of the sack of the city in 1527. Then the great transformation began. Sixtus V employed Giacomo della Porta and Domenico Fontana to plan great new streets across the Esquiline, Viminal, and Quirinal Hills with convergences on the churches of S. Giovanni in Laterano and S. Maria Maggiore, opening out the Lateran and Esquiline piazze and building the Piazza del Popolo on which three long straight streets converged. The Aqua Felice, like the Via Sistina, still bears his name. Obelisks were placed in four of the squares punctuating the junctions and acting as points of focus for the street vistas. The largest in the world (100 ft high) is the red granite one with hieroglyphics in the Piazza of St John Lateran. It is Egyptian, dating from 1600 B.C. – originally from the Temple of the Sun, Heliopolis – and was ordered to be taken there from the Circus Maximus by Sixtus V to replace the statue of Marcus Aurelius which, as we shall see, had already gone to the Capitol. Another obelisk re-erected by Domenico Fontana in those momentous 1580s was the one in the middle of the Piazza di S. Pietro, originally from Nero's Circus.

One of the discoveries of the Renaissance town planners, to which classical architecture lent itself, was how street architecture could be given unity by emphasizing continuity of levels in the frontages, quite different from the diversity and independence of the separate units which went to make up a medieval street.

In 1546 Sixtus v got Michelangelo to design a magnificent approach to the Capitol, the ancient seat of government. The Palace of Senators faces the piazza, flanked by twin palaces, at the centre of which were the first oval of the Renaissance and a Roman statue then thought to be of the Emperor Constantine, the first Christian Emperor, now known to be of Marcus Aurelius. Leading up to the piazza is a grand flight of steps.

Altogether the great work that went on in the later part of the sixteenth century under the patronage of Sixtus v was very successful and a necessary foundation for the great additions of the Baroque age, even if Michelangelo's essay in town planning, later modified by della Porta, was too objective an exercise to give full reign to his introspective genius. Even into modern times Rome was still very much a Sistine city.

CHAPTER NINE

Late Renaissance, c. 1530 - c. 1600

RETURNING now to purely architectural development we come to that aspect of Renaissance art which has relatively recently been channelled off to receive the separate consideration that is its due. Even before Sangallo's Palazzo Farnese, Giulio Romano had begun to practise it as a new classical manner. But before discussing Giulio's work it will be better to attempt first a definition of Mannerism, the style of the Counter Reformation, the movement which was generated in the Roman Catholic world to oppose the Protestant Reformation of the north and to which it supplied an architectural background.

Various impulses were contributing to it in Rome in the early sixteenth century. Chief among them was the feeling of architects of the time that, confronted as they were by the achievements of the great masters of the High Renaissance, only by rejecting certain of their canons could they attempt to do more than go on imitating them and the work of the Ancients.

There was a kind of revolt against the artistic establishment; yet to say this is to suggest that Mannerism is some kind of coherent movement with a programme. This is certainly not, but rather a mood or attitude of the time which embraced a variety of responses to the architectural *status quo*. Nevertheless, some useful generalization is possible. As the High Renaissance went in for the clear articulation of space and form, balance, and harmony. Mannerism favoured ambiguity, illogicality, distortion, and discord, sometimes carried to the point of what can only be called neuroticism when compared with the calm, intellectual stability of the other.

High Renaissance richness and grandeur were replaced by restraint and subtlety. One aspect of Mannerist self-consciousness was its emphasis on academicism and scholarly studies. When Mannerist architects are not being wilfully heretical they are insisting on a strict adherence to the ideas expressed in the treatises

PALAZZO DEL TÈ, MANTUA

on classical architecture. But in general, they are subjective, each seeking his own version of the classical mode.

The first outstanding Mannerist was a pupil of Raphael, Giulio Romano, whose early works in Rome are the Palazzo Maccarani and the Palazzo Cicciaporci. His most famous work, however, is the Palazzo del Tè at Mantua (1526). It is a *villa suburbana*, a one-storey quadrangular building round a central court which recalls Roman prototypes, but with a new careful relationship established between house and garden. It is a splendid work but full of subtleties and odd caprices apparent in the complex rhythms and textures of the façades; subtleties in the way they play sophisticated variations on the same basic theme (notably the severe entrance front which contrasts with the light, open garden front), caprices in such details as broken (and therefore highly illogical) entablatures, the bizarre rustication, varied in size and sometimes omitted altogether, as it is from the attic storey of the Cortile della Cavallerizza at the Palazzo Ducale (1538) in the same city. Here the contrast with the heavily rusticated lower storeys is most marked and there are irrationally twisted columns supported on corbels.

Giulio also employed rusticated columns and other features in an imaginative way which became very popular with Baroque and later neo-Classical architects. Perceiving all its possibilities he in fact carried the art of rustication a stage further than High Renaissance architects, making it yield emotive as well as aesthetic effects in his work which at times is expressionist.

The interior decoration of the Palazzo del Tè resembles Raphael's style, combining painting with stucco ornament, in the Villa Madama, where Giulio had worked, except for the strangely disquieting illusionist painting in the Room of Giants.

His own house at Mantua (1546), now very different from early palazzi, is a sort of Mannerist version of the House of Raphael,

HOUSE OF ROMANO, MANTUA

full of artifice and tensions. Here again are the same capriciousness and contrivance already observed in earlier work.

This time a flatter, stiffly formal façade with sharp detail is not as punctilious as it first appears but is marked by odd discords and irrationalities. The entrance arch is peculiarly depressed and the pediment is no more than the string course inclined above it. The windows are not framed in the orthodox manner but surrounded by continuous banks of decoration and their pediments deprived of proper entablatures. The band above the ground-floor windows disappears curiously behind their keystones. All these are the deliberate solecisms which the taste of the period found a piquant contrast to the style of the High Renaissance. To appreciate the deviations one had, of course, to have a good grounding in the classical conventions so that this was a taste, seeming to some jaded if not decadent, both sophisticated and knowledgeable, negative proof of the widespread familiarity with classical canons. Another of his works at Mantua is the Palazzo Colleredo with the curious 'terms' of its façade.

Like Giulio but in a different way (rustication, for example, has no appeal for him) Michaelangelo Buonarroti, that Titan of the High Renaissance, rejected its style based on the correct use of classical grammar, exemplified in the work of Bramante and Raphael and derived from a study of Vitruvius and Roman remains. Not coming to architecture until he was 70, in a later and different spirit, he sets against its authority his own personality and the individual forms by which it sought expression.

The greatest of all sculptors, he began his first architectural

7*a*. S. Giorgio Maggiore, Venice (1565). A beautifully serene church design by Palladio. Picturesquely grouped with dome, campanile, and a front composed of interlocking pediments.

7*b*. St Peter's, Rome, from the back. In Michelangelo's conception giant Corinthian pilasters 'support' a huge attic. The massive scale and dynamic rhythms are Baroque; the unclassical detailing of the openings typical of Michelangelo and Mannerism.

8. S. Maria della Salute, Venice (1631): a majestic Baroque church by Longhena. The centralized design is manifestly built up to the main dome and lantern through the great volutes giving abutment to the drum.

undertaking in 1521. This was the New Sacristy provided for in Brunelleschi's design for S. Lorenzo in Florence. It was to take the form of a mausoleum for the Medici family, principally as a setting for his famous sarcophagi and statues of Giuliano and Lorenzo de' Medici.

The sculptural style is evident and the aedicules of the blank niches are good examples of the way Michelangelo deviated from the correctness of the High Renaissance for they are without precedent in a number of ways; cramped as they are, they employ attenuated pilasters of an unidentifiable order and with extraordinary pediments. It is by means of such singularities and the contrasts between them that there are developed disturbing dynamic tensions and emotive properties which are visual discords

MANNERIST DETAIL:
MEDICI CHAPEL, FLORENCE

compared with classical harmony. Unfortunately, this highly personal moody and truculent early Mannerist work was never completed.

In 1524 Michelangelo began the Biblioteca Laurenziana, the Medici Library added to S. Lorenzo, with its anteroom and triple staircase. The anteroom has very high narrow Mannerist proportions but its shape owes something to the Pope's refusal to have top lighting. It contrasts perversely with the larger but broader and less disturbing volume of the Library itself on first-floor level. The façades of the anteroom show similar tendencies to those of the Medici chapel.

Illogically he recesses the coupled columns and stands them on console brackets, which would be quite inadequate to support them, while projecting the intervening panels with their blind niches, the pediments of which are supported by highly original tapered pilasters fluted in part only. The pediment over the entrance is 'supported' only by the raising of the thin band which surrounds the door. Even the colour scheme contributes to the Michelangelesque brooding solemnity of mood, the various elements picked out in grey against a white background. The Library has a fine timber ceiling work worth remarking on.

The staircase, divided into three flights in its lower part, is done in heavier forms but is odd and personal in the same highly subjective way. It was completed by Vasari and Amannati in the 1550s.

Discord, distortion, severity, a peculiar individualism – these then are some of the qualities which can be descried in the

PALAZZO DEI CONSERVATORI, ROME

Laurenziana. They are present too in the upper storey which Michaelangelo added to Palazzo Farnese after Sangallo's death in 1546 and to which reference was made earlier.

In the same year he began his essay in town planning – his design for the Capitol which has also been described. In the twin Vatican palazzi on either side of the Palace of Senators, the Palazzo dei Conservatori and the Palazzo Nuovo, Michelangelo introduced for the first time a giant order of Corinthian pilasters on pedestals, which runs up through two storeys thus tying them together. Between these pilasters is an Ionic order of smaller columns carrying straight entablatures instead of arches as hitherto. Like some of the detailing this is a most unorthodox arrangement, a new variation of combining orders on different scales, giving a magnificent amplitude to the building as a whole while cleverly retaining the all-important human scale in the lower storey. The very impressive giant order was much taken up after Michelangelo in Baroque and later classical architecture. His work on the Capitol was completed by Giacomo della Porta.

When in 1546 Pope Paul III asked Michelangelo to follow Sangallo in the work of constructing the new St Peter's he declined at first with typical independence and only agreed on the condition that he should receive no salary for his work.

Rejecting the proposal for a nave, worked on by Raphael and Sangallo, he returned once more to Bramante's centralized plan of forty years earlier which he simplified and clarified into a compact Greek cross with the corners filled in and a square ambulatory round the central space. Apses were to be added to three arms as before but rounded externally and the absolute symmetry of the design was to be broken by the addition of a portico entrance. This was in fact never built and later in the mid-seventeenth century Maderna was to add the nave and a wide, somewhat pompous, façade.

Outside, however, Michelangelo used again a giant Corinthian order of pilasters, the largest in the world, supporting a huge attic with odd windows and many and varied niches. The entablatures and cornices, running horizontally, bind the parts of the building together, but as they advance and recede they introduce a three-dimensional movement, an effect of plasticity which is new.

The drum has projecting pairs of columns and a broken cornice which give a similar impression of dynamic sculptural rhythms.

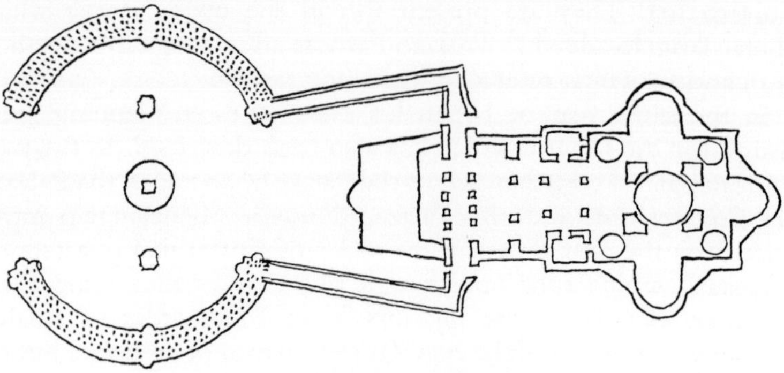

S. PIETRO, ROME

Already this gigantic and essentially un-Antique composition, Michelangelo's finest architectural work, is pointing forward beyond Mannerism to the Baroque of the next century. It is a measure of the genius of Michelangelo that he could not only comprehend the High Renaissance ideals of Bramante's original intentions for the great church but reach out through the style of the later sixteenth century to fertilize the imagination of the seventeenth. He strides across the century like a Colossus.

Above the drum rises the enormous dome on pendentives supported ultimately only by the four massive piers of unprecedented scale begun by Bramante. Michelangelo designed an elongated ribbed dome, meant to dominate the composition outside as well as inside, but he died before it could be finished. This was done by Giacomo della Porta and Domenico Fontana, the ablest engineer of his day, whose work at the Vatican Palace has been referred to. They gave it a more pointed profile than Michelangelo intended and completed it with a lantern.

Inside the vast interior, so grand a setting for the glorious music of Palestrina and Frescobaldi, the triumphal arch motif once again provides the unit of bay design, while the arms of the cross are barrel-vaulted, as is Maderna's nave. Unfortunately the latter interferes with the spatial effects under the dome, the lower part of which is partly obscured from outside by the façade which intervenes between it and the spectator. Here among the other works of art is one of Michelangelo's noblest sculptures, an earlier Pietà (the later one is in the Duomo, Florence); but the decoration with its rich marbles and gilding is the work of Maderna. Bernini did the great colonnades encircling the piazza, the approaches to which Michelangelo had remodelled on more symmetrical lines; but as the piazza is a work of the Baroque, description of it is postponed until the next chapter. Ten architects, in fact, were employed altogether on St Peter's and the best view of Michelangelo's contribution is to be seen from the back. There the complexity, the dynamic upward striving, and the vastness of his conception can best be appreciated.

Another church in Rome where the work of Michelangelo may be seen is S. Maria degli Angeli (1559). This he adapted from the ruins of the Baths of Diocletian, giving it an interior ennobled by huge columns, cornice, and a wonderful spatial effect. It was, however, modified by Vanvitelli in the middle of the eighteenth century. Finally there is a posthumous work, the Porta Pia gateway, where once again the forms and imagination of the Baroque are anticipated, for example in the double pediment, one of which is broken. After all the innovations of Giulio Romano an Michelangelo there could be no return to the old ways; a new freedom, if not a new licence as some of the older generation would have had it, had burst the chains of orthodoxy.

In the early sixteenth century in Venice we come to two architects who began as Bramanteans and developed, amid the influences of that highly individualistic city, in their own direction. They are Jacopo Sansovino and Michele Sanmicheli.

Sansovino, like Michelangelo, was a sculptor as well as an architect. He fled from Rome on its sack in 1527 and thereafter worked for the Venetian Republic. His Libreria Vecchia (1537) in the Piazzetta has a lower storey with a very orthodox Doric order applied to a pier and arch system, then an upper storey with an Ionic order carrying a heavy attic crowned with a balustrade punctuated with statues. Despite the heavy correct High Renaissance feeling, what strikes one about the façade is its richness of texture and ornament. The garlanded frieze, for example, is clearly designed to satisfy the same kind of taste as that earlier Gothic ornament so characteristic of Venice. But more important than this is the way the intercolumniations of the Ionic order are filled with arches supported by smaller Ionic columns arranged on either side of the main ones to produce a rich and complicated contrapuntal effect.

LIBRARY OF S. MARCO, VENICE

Near-by Sansovino's immensely weighty and suitably muscular Mint, La Zecca, is contemporary with the Library; here rusticated columns recalling Giulio Romano's work were first introduced to Venice. On the other side of the Library the Loggetta (originally 1540) was designed to relate the complex horizontal front of the Library to the great plain vertical of the Campanile. It is a charming and highly ornate little structure.

Other works in Venice by Sansovino are the churches of S. Giorgio dei Greci and S. Martino (1514), the Scala d'Oro (Palazzo Ducale), and the splendidly proportioned Palazzo Corner della Ca' Grande (1537). The same basic palace type endured in Venice from the fifteenth to the eighteenth century but with growing symmetry and increasingly rectangular window shapes. In the Palazzo Corner Sansovino achieves the first really regular design, one taken up by Longhena in the next century. The high rusticated basement with triple openings, mezzanine windows above its principal ones, and Mannerist detailing, is succeeded by two storeys of round-headed windows between coupled columns in the High Renaissance manner but with windows in the top frieze beneath the cornice. There is still a tendency to emphasize the centre of the façade.

PALAZZO CORNER, VENICE

The lower storey is similar in style to that of the Palazzo Canossa, Verona, the work of Sanmicheli, also dating from the 1530s. Here is the undoubted influence of the Mannerism that we first noted in Giulio's Palazzo del Tè. The rusticated basement has a similar triple-arched entrance and additional mezzanine windows; the *piano nobile,* coupled pilasters and round-headed windows. And yet his Pellegrini chapel is Roman, obviously based on the Pantheon – unless the tall, narrow proportions are Mannerist after all.

Two more palazzi in Verona by Sanmicheli and of the same period are the more Bramantesque Palazzo Pompei, and the very elaborate Palazzo Bevilacqua; both harking back to that very influential design, the House of Raphael. But the Palazzo Bevilacqua shows very strongly the Mannerist influence of Giulio. Its richly rusticated basement and columns, prominently carved keystones, and complex rhythms of bays and openings all point to this. To the *piano nobile* there is a long balustraded balcony. This device which effectively ties together a façade from end to end is also present in his Palazzo Grimani in Venice (1549).

This powerful and strongly modelled design has a robustness and gravity that is in marked contrast to the gaiety of Late Gothic palaces in Venice. The heavily rusticated Gran Guardia Vecchia,

PALAZZO CANOSSA, VERONA

Verona (1609), closely resembles Sanmicheli's style in the buildings just described; it is by his nephew, Dom Curtoni.

Sanmicheli was a much travelled architect. He built Montefiascone Cathedral near Orvieto in his early days and later worked much in the Veneto and abroad on fortification at which he was expert. Like those of Vauban and the early nineteenth-century engineers his military works often had remarkable architectural qualities. This can be seen at its best in the fortified gates at Verona, the Porta Nuova and the Porta del Palio. One can observe here how appropriate the technique of rustication was for designs requiring a massive strength.

Of the Florentine Mannerists Giorgio Vasari, who competed with Michelangelo and others for the completion of the Palazzo Farnese, is better known for his *Lives of the Most Illustrious Painters, Sculptors, and Architects*, one of the first works of art history, published in 1550. But his chief architectural work is the Palazzo degli Uffizi (1560) now the gallery of that name, in Florence.

It was intended to serve as a great office building for the administration of Cosimo I and as such was one of the first of its kind. It consists of two tall blocks, their storeys not clearly differentiated, separated by a long narrow courtyard but joined by a façade and loggia overlooking the River Arno. Clearly there are Mannerist characteristics here and in the capricious and attenuated detailing. Both Vasari and his successor at the Uffizi, Bernardo Buontalenti, were subject to Michelangelo's influence. Indeed it was the later who had advised Vasari to take up architecture in the first place.

Another sixteenth-century Florentine was Bartolomeo Ammanati who built the bridge of S. Trinita (1566) and whose work was always competent, if sometimes a little pedestrian. The Pitti palace in Florence with its huge astylar façade goes back to the time of Brunelleschi in the lower parts of its central block but as it is now, the largest palace in Italy after the Vatican, it dates largely from the sixteenth and seventeenth centuries. Some of these later extensions were carried out by Ammanati, again for Cosimo I, notably the wings on the side of the Boboli gardens with their rusticated columns (perhaps an allusion to those of the Venice Mint by his master Sansovino) and the central and lateral cortili.

The Palazzo della Signoria, Lucca (1577), is usually ascribed to Ammanati. It has an interesting façade in which the impression of the orders is less prominent than the total effect of a surface modelled in a sculpturesque manner.

And what of Genoa? Though it was one of the most important Italian cities it was little influenced by Renaissance ideas until the

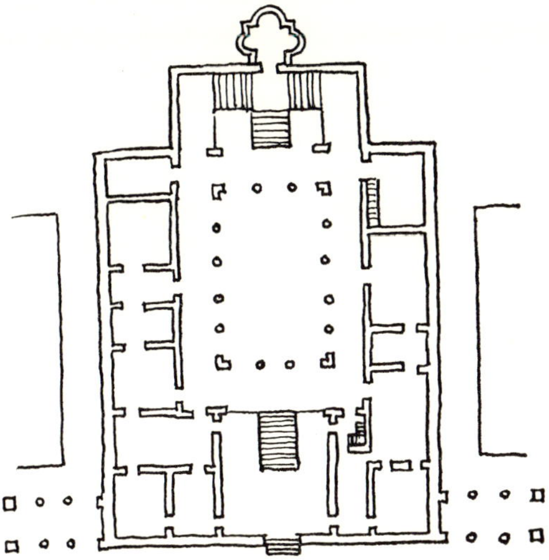

PALAZZO MUNICIPIO, GENOA

sixteenth century was well advanced, when Galeazzo Alessi, a sensitive and unpedantic architect, produced some outstanding Mannerist buildings both there and in Milan.

To Genoa belong the great church of S. Maria di Carignano (1552), the plan of which is similar to Raphael's proposal for St Peter's, the Palazzo Cambiaso (1565) and various ville in the district. The Palazzo Doria–Tursi (Municipio), 1574, a dignified and magnificently planned composition with fine cortile and terraced gardens on its characteristic sloping site, is by a follower by the name of Rocco Lurago.

Notable among Alessi's Milanese work is the Palazzo Marino (1558) which was to become the Municipio. An interesting feature of this building is its courtyard elevation which displays more than a dash of northern fantasy, Flemish and German, in its abundant decoration in bold relief and terms replacing orders on the second storey. Once again there is an exchange of ideas between Lombardy and Germany, but rare at this time, especially in the reverse direction. He also built the church of S. Vittore al Corpo.

Pellegrino Tibaldi also had some large commissions in the second half of the sixteenth century. He worked at Milan on the façade of the Cathedral in 1560 and the Arcivescovado in 1565. At Bologna he built the Palazzo Magnani–Salem and the Palazzo Arcivesovile, both about 1576. His churches may be seen at Milan (S. Fidele, 1569, and S. Sebastiano, 1576), Turin, Genoa, and Novara and he built the Collegio at Pavia as early as 1546.

Mannerists of the later sixteenth century, whilst forming their own individual versions of classicism, were much more inclined to have regard to academic correctness than to indulge in the capricious irregularities of earlier ones. Sebastiano Serlio, for example, pupil of one of Bramante's pupils, published eight books on architecture which, translated into several European languages, became standard authorities and source books for later architects, handing on to them Bramante's ideas as modified by the later sixteenth century. It was he who rigidly 'fixed' the proportions of the Vitruvian orders and who developed his personification of them to such an extent that, from now on, a common way of using them was in a representational way, for a purpose and context thought appropriate to their individual characters – Doric masculine, Ionic matronly, Corinthian virginal.

Giacomo Barozzi Vignola too produced a similar work, nar-

S. ANDREA, ROME

rower in scope but more scholarly and not much less popular. Again there were engravings of the orders together with illustrations of his own work. He also wrote a book on perspective for Vignola. He was a painter by training who had worked in Rome and at Fontainbleau (1541–3) for the French king, François I; and in his architectural work, as in some of Michelangelo's (which probably influenced him; it was an influence which few who came after him could escape) we can discern not only Mannerist elements but also seeds of the Baroque style of the next century.

For example his small centrally-planned church of Sant' Andrea, Rome (1550), perhaps based on Roman mausolea, is the earliest example of the elliptical dome which became much favoured by Baroque architects; whilst his Santa Anna dei Palafrenieri (1572) is the first oval ground plan, also to be much followed in the seventeenth century.

More conventional in plan, in that it represents a new version of the traditional Latin cross, deriving from Alberti's Sant' Andrea, Mantua (a Greek cross combined with nave and side chapels) is Vignola's Gesù, Rome (1568), designed as the principal church of one of the new orders created at the Counter Reformation, the

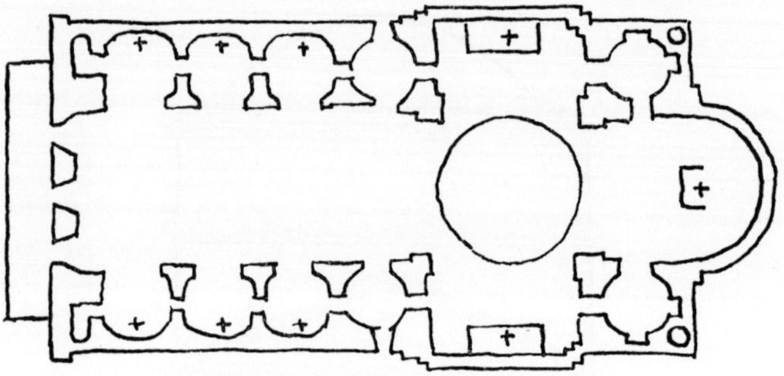

IL GESÙ, ROME

Jesuits: Vignola's nave, however, is wider (as wide as the shallow transepts) and internally circular chapels fill in the outer angles of the crossing. The Jesuit order was to be a very active and powerful agent in the increased church building that was now taking place

IL GESÙ, ROME

and both Vignola's plan and his design for the front of the Gesù, being adopted by the Jesuits, became standard solutions for most Baroque churches of the seventeenth and eighteenth centuries, as far afield as Peru.

Again it goes back to Alberti and his use of the triumphal arch motif but the present front is actually by della Porta (*c.* 1575) who devised a more complex and refined development of Vignola's, with less emphasis in the centre, and scrolls to hide the roof at the sides and relate them to the higher central nave, as Alberti had done at S. Maria Novella, Florence, a hundred years before.

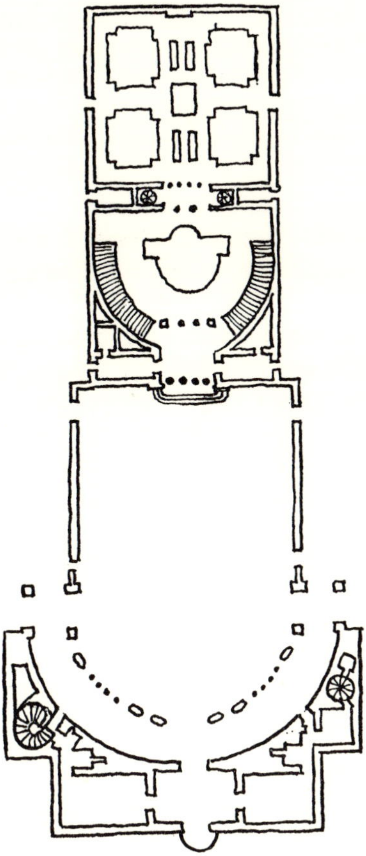

VILLA GIULIA, ROME

Della Porta has already been mentioned as reponsible for the revised design of the dome of St Peter's after Michelangelo's death. He looks forward to the Baroque in a third work: the two-towered front of the Greek church of Sant' Anastasia, Rome, which anticipates Borromini in the next century. He also designed the façade of S. Maria dei Monti (1579), a representative church of its day, and laid out at the Villa Aldobrandini, Frascati (1598), a wonderful synthesis of Mannerist architecture, sculpture, and classical garden.

Returning to the Gesù, apart from its very influential plan and façade, it was a seminal design in other respects too, such as in its immense forward-thrusting nave cornice and its more generous use of light, especially in its manipulation of light in the interest of dramatic effect. The decoration, however, fully Baroque and a hundred years later, is misleading since Vignola's original scheme was austere and restrained. Mannerists of the Counter Reformation believed, as Palladio put it, that 'of all the colours, none is more suited to churches than white, since the purity of colour, as of life, is particularly pleasing to God'.

Another of his churches, away from Rome, is S. Maria degli Angeli, Assisi (1558), but perhaps in Rome Giacomo del Duca's Michelangelesque drum and dome on S. Maria di Loreto, dating from the seventies, was a more influential piece of ecclesiastical architecture.

Of Vignola's important secular works his Villa Giulia (1550), now a museum, was built for Pope Julius III as a *villa suburbana.* There is Mannerism here in the way the straight and somewhat severe entrance façade contrasts with the concave garden front,

VILLA GIULIA, ROME

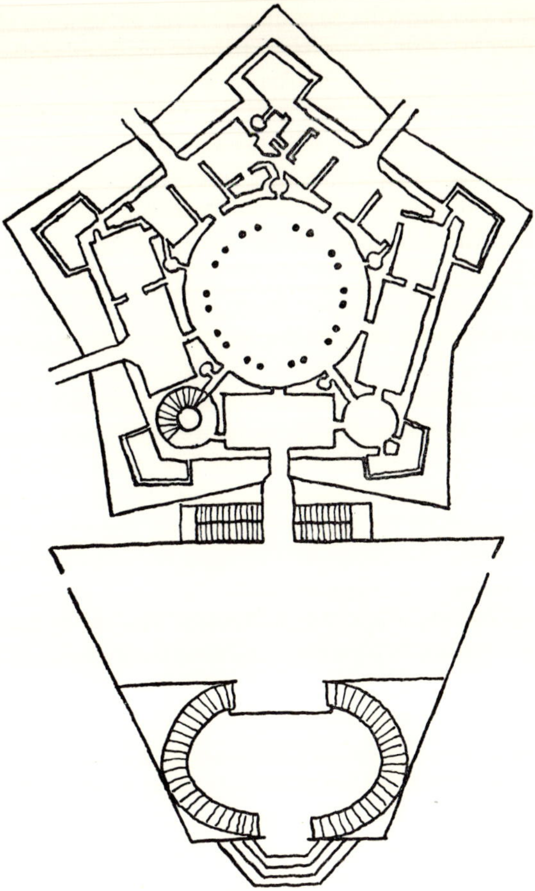

CASTELLO FARNESE, CAPRAROLA

the colonnade of which employs the straight entablature which Michelangelo used in his Capitoline palaces. This semi-circular shape is repeated in a second court with a nymphaeum at the centre, and the long vista right through the loggias to distant walled garden is also Mannerist. The garden and nymphaeum are the work of Ammanati and Vasari helped with the villa itself; both of them were Florentine Mannerists.

The classical Italian garden at its sophisticated best is a considerable achievement. Laid out with geometrical art and related architecturally to the villa to which it is an extension, it is diversified with flower beds, cypresses, fountains, pools, cascades, and statuary – just as the Romans had adorned theirs with works of Greek sculptors. Apart from those already mentioned – the Boboli in Florence and the Villa Giulia – perhaps the best known are the influential Farnese gardens, unfortunately destroyed in the last century, laid out by Vignola on Palatine Hill with ramps and steps leading through alternately enclosed and open spaces to pavilions at the top, and the gardens of the Villa d'Este, Tivoli (1549), with their famous water features. The latter were laid out by Pirro Ligorio the architect of the superb Casino di Pio IV (1558) in the Vatican gardens, a Mannerist design of exquisite elegance.

Among the great papal families who provided most of the architectural patronage, the Farnese were prominent and it was for Cardinal Farnese that Vignola took over the great villa-castle at Caprarola near Viterbo known as the Castello Farnese. The unusual fortress-like pentagonal plan and circular cortile in the High Renaissance style had already been laid out by Sangallo and Peruzzi, but from 1559 Vignola began the house as a high, massive, elaborately rusticated building. The flat pilaster shapes, vertical divisions, and quoins of the first and second storeys are hallmarks

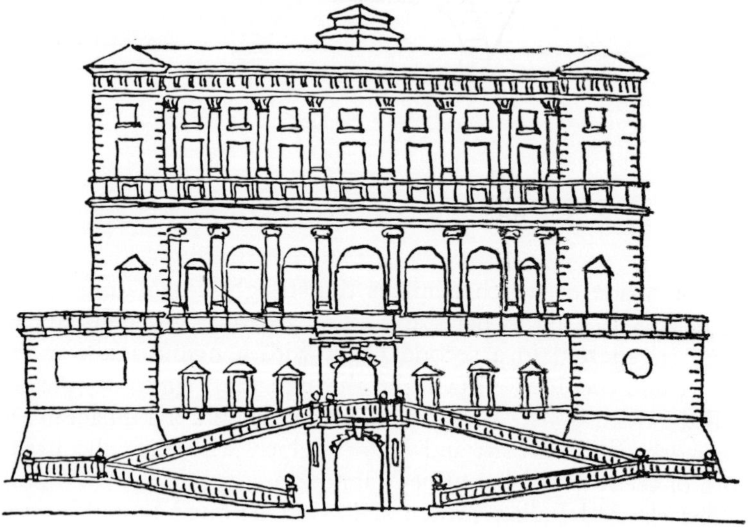

CASTELLO FARNESE, CAPRAROLA

of his style, owing something to Giulio. The entablature with its consoled frieze, however, is his own original creation that was later much copied. The spiral staircase is in the manner of Bramante. The gardens are among the most outstanding in Italy.

About the same time as the work at Caprarola was begun, Vignola was engaged on the Palazzo Farnese at Piacenza.

The prince of late sixteenth-century architects and the first professional in the modern sense was undoubtedly Andrea Palladio in whose work we see again the move away from unorthodoxy towards a greater respect for academic classicism. Behind this lies Palladio's great respect for Vitruvius and a ten-year study of Roman remains. Like Serlio and Vignola, moreover, Palladio helped to transmit to succeeding generations his conception of classical architecture by publishing his *I Quattro Libri dell' Architettura* (1570) in which his own designs (some of them very influential but like the Villa Mocenigo, a four-wing design, never built) were juxtaposed with those of the Ancients so that what was really disseminated was not just a pure classicism but his particular interpretation of it. Thus it was by no means antiquarian Roman; it showed an awareness of both Bramante and Michelangelo and what emerges is a classical style that has the discipline and clarity of the Ancients but blended with it here and there an unobtrusive Mannerism; though recently it has been insisted that Mannerism is a term misleading when applied to Palladio; and he certainly draws on Byzantine and Gothic structural principles. Palladio's books, more scholarly than Serlio's and more comprehensive than

THE BASILICA, VICENZA

Vignola's, appeared in many translations, notably in English. In Britain his work was known from the time of Inigo Jones who introduced his style and he gained the reputation of being the greatest and most characteristic virtuoso of Renaissance architecture. In particular, he dominated the work of Lord Burlington and his circle in the first half of the eighteenth century.

Palladio worked mostly in the north-east, in and around Vicenza in the Veneto. There in 1546 he remodelled the medieval Basilica for the Council of the Four Hundred. Given the inner hall, Palladio contrived to screen it with enveloping arcades, perhaps taking his idea from the Gothic arcades of the town hall at Padua; but the final appearance is more open and 'modelled', very Roman and much closer to Sansovino's Library in Venice, if plainer, in the Serlian manner. Thus the façade is a two-tier one with a ground-floor loggia of Doric upon which is superimposed an Ionic order. The design is given necessary strength and solidity at the corners by doubling the columns; but what also strikes one is the width of the arcades, an arrangement determined in the first place by the width of the original bays.

Palladio, however, cleverly turns this to account by using the arch-lintel construction which became widely known in the eighteenth century as the 'Palladian' motif, though in fact it derives from Bramante via Serlio. Between the larger columns he introduces smaller ones supporting short entablatures from which spring smaller arches. This has the desired effect of filling in or narrowing the intercolumniation. The device is similar to, but not identical with, the so-called Venetian window or Serlian motif which goes back to Raphael, was employed by Scamozzi in Venice, and also achieved great popularity in the eighteenth century.

Another feature of the façade is the way the entablatures break about the main columns and the vertical lines are allowed to carry up to the statues which provide accents at intervals along the top balustrade. With means such as these Palladio preserves excellent proportions and at the same time provides a rich play of light and shade throughout the design, which makes an interesting contrast with the elegant campanile next to it.

In Vicenza too are a number of palazzi by this architect. The Palazzo Chiericati (1550) obviously owes somethng to Bramante but it shows Palladio's more restrained style and his way of

VENETIAN WINDOW
PALLADIAN MOTIF

opening up a façade by using the loggias that were formerly used for courtyard elevations for there is no internal cortile. It is true that this may have been partly due here to the fact that the palazzo faces a square and was to have been part of a complete piazza design with colonnades in the manner of the Forum but the effects are exploited so much elsewhere in his work that it is evident that this particular type of contrast between solid and

PALAZZO CHIERICATI, VICENZA

void was greatly to his taste. As it is one of the most with Serlio, marked characteristics of his style.

The Palazzo Porto (1552) is designed as two identically planned blocks (for family and guests) with a Roman atrium between. The façades derive from Bramante's 'House of Raphael' type and recall Sanmicheli's style in Verona in the 1530s; but the symmetry of the planning, expressed externally, and the way the rooms are not only harmonically proportioned (now in a much more complex way than at the Early Renaissance) but are also related in size and shape are especially typical of Palladio. To a humanist this proportioning, of course, imitated the Order of Creation.

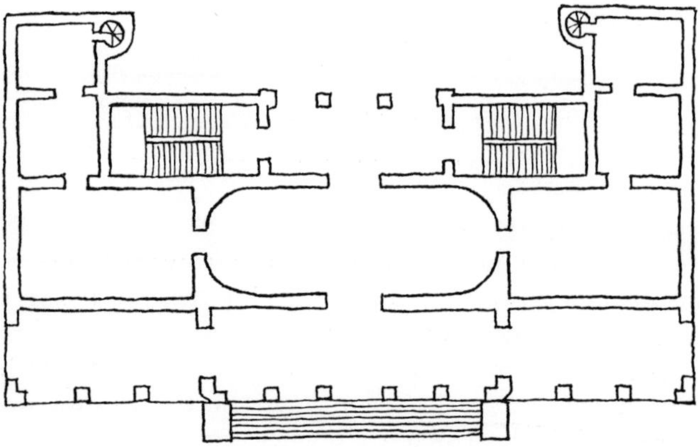

PALAZZO CHIERICATI

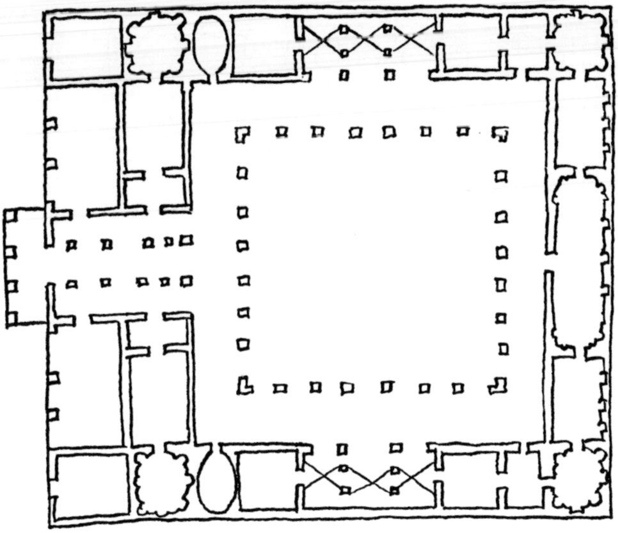

PALAZZO THIENE, VICENZA

The unfinished Palazzo Thiene (1556) shows him experimenting with Mannerist textural effects through rustication, like Giulio – the cortile is monumentally 'Roman' and the plan, with its symmetry and varied room shapes, Palladian. In some late palazzi he employs Michelangelo's giant orders: columns in the Palazzo Porto–Breganze fragment, pilasters in the Palazzo Valmarana (1566). The façade of the latter is a 'plane-and-pilaster formula' admirably adapted to the narrow street site.

Palladio's main field was domestic architecture but before leaving town for countryside to consider the villas for which he is most renowned we should first look at two beautiful churches he built in Venice: S. Giorgio Maggiore (1565) and Il Redentore (1576), among the finest classical churches ever designed and with a calm serenity untypical of that city.

The former is a cruciform monastic church picturesquely set on its small island across from the Palazzo Ducale. It has a nave extending beyond its domed crossing or 'tribune', and between chancel and monks' choir – a distinct unit – are columns that show how Palladio used them in interiors to obtain a characteristic open screen effect. This is more noticeably developed in Il Redentore where an 'apsidal' screen of Corinthian columns behind the high

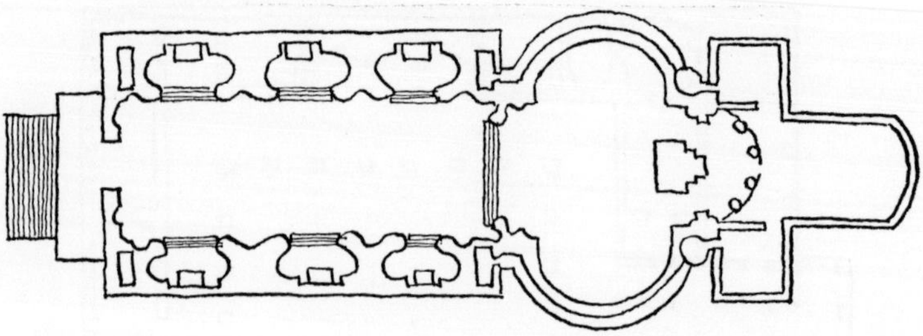

IL REDENTORE, VENICE

altar separates the choir beyond yet allows a flow of space and a glimpse of vistas between, refusing to impose that clear-cut distinction which had been preferred earlier. Both plans show a concern for the liturgical requirements, and planning sequences and structure recall Palladio's studies of Imperial Roman baths. Especially Palladian is the way in which he floods his churches with modulated light reflected by the painted stucco interiors that were a Venetian innovation. His use of light architecturally more than anything else reveals his ability to fuse the intellectual and the sensuous, which is so much part of his special achievement.

The eastern parts of this otherwise basilican church are a very complex piece of planning but the nave and side chapels with their triumphal arch motifs are of a design that we have noted before, except that her pilasters are replaced with half columns.

Both these late churches by Palladio have façades which, in two ingenious variations, interlock two types of temple front. The idea seems to begin in another Venetian church by Sansovino for which he designed the façade, S. Francesco della Vigna – his first ecclesiastical job – and it is his solution to the problem of relating sides to middle in the classical church front.

The elegant cloisters he did for S. Giorgio contrast with the heavier Roman ones provided for the Carità, also in Venice. The centrally planned chapel of the Villa Maser, however, seems almost to anticipate the Rococo in its ornamental feeling, as well as owing something to the Pantheon.

Palladio's villas are not of the *villa suburbana* type; situated in the Veneto favoured as a retreat by the rich merchants of Venice, they are country houses of the kind that was intended to be the

S. GIORGIO MAGGIORE, VENICE

centre of an estate, now that in the sixteenth century a new agriculture had to make good a decline in mercantile trade.

Though there is no 'typical' Palladian villa it was a type that he was to make particularly his own, though some of its characteristics no doubt owed something to what he had learned from others. Among these were his master Trissino who, following the Farnesina, had built the villa at Cricoli, and gone in for symmetry and mathematically proportioned rooms related to one another in harmonic sequences of size and shape – as we have seen, a Palladian practice; Sansovino whose Villa Garzoni at Pontecasale has a 'Palladian' double loggia in the centre of its symmetrical High Renaissance façade; and Sanmicheli who seems to have invented, in a last work, the idea of the main block being linked to dependent blocks by quadrant colonnades, an arrangement used by Palladio and passed on especially to the English Palladians who employed it widely in their eighteenth-century country houses. Particularly Palladian was the manner in which he successfully integrated the service elements with the villa proper into a single complex arranged in a hierarchy of functions.

VILLA GARZONI, PONTECASALE

Palladio's first villa, the Villa Godi at Loneda, has the cubical form of later ones but is without the high 'temple front' portico characteristic of them (and which he mistakenly believed was a feature on Roman houses) such as the Villa (Capra) Rotonda (1550). This is more formal than most, a *villa suburbana,* its symmetry absolutely uncompromising in design, its arrangement of rooms centralized on a low-domed circular hall and enclosed on its four sides with identical façades, each with its pedimental windows and Ionic portico. It stands on a hill and the way the dependent parts build up to the centre of the design well illustrates his hier-

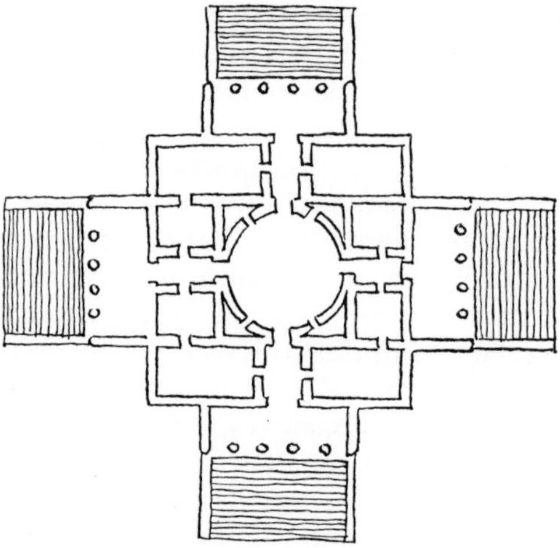

VILLA ROTONDA, NEAR VICENZA

VILLA ROTONDA, NEAR VICENZA

archical arrangement of elements in a design – despite the absence of service buildings here – probably suggested to him initially by his study of the Temple of Fortuna complex on the hillside at Praeneste (Palestrina). Tradition and novelty are blended here in a way which might be called Mannerist. Be that as it may, it is a dignified and noble conception yet at the same time elegant and infused with the feeling of cheerful ease which Palladio succeeded in bringing to his designs. He is intellectual but never dryly pedantic, whatever some of his imitators became, and always an artist of great subtlety and warmth.

The same clarity and restraint may be seen in Palladio's unfinished Villa Trissino at Meledo where the plan illustrates the type where the central block is connected to the separate 'wings' or dependent blocks by means of curving colonnades or screens in the manner already referred to. They seem to reach forward and embrace one as the entrance is approached and at the same time extend the house into its surroundings. Here is the origin of that relationship between the architecture of the country house and the landscape in which it stood, a relationship so fully explored by English designers in the eighteenth century as one of the main aspects of the Picturesque. Palladio's appeal to their clients, of course, resided in the fact that his villas served a socio-economic set-up not dissimilar to their own. The external stairs leading grandly to the portico entrance and the *piano nobile* were a feature to be imitated countless times in the centuries which followed.

The Villa (Foscari) Malcontenta (1560) by the Brenta Canal is a high cube with an impressive Ionic-pillared portico, while his

Villa Maser of about the same date is also a simple design much enhanced by the wonderful illusionist frescoes by Paolo Veronese, architecture and painting combining in a manner that anticipates the Baroque. Internally, Palladio, like Serlio, continued the use of the traditional square newel staircase round an open well but they both introduced a new oval-shaped newel stair and adopted the practice of cantilevering the steps out from the wall so that they required no outside support. An interesting constructional feature of Palladio's work is that instead of the more usual stone and marble (except for carved stone detail) he uses brick even for the columns in the fashion of north Italy but renders it with stucco to gain an effect similar to stone with the added advantage that it can be tinted and therefore introduces an element of colour.

His Loggia del Capitaniato is a richly decorated late work and is an ornamental version of the theme of Michelangelo's palaces on the Capitoline Hill. It is a civic loggia with council chamber on the *piano nobile,* characteristic of his latest style in its Imperial richness and sensuousness that reminds us Palladio was the contemporary of Tintoretto and Veronese. The latter did the superb frescoes in his Villa Barbaro at Maser.

In 1580, the year of his death, Palladio designed the still-used, wooden Teatro Olimpico, Vicenza, for the Humanist Academy of which he was a member, a rare and interesting early theatre based on Roman prototypes with a semi-circular covered auditorium and a permanent stage and perspective backdrop, the illusionism of which reminds us how close we are to the Baroque.

The perspectives were in fact by his pupil Vicenzo Scamozzi who altered the dome of Palladio's Villa Rotonda.

Scamozzi was an academic Mannerist at the time Baroque was developing and he also followed his master by producing a large architectural manual in 1615 which did much to promote classicism in the eighteenth century, and by building a number of villas such as the Villa Pisani, Lonigo (1576) (his best) and the Villa Molin, near Padua (c. 1597) where he built S. Gaetano in 1581. He finished off the façade of Palladio's S. Giorgio Maggiore in Venice and designed the large, dignified Procuratie Nuove (1584) on the south side of the Piazza S. Marco, basing it on Sansovino's library, lengthened and given a third storey.

Scamozzi's centralized plan for the fortified town of Palma Nova is a remarkable example of Renaissance fortification with

SCAMOZZI'S PLAN FOR PALMA NOVA

low, pointed bastions in accordance with the new dynamic concepts of defence which came in with Renaissance artillery. Here gunnery theory and aesthetic planning came together to produce attractive, symmetrical schemes that became an international style of planning in Europe and in trading stations abroad. The cathedral at Palma Nova (1603) is also by Scamozzi.

CHAPTER TEN

Baroque

MANNERISM is the style associated with the Counter Reformation, but about the time the success of this became assured in the early seventeenth century a new style began to emerge that is not characterized by Mannerist tensions or insistence on academicism. It was a style that may be taken both as a relaxation of Counter Reformation severity and as a rejection of restrained Classicism in favour of fuller, more expansive forms, stronger rhythms, dramatic and emotional qualities of a freer kind. The Catholic Reaction is expressed by the joyful energy of a new style.

In a general way, of course, Baroque evolved from classical Renaissance architecture but in an original way, frequently quite unclassical, rejecting rationality and the antique grammar of design as expressed in staid conventions and rules in a search for grand extravagant effects and excitement.

Michelangelo was mainly a Mannerist in his architectural work but Baroque rejected Mannerism as too inhibited and austere and instead found its inspiration largely in the Michelangelo of St Peter's where his bold sculptural moulding of walls as if they were composed of some plastic substance, his dynamic handling of mass and space, and his emphasis on drama, grandeur, and picturesqueness all became leading *motifs* of the Baroque style. Whereas Mannerists were content to manipulate the classical elements, Baroque architects manipulated whole walls and roof surfaces and developed a new sense of spatial flow: Renaissance interiors are composed of separate static spaces but in typically Baroque buildings there is a continuous movement of space with rhythmic sequences and dramatic culminations.

Among the chief elements of Baroque, then, besides a new freedom and complexity in planning with varied shapes, often based on the ellipse, are curving façades, curving spaces and forms. There are emphatic projections and recessions, orders of columns and pilasters (often of giant proportions or twisted) doubled and clustered together with broken cornices, broken pediments, wavy scrolls and volutes assembled in rich complicated designs full of variety, striking effects, and sensuous appeal. With such elements considerable nobility was often achieved; impressiveness always. If occasionally there were lapses into vulgarity there was never meanness.

Another hallmark of Baroque architecture is its love of luxurious decorative effects in which strange exotic and even fantastic forms and details are indulgently piled on in a manner which appears to have no logic except the typically Baroque one of uniting all into a single composition in which structure and decoration merge. In Baroque architecture, decoration is not something added, as in antiquity and during the Renaissance; it is the principle which lies behind an entire design. No detail stands alone; all are part of one great design, unified, integrated so that their impact is felt at its most powerful.

Baroque sometimes has the defects of its virtues, however, and decoration can run to excess. Occasionally, too, its exuberance and its sensuous qualities are too overpowering for Anglo-Saxon taste. But this, it should be remembered, is just the effect at which the designers of interiors like this were aiming, using all the skill of the decorative craftsmen at their disposal to capture the heart of the beholder by wooing his senses. Thus light is often used dramatically and emotionally bursting forth in sudden explosions, while paintings, colour, and gilding are freely applied to enhance walls and ceilings. Typical of the latter are the great compositions full of crowded turning figures bursting through into what appears to be the open vault of the sky, an effect obtained by perspective painting going back to Correggio's magnificent design (1526) for the dome of the gloomy medieval cathedral at Parma. The apotheosis is reached in Andrea Pozzo's ceiling for S. Ignazio, Rome, a quite astonishing achievement.

Yet another feature of Baroque is its penchant for illusionism, *trompe l'oeil* effects, as exemplified by its optical tricks and use of simulated materials. No modern 'puritanism' represses its impulses in this direction. One of its commonest optical devices is to increase the appearance of depth by exaggerating perspective in a way that was noted in the early work of Bramante at S. Maria presso S. Satiro, Milan, and in the way Michelangelo positioned his twin Capitoline palaces on either side of the Palazzo Senatore.

But the practice does not reach its apotheosis until the Baroque period when both the individual parts of buildings and sometimes whole groups of buildings, squares and steps were frequently arranged scenographically to create an impressive *mise en scène* or stage-set effect. It is no accident that the seventeenth century also saw the development of similar vistas and scenic effects in connection with the actual stage sets required by the new Italian operas with their perspective architectural backcloths. Indeed, in the context of theatrical design Baroque and Rococo (a lighter decorative development of it) have survived unchallenged later than any other form of Classical architecture, even into the twentieth century, if in a somewhat debased form in the swelling balconies and gilt stucco of innumerable opera houses and theatres all over Europe. It was Venice in the seventeenth century which first introduced semi-circular tiers of boxes.

Realistic figure sculpture, too, with astonishingly rendered textures, plays an important part in Baroque decorative schemes, forming links between the spectator and the architectural setting as well as usefully serving to disguise awkward points in the design.

The beginnings of Baroque may be traced from about 1600. They occur in Rome, naturally enough, having in mind the influence of Michelangelo and the church-building activity of the Jesuits in the early seventeenth century. Until quite recently, in fact, within the circuit of its walls Rome was largely a Baroque city in character. The style reached a peak there from 1630 to 1670 before it travelled north later in the century to Lombardy and the Piedmont. There it swept on irresistibly, extending well into the eighteenth century, to capture the other Catholic countries of Europe and eventually reach as far as the new world possessions of Spain and Portugal.

The first great master of the Baroque architecture was Giovanni Lorenzo Bernini, also its greatest sculptor. A Neapolitan with an ardent southern temperament, he arrived in Rome in 1605. His skill and universal talents rapidly earned him the patronage of the princes of the church so that commissions soon began to flow in.

His sculpture with its swirling movement, and radiating energy may be seen in the Villa Borghese (Apollo and Daphne, and David), in his splendid fountains to be mentioned later, and in what is perhaps his masterpiece in this medium, his S. Teresa in the chapel of that name in S. Maria della Vittoria where he combines realism and illusion in a magnificent *tour de force* of Baroque theatrical emotionalism.

Bernini's most famous architectural works are the immense double colonnades curving round to enclose the magnificent piazza in front of St Peter's with its central obelisk and fountains. These magnificent ranges of Doric columns, four deep, supporting a huge entablature and over sixty huge statues of saints, vigorous and grand yet open in feeling, were designed with a deliberately scenographic intention of building up Maderna's façade (1606) to increase its apparent size and importance. Maderna had already added a nave, thus reverting to an earlier idea than Michelangelo's plan for the great Basilica – which is marked by a new Baroque lightness and spatial fluidity. This great piazza, a splendidly integrated forecourt where the huge crowds gather for the papal benediction, is an extraordinarily complex thing, despite its apparent simplicity, with allusions to the atrium of the Early Christian churches, to Michelangelo's oval on the Capitol, and to Palladio's open colonnades; while the monumental size and *mise en scène* effect are wholly Baroque characteristics.

Inside St Peter's, besides the papal tombs and florid throne of St Peter, Bernini devised the huge 85 ft baldacchino (1633) to give emphasis to the high altar at the crossing, in the manner of the Early Christian ciborium. Its four great twisted 'Solomonic' columns derive from the fourth-century Basilica of Constantine and are made of bronze taken from the Pantheon. In the rest of the decoration of St Peter's with its sumptuous use of coloured marble, gilt stucco, bronze, and statuary we see the first great opulent Baroque interior.

At the side of the Basilica of St Peter's, necessarily cramped between it and the near-by Vatican Palace is his Scala Regia (*c.* 1665). A good illustration of Baroque illusionism, its width narrows inwards to produce the optical illusion of appearing longer than it actually is. The device is managed by using a colonnade of diminishing proportions and making the walls of the long tunnel-vaulted staircase converge inwards towards the palace, to which it is the principal entrance. A typical scenic effect is the way Bernini ingeniously contrives to overcome the awkward change of direction by introducing the dramatic climax of an equestrian statue at the angle, and there is clever use of concealed lighting for its dramatic possibilities. The gorgeous decoration, richly satisfying, is typical of his assured manner.

In the same year as he built his church at Castel Gandolfo Bernini began his finest church of all. S. Andrea al Quirinale, Rome (1658). This impressive design follows in the tradition of the centralized plan adopted for many Renaissance churches but it is a wonderful realization of his idea of a church as a setting for luxuriant Baroque painting and sculptural decoration – what has been called religious theatricalism – and it is almost a pure oval in plan, a shape that was typical of centralized Baroque churches, where it was introduced as an alternative to the circular or Greek cross plans of the earlier period, but not confined to it.

The oval plan actually appears for the first time in Sebastiano Serlio's book, *Churches* (1547), the long axis corresponding to the longitudinal nave. This was to be the usual position adopted for the oval plan in the many subsequent variations on the theme. It was followed in S. Anna dei Palafrenieri, Rome *c.* 1570, by Vignola and then by Maderna in his S. Giacomo al Corso (1594), and much later by Rainaldi in his S. Maria di Monte Santo (1662) (on which Bernini also worked).

But Bernini's S. Andrea al Quirinale was not like these and represents a rarer and more interesting development where the long axis of the oval is parallel to the entrance. Its plan is, in fact,

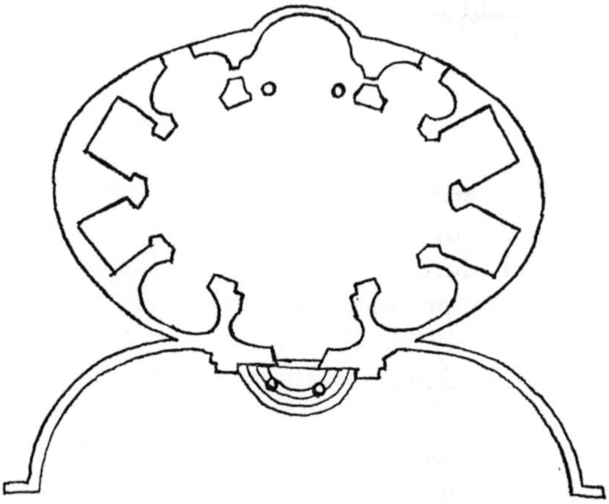

S. ANDREA AL QUIRINALE, ROME

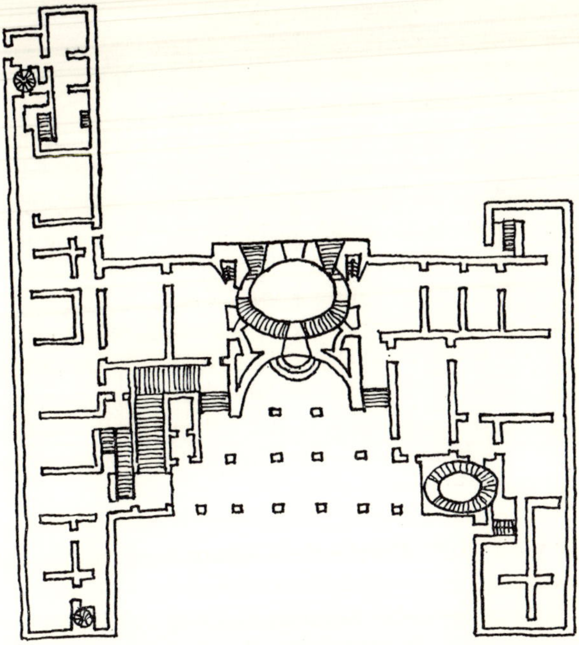

PALAZZO BARBERINI, ROME

a very regular and straightforward ellipse with radial chapels scooped out all round except for the entrance and high altar facing it. The effect is most harmonious and almost musical. Another of Bernini's churches is to be seen at Ariccia (1662) but for a moment let us put Baroque churches aside and turn to palaces.

High Renaissance Rome had carried forward the Florentine idea of the quadrangular palace, still fortress-like in its solidity despite its richly modelled façades with orders and pedimented windows, and the type still continues during the Baroque period. But the Palazzo Barberini (1624) is an exception in that it has a quite new open quality which seems to reflect some of the lightness and breadth of late sixteenth-century Palladian villas and Genoese palaces. The conception of Carlo Maderna, the principal architect of the earlier generation who had completed the nave and façade at St Peter's (1606) as described and built the Palazzo Mattei (1598), the plan of the Palazzo Barberini is something like

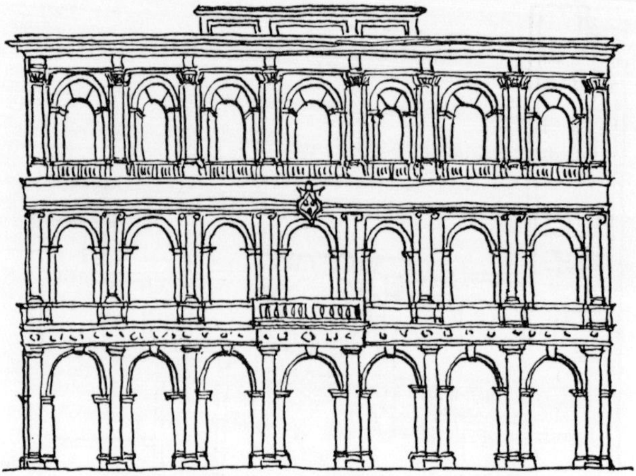

PALAZZO BARBERINI, ROME

one half of Bramante's Cortile de S. Damaso at the Vatican, with centre loggias and short projecting wings.

The elevations appear to be related to the cortile of the Palazzo Farnese by Antonio de Sangallo the Younger and the main façade is ascribed to Bernini but the rich Baroque ornament added to the orders and the perspective effect of the top storey windows are probably the work of Borromini who did much of the detailing. Inside there is an oval *salone* and a newel staircase of oval shape, types which first made their appearance in the domestic architecture of Palladio and other north Italians. The principal staircase, though not oval, is more aîry and of more generous proportions than in the previous century so that here again is a lighter, freer, more elegant spirit to add to the force and fervour of Baroque.

Bernini's Palazzo di Montecitorio (1650), now the Chamber of Deputies, was finished by Carlo Fontana who built the Palazzo Bolognetti (1700); but a much greater work was Bernini's Palazzo Chigi-Odescalchi (1664), unfortunately much altered, where the centre bays with their giant Composite pilasters stood forward from rusticated wings in a manner that came to be much copied for its grand effect. The inspiration is both Bramante's 'House of Raphael' and Michelangelo's Capitoline palace design.

Francesco Borromini was a contemporary of Bernini, his rival, and the second great name in Roman Baroque. Unlike Bernini he was unstable and introverted. He trained primarily as a mason, working first with Maderna and later with Bernini himself whose impetuosity he shared but whose unorthodox approach and originality he exceeded to the point of eccentricity.

Characteristic of Borromini's work are even more than ever dynamic forms and dramatic gestures, extravagant effects of multiple curving lines and scrolls, though like Maderna's, it also has something of the northern breadth and openness about it at times.

S. Agnese di Piazza Navona (1652) is a very fine High Baroque composition. Begun by Carlo Rainaldi on a centralized Greek cross plan it was taken over by Borromini who changed it to a variation on the oval theme, which placed the main axis parallel to the entrance façade. The result, however, is much more complex. than Bernini's S. Andrea al Quirinale for the central octagonal

S. AGNESE IN PIAZZA NAVONA, ROME

space is here extended out into chapels and niches to arrive at the broken but roughly oval shape we see now.

The façade, in the twin-towered north Italian manner, is very much a three-dimensional design with bold projections and convex curves which make it a particularly good example to analyse for its Baroque characteristics. Here most of the elements are still classical as in Renaissance architecture but they are used in strikingly original ways and combined with others, such as the oval windows over the doorheads, which are not classical. The façade with its 'temple front' porch entrance flanked by double pilasters, is concave in the centre and from it, on either side rise the two towers. They are square at the first stage and round at the second, the two stages being related by a most unorthodox broken entablature. The whole group of forms of which the building is composed is dramatically conceived and dominated by the lanterned dome which rises from the high drum, again with doubled pilasters and boldly broken entablature. Altogether this is a complex and richly orchestrated design.

Borromini's S. Carlo alle Quattro Fontane is both earlier and later than S. Agnese. The plan dates from 1633 but its façade was not completed until thirty-four years later, just before he died. His first great work, this astonishingly complex plan for a church as small as this, is a wonderful variation of the oval of the 'longitudinal' type. Instead of the clear articulation of space familiar in Renaissance architecture here is a plan shape in which what

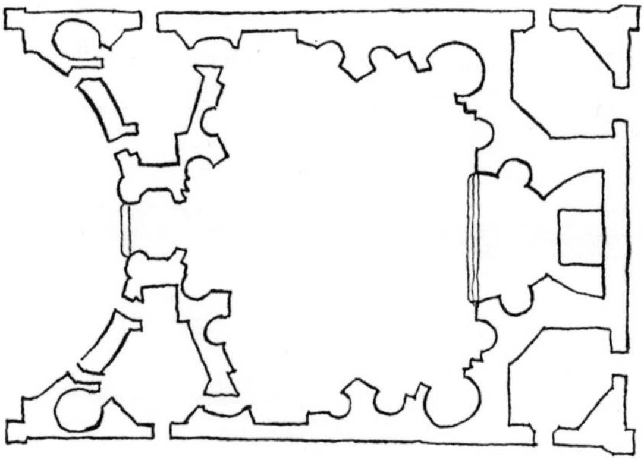

S. IVO, ROME

appear to be parts of five ovals (the centre space and the surrounding chapels) are fused together under a honeycomb dome in a rhythm of broken curves which flows round the undulating walls (the first time since Hadrian) in a distinctly sensuous movement. The basis of the plan, however, is actually equilateral triangles showing that a more regular geometry sometimes underlies the more obvious freedoms of Baroque, though not nearly so rigid a geometry as the Renaissance favoured. Baroque can be at once sensuous and intellectual.

The façade (1667), oddly placed across one corner as it were, is another brilliant exercise in Baroque rhythms, the storeys swaying in and out contrapuntally. Inside S. Carlo one observes the typically Baroque use of exaggerated perspective for the niches, as in Borromini's top-storey windows of the Barberini palace. Despite a fertile imagination which enabled him to introduce new ornamental motifs his interiors show a preference for white stucco effects rather than the polychrome richness of Bernini.

Borromini, despite his retarded beginning as an architect, enjoyed great success. He also built the churches of S. Filippo Neri (1637) on an awkward site, the façade of which cleverly serves for both chapel and conventional buildings, the superb S. Ivo della Sapienza (1642), with triangular planning again, yet a single unified space; and a most extraordinary lanterned, well-lit, drumless dome, and S. Maria dei Sette Dolori (*c.* 1655). At times he hints, in his highly personal style, at the Gothic in his use of a form or the emphasis he gives to dynamic structure.

In the 1640s he remodelled the interior of the ancient basilica of S. Giovanni in Laterano giving it its present Baroque appearance, except for the severe façade with loggia and the Corsini chapel which are the work of Alessandro Galilei (1732). Mention has been made of his contribution to the Palazzo Barberini and he again worked where Rainaldi had worked on the grand saloon of the Palazzo Doria-Pamfili (1650).

Borromini's last complete work was the Collegio di Propaganda Fide which shows him now very far away from the conventions of High Renaissance architecture. Its unorthodoxy is extreme and was recognized as such even in his own day, so that few wished to follow him in this new development. Another feature which the Collegio displays is a heavy rather melancholy monumentality not hitherto a marked feature of his highly expressive work. In 1667 he committed suicide.

Despite the very interesting and characteristic Baroque churches on a centralized plan which we have been describing, most, as explained at the end of the last chapter, followed Vignola's Gesù. It became an archetype of these which combined the longitudinal nave (with side aisles replaced by chapels) with centralized eastern parts consisting of short transepts, centre space, and chancel. Over the crossing was a dome and there was an entrance façade harking back to the triumphal arch motif.

An interesting example of what happened after the Gesù is S. Giovanni de' Fiorentini (1588), for which no less an architect than Michelangelo had devised a central plan. But Giacomo della

S. SUSANNA, ROME

Porta and Carlo Maderna abandoned it deliberately for a longitudinal nave in the manner of the Gesù, even if they divided the nave into aisles and deepened the transepts.

Maderna's S. Susanna (1597) is one of the earliest of the countless Baroque versions of the Gesù type proper but while retaining classical correctness in its two storeys of columns it has developed a richer and more plastic design with strong vertical emphasis. His S. Maria dello Vittoria (1605) also follows in the same tradition. S. Ignazio (1626) shows it again, richer and more expansive, employing more columns and unorthodox use of motifs. Thus the trend continues, getting progressively more crowded and excessive, until it reaches a culmination in the grand and powerful façade of SS. Vicenzo ed Anastasio (1646) by Martino Longhi the Younger, Borromini's S. Carlo (1667), already described, and the façade of S. Maria della Pace (1656) by Pietro da Cortona.

Once again in Cortona's façade numerous columns and pilasters add to its complexity and richness. In addition the front, with

PORTICO, S. M. DELLA PACE, ROME

its projecting convex centre and semi-circular portico, is opened out into straight wings at ground level while above this concave curves reach back and in, an effective counterpoint of forms.

In the small piazza he shows the Baroque architect's theatrical affinities and readiness to create a more intimate *mise en scène* than St Peter's piazza, treating the space as an auditorium, the flanking buildings as boxes, and arranging the side approaches as though they were stage entrances with dramatic views.

Cortona, trained first as a painter, had already built what is perhaps his masterpiece SS. Martina e Luca (1635) a Greek cross with semi-circular apses under a fine coffered dome, magnificently unified into a total and highly individual Baroque building. It is elaborately decorated with many undulations, and especially significant is his use of giant columns internally, not to articulate but to suggest the plastic character of the wall masses. Like Borromini he preferred white interiors. In this he differs from Bernini as he also does in dispensing with statuary as part of his decorative scheme. The seven years from 1640 he spent decorating the Pitti Palace in Florence where his frescoes like his fine ceiling in the Palazzo Barberini show him as perhaps the best decorative painter of his time.

Two years after SS. Martina e Luca he designed S. Maria in Via Lata which shows a shift in the direction of High Renaissance monumental simplicity and *gravitas*, and added the dome to the handsome church of S. Carlo al Corso (1668) by the Longhi, father and son, which shows the same development to a grand serenity characteristic of the earlier period and rare in the more restless Baroque.

Carlo Rainaldi's style is a highly individual version of Baroque modified in the direction of Mannerism. His S. Maria in Campitelli (1663) has a singular double-cross plan; and he was also responsible for most of the twin churches of S. Maria in Montesanto and S. Maria dei Miracoli in the Piazza del Popolo (1662), besides the Palazzo Salviati.

Baroque architecture in Rome dating from the first half of the eighteenth century also includes the façade of the basilica of S. Giovanni in Laterano already mentioned (as well as the interior by Borromini), the Palazzo della Consulta (1736) and the façade of S. Maria Maggiore (1741), by Ferdinando Fuga who rebuilt S. Apollinore in 1750. These façades show his elegant and sophisticated version of the Baroque manner; later it became duller and heavier.

Under Popes Urban VIII and Alexander VII Bernini had been concerned with developing the work begun by Sixtus V in making Rome a great pilgrimage city with great streets focusing on piazze marked by churches, obelisks, and fountains. Rome has always been a city of fountains since Imperial times and mention must be made of some of the finest, the Baroque designs by Bernini – the Triton in the Piazza Barberini, the one in the Barberini gardens, the Four Rivers in the Piazza Navona, and the one in the Piazza di S. Pietro. The Fontana di Trevi (1735) by Nicola Salvi is a wonderful composition inspired by Bernini's earlier ones in which a classical structure, rocks, fountains, and water deities are all brought together in an extraordinary fantasy.

Rome, too, is a city of flights of steps connecting different levels, some great stairways, some narrow steps. One of the most celebrated Late Baroque essays in these is the Scala di Spagna (1723) by Francesco de Sanctis.

Generally speaking, however, Baroque in Rome had passed its peak by the end of the 1670s and began to revert to a Neo-classical Baroque style partly under French influence, for by the eighteenth century the architectural initiative had largely passed to Paris where Louis XIV's architects Louis Levau and Jules Hardouin-Mansart had established an equally grand but more restrained mode, full of clarity, elegance, and precision.

Florence, already so rich in architectural work of the Renaissance has little Baroque to show; but the Boboli gardens are an interesting example of how the style affected Italian gardens.

So far nothing has been said of Baroque in north Italy, whence it spread from Rome, culminating in the impressive work of Guarini and Juvara in and around Turin. But first the other cities of the north. Following the splendid palaces of Alessi in Genoa came those of Baccio di Bartolommeo Bianco – the Palazzo Balbi-Senarega (1609), the Palazzo Durazzo-Pallavicini (1620), and the Palazzo dell' Università (1623) which was begun as a Jesuit college. All three, in the Via Balbi, named after the powerful family for whom the palaces were built, are nobly planned and capitalize scenographically the steep slope on which they are sited, especially the Università with its four levels of colonnaded courtyards and magnificent staircase. The Baroque period did not see the introduction of any new types but it used them dramatically and developed existing ones, including the grand ceremonial type devised by Spain and known as the Imperial. Spain showed more creative imagination than Italy in this respect but Genoa was something of an exception going in for broad spacious designs especially of the T-plan type. It is a fine city for Baroque palaces.

Bianco also built the near-by Villa Durazzo (1620), a pleasing and impressive work; but the huge and prominent Albergo dei Poveri, building in Genoa from 1655 to 1675 under four different architects, is not of a very distinguished quality.

Venice, in S. Maria della Salute (1631) by Baldassare Longhena, possesses one of the most majestic of all Baroque churches. Magnificently positioned in relation to the Dogana (Custom House), the open square, and the waters of the Grand Canal, with its broad flight of steps leading up to the complex entrance

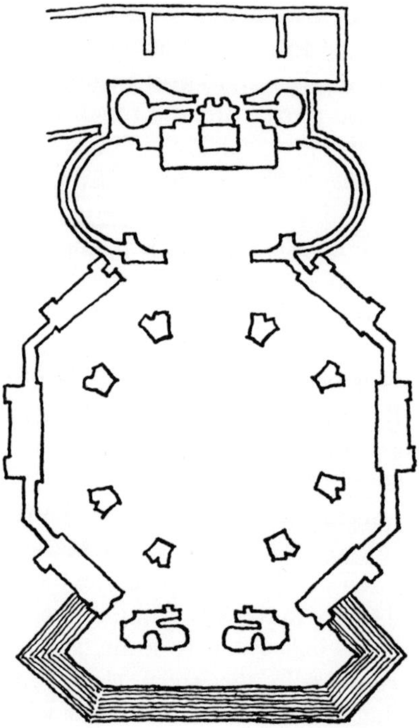

S. M. DELLA SALUTE, VENICE

façade, the design shows a grand appreciation of the scenographic opportunities of the site. In addition to the usual motifs of triumphal arch and temple front there are huge volutes around the octagonal drum, giving abutment to the powerfully conceived and dominating main dome. Underneath this the central space is octagonal too, with ambulatory and six side chapels opening out from it in dramatic vistas. Over the chancel is a second dome which, with the cupolaed turrets and lanterns, adds to the rich and picturesque exterior.

Longhena was the pupil of Scamozzi and worked on S. Maria della Salute throughout his career as the chief Baroque architect in Venice. He was also influenced by the great Palladio (witness the interior vistas) as well as Sansovino and Sanmicheli, as may be divined from his heavily rusticated palazzi on the Grand Canal – the Palazzo Rezzonico (1650) although not the top storey, and the Palazzo Pesaro (1679). Once more in his work one observes the typical Venetian preference for an enriched style even more than for the powerful masses that were essential to Baroque.

Longhena also built the conventual buildings of the monastery of S. Giorgio Maggiore (1643), with its magnificent Baroque double staircase, unusually spacious for Italy and very influential; and the church of S. Maria di Scalzi (1649) to which was added an extravagant façade by Guiseppe Salvi who built another, for S. Salvatore in 1663. Longhena's little church of the Ospedaletto (1670) shows in extreme form his leaning towards fantasy and excess in sculptural detailing.

On the mainland, of the Baroque villas, as distinct from the earlier ones by Palladio and Scamozzi, perhaps the finest is not one of those attributed to Longhena but the Villa Pisani, Strà (1735), by F. M. Preti and G. Frigimelica. Like S. Simeone, Venice (1718), it showed the spirit of Palladio was still very much alive in the Veneto even at this late date.

In Milan the most prominent early Baroque architect was Francesco Maria Ricchino, though there is not a great deal of Baroque architecture in that city. Among the best of his works are the Palazzo di Brera (1651), once a Jesuit college, now the famous art gallery, with its commanding façade and its grand and dignified cortile arcaded with coupled columns. Its proud restraint is really Mannerist rather than Baroque however.

Ricchino also probably did the Collegio Elvetico (1627), now the Archivo della Stato, with its concave façade, and the Palazzo Annoni (1631). A few churches are by his hand, S. Guiseppe (1607) departing from Mannerism in its plan based on two centralized units and its aedicule façade, and S. Giorgio, a small attractive octagonal design being his best surviving ones. He also restored some earlier churches and in 1621 built the splendid central great court in the Ospedale Maggiore by the quattrocento architect Filarete, to whose style he was careful to accommodate his design. He finally completed Tibaldi's west front of the great Gothic cathedral in 1638.

In the small town of Mondivi, west of Savona, there is notable work by Francesco Gallo in the cathedral and especially in the near-by church of the Madonna di Vico.

We come now to consider the most Baroque city of North Italy – Turin in the Piedmont. The style was, however, late in arriving and as part of Savoy had been in French occupation and there were dynastic ties the variety of Baroque to be found there bears some signs of this connection. The outstanding names here are Camillo Guarino Guarini, who first put Turin on the architectural map, and, half a century later, Filippo Juvara.

Guarini's churches here and abroad (as at Lisbon and Paris, for he gained an international reputation) reveal a great inventiveness

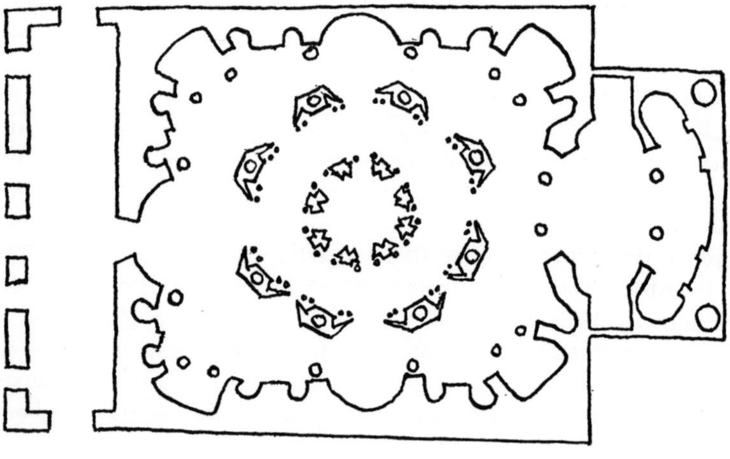

S. LORENZO, TURIN

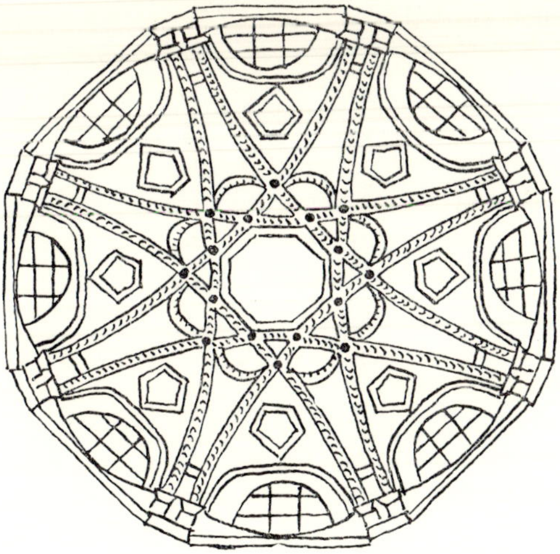

DOME OF S. LORENZO, TURIN

and an extravagant complex spatial use of oval shapes and undulating curves that show him continuing in the expressive manner of Borromini. In his highly creative centrally planned S. Lorenzo (1666), for instance, one of the most magnificent of late Baroque churches, the arches and balconies sway out to the central space above which rises an octagonal 'open' dome with interlaced semi-circular ribs that suggest the 'Saracenic' architecture which he must have encountered on his previous travels in Iberia and Sicily, where he built a church at Messina. The swaying forward of the arches was to appeal greatly to the Baroque architects of Southern Germany and Austria, while Guarini also built vaults with interlaced groins recalling similar Gothic and Islamic structures. Both aesthetically and structurally he was a pioneer.

Guarini also had a preference for centralized plans and curved forms even when he employed a longitudinal nave, introducing bays of an oval shape. This can be seen in his influential church of the Immaculate Conception (1672) for the Mission of St Vincent, with its double circle plan. For a longitudinal design it reveals an astonishingly dynamic interweaving of space which much affected the architecture of south Germany and Austria. Behind his sinuous shapes and lines and imaginative flights there exists a firm intellectual structure for Guarini was a mathematician of

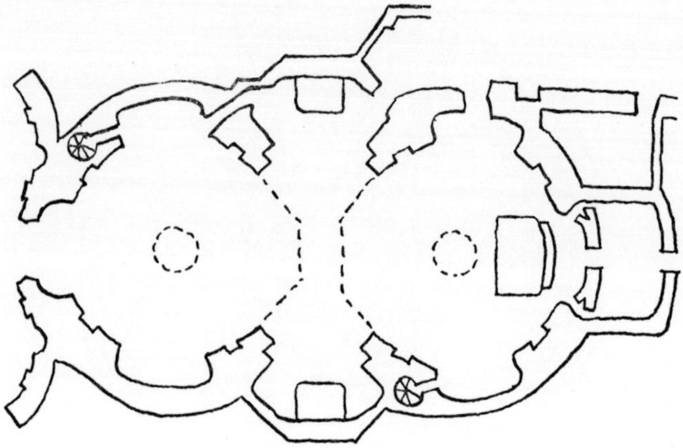

CHURCH OF THE
IMMACULATE CONCEPTION, TURIN

note besides a priest. The Capella della SS. Sindone (1667), like S. Lorenzo, has a bizarre conical dome built of segmental arches, diminishing upwards, a mysterious distribution of light being obtained filtering through the grids.

In 1678 Guarini built the Collegio dei Nobili which is reminiscent of Borromini and a year later began the enormous Palazzo Carignano (1679) with its plenitude of curves. Here with great *brio* and success he applies to a palace front Borromini's principle of the undulating façade which here reads at the centre concave, convex, concave. It is a design of considerable skill and boldness, as is the interior with its chief central apartment, a characteristic oval, reached by two splendid Baroque staircases, both salone and stairs among the very finest in Italy. The detail of the curious 'eared' window pediments is characteristic.

Guarini spent the last part of his life in Turin, dying in 1683. Juvara did not arrive there until 1714, when he came on the invitation of the King of Savoy, having trained in Rome under Carlo Fontana, an assistant of Bernini who practised a somewhat derivative academic style well exemplified by the façade of S. Marcello al Corso, Rome (1682). He had already earned a reputation as a stage designer. Juvara followed Guarini on the Santuario della Consolata, designed the façade of S. Cristina and constructed the domes of S. Andrea Mantua and the late fifteenth-century, transitional, Como Cathedral (1731), for his work in Italy is not altogether confined to Turin.

One of the greatest of all Baroque churches is his Basilica della Superga, Turin (1715), but it is a restrained Baroque, moving away from the sumptuousness of Rome and the Rococo proclivities of Guarini towards the Neo-classical of the second half of the century. The chapel of the Veneria Reale (1716) is also a grandiloquent work; but other fine churches such as the Chiesa del Carmine (1732), which has Rococo spatial, structural, and decorative qualities, S. Filippo Neri (1715) and S. Croce (1718) were badly damaged in the war.

Juvara did several palazzi in Turin such as the Palazzo d'Ormea (1730) but more important are the four great works he did as royal architect – the Veneria Reale (1714), the Palazzo Madama (1718), somewhat Berninesque, the incomplete Castello di Rivoli (1718) and above all the X-plan hunting palace, Castello Reale, at Stupinigi (1729) with its ramifying but symmetrical lay-out.

LA SUPERGA, TURIN

Again we see in this great creation the restrained classicism that is most characteristic of Juvara's work. It is a Baroque total-work to which numerous painters, sculptors, and stuccoists have all contributed, especially to the great hall with its echoes of transalpine influence; for Juvara also extended his concern for interior effects to the furnishings which he himself designed.

Lacking the originality of some earlier Baroque architects, Juvara was nevertheless a brilliant exponent of an elegant restrained form of Late Baroque. Prolific in decorative invention and in his output generally (it also included the laying out of some new quarters in Turin and the domes of Alberti's Sant' Andrea, and Como cathedral) he gained a name abroad and was invited to Spain and Portugal to fulfil important commissions. Like Lombard masons of the time, Baroque architects from the north of Italy were widely travelled and this helped to disseminate the style in other Catholic countries.

There is not a great deal of good Baroque architecture in north Italy outside the largest cities but Bologna has S. Paolo (1611) by G. A. Magenta and E. Fichi, and S. Maria della Vita (1687) by C. B. Bergonzoni, the dome of which, dating from a hundred years later, is by Bibiena, one of the well-known family of painters-designers-architects who flourished in the eighteenth century. Parma has S. Antonio Abbate (1712) by Ferdinando Bibiena and the Palazzo Municipale (1627) by G. B. Magnani.

CASTELLO REALE, STUPINIGI

Finally there is the very individual and ornate Baroque architecture of southern Italy and Sicily, and once again these regions reveal the cultural influences they have been subjected to through political domination by foreigners, this time the Spanish who ruled them from 1503 as the Kingdom of Naples, apart from a period of twenty-seven years at the beginning of the eighteenth century.

Naples itself built a great deal in the Baroque style including the monastery known as the Certosa di S. Martino (*c.* 1630) by Cosimo Fanzago, with its fine Baroque church but rather Renaissance-style cloister, and another later church by this architect, S. Maria Maggiore (1657). The Palazzo Reale (1600) by Domenico Fontana was enlarged in the mid-eighteenth century about the time Ferdinando Fuga, mentioned earlier for his work in Rome, built the Reclusorio and the Chiesa dei Gerolamini. Fuga's large Neapolitan work, however, lacks the originality and verve of his best Roman.

The charming small town of Lecce in Apulia is a museum of Baroque churches and small palazzi, mostly by Giuseppe and Francesco Zimbalo. The deliciously elegant and ornate façade given to Riccardo's S. Croce by one of the Zimbali shows that there is nothing sombre or ponderous about them at their best; they were the creators of a very original decorative style. The church of the Carmine (1706) is attributed to their pupil Giuseppe Cino. But more than for these fine examples of Baroque architecture, Lecce is celebrated as the first town where the whole urban design is organized as a real-life stage set, as it were – a treatment that was to be extended to the Sicilian cities rebuilt after the earthquake of 1693, notable at Ragusa and Noto.

The Piazza del Duomo, Palermo (1761), gives a good idea of this kind of urban lay-out developed by Late Baroque. G. Amato built the Chiesa della Pieta (1686), after remodelling the Norman church of S. Salvatore (1628). Sicily has a large number of Baroque buildings very singular and extravagant as a rule. Siracusa, Ragusa, Catania, and Noto have many examples, partly as a result of the necessity to rebuild after earthquakes, though the same phenomena also resulted in the destruction of some earlier ones. At Siracusa the Duomo was given a Baroque façade in 1730 by A. Palma; it is a church which has been many times transformed, starting as a fifth-century Doric temple, becoming a

Christian church in the seventh century, a mosque in the ninth century, and then once more a Christian church.

Notable work at Catania is the façade of the Duomo (1730) and the Palazzo Municipale (1732) and the Collegio Cutelli (1754), all by Giovan Battista Vaccarini. Though another pupil of Carlo Fontana we can see in Vaccarini's work, as in that of Guarini, elements of the Rococo that was to be one of the characteristic developments of the Baroque style in the eighteenth century, especially in Central Europe where the influence of the Italians was greatest. Generally, however, Vaccarini's work is rather more restrained than was usual in southern Italy and Sicily at this time. A characteristic of the south is a lavish use of marble inlay decoration that is almost like marquetry.

CHAPTER ELEVEN

Rococo, Neo-Classicism, Revival c. 1750 – c. 1900

BY THE middle of the eighteenth century in Italy was more or less played out and a Neo-Classical style under French influence was taking its place. The tendency towards this has already been noted in Juvara's La Superga, for example; while at the same time the Rococo elements in Guarini, the earlier Lombard Baroque architect, were not very greatly developed in Italy where there is a noticeable absence of this light, curvaceous, ornamental style; with the exception of a few examples such as the façade of the old basilican church of S. Croce in Gerusalemme, Rome (1741) and the Basilica of S. Trophimena, Minori, Savona.

The former is by Domenico Gregorini and Pietro Passalacqua but a better-known Roman Rococo architect is Filippo Raguzzini whose great work is the stage-like set of the buildings in the Piazza S. Ignazio facing the church of that name, with their elegant and sophisticated concave façades, segments of three

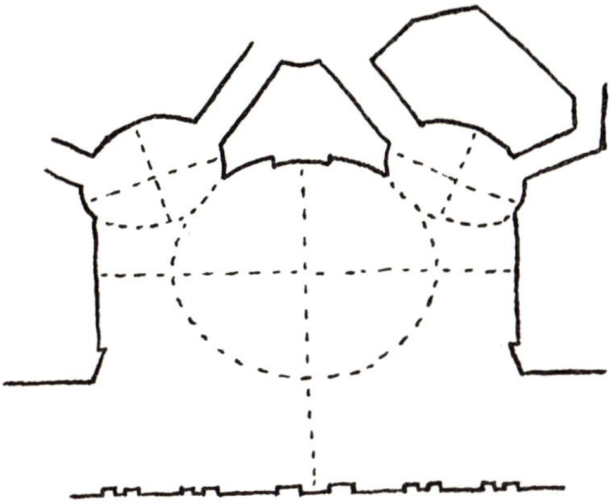

PIAZZA S. IGNAZIO, ROME

related ovals. Similar surface characteristics, a long way from the muscularity of Baroque, are observable in his façade of S. Maria della Quercia (1727).

A Turin architect of the period was Bernardo Vittone, a pupil of Juvara but also a follower of the more dynamic Guarini. His small but delightful S. Chiara, Brà (1742), manifests a new light airiness and gaiety and a unification of space (especially vertically, despite the complexity of its upper parts) that mark its particular spatial and decorative qualities as Rococo rather than Baroque. His preference for light but complex structural systems, diffused clear lighting, and delicate pale colour effects can also be seen in his S. Michele in Rivarolo Canavesi (1759), not far from Turin. Again brick-built, this is a domed octagon with choir and oval sacristy attached, and a concave façade. That Vittone was structurally inventive is shown by his use of the three-vaulted dome (after Guarini) and pendentive-squinches, as in S. Maria di Piazza, Turin (1751) with its superbly domed nave and choir, one of the finest Rococo works in Italy despite its Juvaresque Neo-Classicism.

Neo-Classicism begins in Rome in the middle of the eighteenth century with the Caffè Haus of the Villa Albani by Carlo Marchioni, reflecting the classical taste of the collection of antiquities which the villa housed; and Antonio Asprucci did the fine interior of the Villa Borghese (1777) and the follies in the park there. But the greatest name in Italian architecture associated with this development in the second half of the century is that of Luigi Vanvitelli, son of a Dutch painter, whose most famous achievement is the vast and magnificent pile of Caserta, 18 miles to the north of Naples (1751). It was the Palazzo Reale built for the Spanish Bourbon King of the Two Sicilies and was intended to

CAFFÈ HAUS, VILLA ALBANI, ROME

be a kind of Versailles, grandiloquently planned round four courtyards, not only a royal home complete with chapel and theatre but a centre for the court and central government building for the administration of the kingdom.

The elevations, with their carefully proportioned superimposed orders and restrained use of curved forms, clearly show the Neo-Classical inclination of the period; though the great octagonal central entrance and majestic ceremonial stairway are Baroque in scale and scenic effect and some of the best interiors, well up to their architectural frame, are in the cool French Empire style – the Sala di Astrea and the Sala di Marte designed in 1807 by Antonio de Simone for Joseph Bonaparte. Following Simone, Gaetano Genovese did a splendidly rich white and gold throne room in 1839.

In the gardens at Caserta, too, a change of style may be observed. Instead of the former terraced plans, there are new long vistas in the French manner of Le Nôtre, but there is still an impressive use of water effects, moving and not static in the French manner, in the most magnificent cascade.

Vanvitelli had worked in various places, including Rome (the convent of S. Agostino), and Ancona (the Lazzaretto, 1733) before coming to Naples; but it was there that his best work was done including such different works as the Acquedotto Carolino (1752), the Piazza Dante (1757), and the church of SS. Annunziata (1761).

In Venice Giorgio Massari carried on Longhena's tradition giving a façade to the Gesuati that is both Baroque and Palladian. The Venetian contribution to Neo-Classicism, however, embraced the writings of Carlo Lodoli whose ideas were widely influential during the eighteenth century.

Notable works of the period in Milan are the great opera house, La Scala (1776) by Giuseppe Piermarini (though its sumptuously decorated interior is the work of Alessandro Sanquirico and dates from 1830), and the Palazzo Serbelloni (1794) by Simone Cantoni and the Palazzo Rocca-Saporiti (1812) by Giovanni Parego. The former was executed in a restrained French manner of the time and when Napoleon arrived in Milan he added the Forum Bonaparte (1806) by Giannantonio Antolini and an imitation Roman triumphal arch, the Arco della Pace (1807), by Luigi Cagnola.

Pleasing past-Napoleonic work is the pair of gatehouses at the Porta Venezia (1826) by Rodolfo Vantini and, some few years later, the small but rather exquisite Palazzo Lucini (1831) by Ferdinando Crivelli is an excellent High Renaissance pastiche – not, as one might expect, frequent in Italy at this time. Opposite is the Casa di Risparmio (1872), a rusticated example of the Italian Renaissance version of that arcuated mode called in Germany *Rundbogenstil*.

Though Italian architecture of the past still had great prestige in Europe at the beginning of the nineteenth century it is evident that Italy was by now no longer the main source of original architectural ideas. The initiative had passed to France, Germany, and Britain, and for the first time for several centuries Italy found herself at the receiving end. Though this situation may indicate a lack of creativity, nevertheless Italian architecture of the nineteenth century has perhaps not received its due. Judging by the standards of earlier and greater work perhaps we have come to expect too much. For much of the period the country was disturbed by war and revolution, and there are marked differences between the architecture produced there and that of other European countries.

S. Carlo (1844) is one of the few notable buildings of the mid-century in Milan, its dome based on that of the Roman Pantheon, a very archetypal work much followed in the nineteenth century. The middle years also saw the expansion of the railways and the monumental main station at Milan (since rebuilt) was the work from 1857 of Buchot and entirely French Beaux Arts in character.

So far nothing has been said of that European movement which emerged in the second half of the eighteenth century and continued into the nineteenth known as Romantic Classical. To its formation the work of the great Venetian etcher and designer, G. B. Piranesi, contributed. Though he was not a builder, he was the last Italian designer to exert an international influence until modern times in his architectural etchings, e.g. *Carceri d'Invenzione* (*c.* 1740) showing fantastically composed, gigantically scaled, and dramatically rusticated classical buildings, as well as his more orthodox reproductions of ancient architecture.

Romantic Classical was to take various forms but particularly Neo-Greek and though Piranesi was a great admirer of Roman antiquities he also published posthumously a fine set of etchings of the ancient Greek temples of Paestum and experimented with other sources, such as Egyptian art, in his decorations for the Caffè Inglese, Rome (1760).

Michelangelo Simonetti had built the Museo Pio-Clementino at the Vatican in 1769, and based on the type established by this was Raffaelle Stern's new tall and spacious extension to the sculpture museum, the Braccio Nuovo (1817) in the Romantic Classical tradition. Museums in the Romantic Classical mode were very much of the period, as witness Smirke's Neo-Greek British Museum. Other Neo-Greek features in Rome by Luigi Canina may be seen in the Borghese Gardens.

But what has been called the finest Romantic Classical building in Italy is to be found at Padua, the Caffè Pedrocchi (1816) by Giuseppe Japelli, a pupil of Selva and Antonio Gradenigo. Certainly it is a noble design. With its central raised Corinthian loggia, and projecting flat Doric porticoes on either side it makes good use of contrast between solid and void, while the finely conceived ornament is applied with discrimination and restraint. Oddly enough, Japelli added a Neo-Gothic wing to the caffè in 1837 for he was very much an eclectic capable also of the 'Palladian' villa and 'English' park at Saonara (1817), as well as the Neo-Rococo Teatro Verdi (1847), also in Padua.

In Genoa there are C. F. Barabino's Romantic Classical Teatro Carlo Felice (1827), and his long colonnaded Campo Sant di Stazlieno (1835) has a chapel the design of which again owes

CAFFÈ PEDROCCHI, PADUA

S. FRANCISCO DI PAOLO, NAPLES

much to the Pantheon. So does the church at Possagno, known as the Tempio Canoviano (1819) after the famous sculptor Canova who commissioned it from Selva, and who may have had a hand in its fine Romantic Classical design.

Naples has far better work to show from this time than either Rome or Genoa. An able Romantic Classical architect was Pietro Bianchi who built S. Francesco di Paolo in 1816. Its central plain rotunda and shallow dome, repeated immediately at each side by smaller domed structures, is fronted by a pedimented portico from which extend curving colonnades embracing the piazza in the Baroque manner of Bernini. Despite its obvious indebtedness to the Pantheon, this time on a much larger scale, S. Francesco has the clean-cut quality and scale of a typical Romantic Classical design.

Generally, however, this mode which proved so popular in western architecture from Edinburgh to Washington D.C., in the early part of the nineteenth century was not so popular in Italy which preferred as a rule to go in for some kind of academic revival of its own past classical styles.

Thus in Naples there is Antonio Niccolini's new front (1810) for the San Carlo Opera House (interior 1841) with its mixture of Neo-Roman and Mannerist elements in its heavily rusticated lower storey (rather too high for good proportions) and its fine great arched openings; and above an open loggia carrying a straight entablature, glazed behind, with a balcony the whole width of the façade in front of it.

9. Italian Rococo observable in the elegantly swaying façade of this palazzetto in the Piazza S. Ignazio, Rome (1727). This is only one element in a scenographic grouping of buildings facing the church.

10*a* Palazzo Reale, Caserta (1751) by Vanvitelli. A Neo-Classical 'Versailles' for the kings of the two Sicilies. Compare the evident restraint and rectilinear qualities with the exuberance and curved forms of Baroque.

10*b*. The ceremonial Staircase of Honour at Caserta is more Baroque in feeling than the exterior elevations, with effective spatial movement and controlled grandeur.

11. Gran Madre di Dio, Turin (1818). Bonsignore's clean-cut, shallow-domed Romantic Classical church for the new quarter of the growing city is clearly inspired by the Pantheon, a popular source at this time.

SAN CARLO OPERA HOUSE, NAPLES

The Royal Palace, too, was extended and remodelled (1837) and its long quay façade tidied up and made more orderly by Gaetano Genovese whose work we have noted at Caserta.

Turning again to the north of Italy we find in Venice that the Napoleonic occupation which dealt the *coup de grâce* to the old republic was marked by the replacement of Sansovino's S. Zimignan by a work of G. M. Solis in the Piazza S. Marco, better calculated to accord with the fifteenth- and sixteenth-century façades of the Procurazie.

Before and after this is the opera house, La Fenice, its façade by Giannantonio Selva, already mentioned, dating from 1786; the delicious Neo-Rococo interior is by the Meduna brothers, as late as the 1830s.

Away in the extreme north-east at Trieste, Matthäus Pertsch had done the façade of the Teatro Verdi in 1798 but eight years later began what was to be not only one of the best buildings in Trieste but in the whole of Italy in the opening years of the nineteenth century. This is the Palazzo Carciotti with its raised portico and small dome above. It is the best of the various early nineteenth-century palaces lining the Canale Grande at the head of which is the fine spacious church of Sant' Antonio di Padova (1826) by Nobile.

S. ANTONIO DI PADOVA, TRIESTE

It is time now to consider the early nineteenth-century architecture and town planning of Turin, the old capital of Savoy which had begun its career as one of the great industrial cities of Europe. In the broad arcaded streets and large piazze of the new quarters, such as the Piazza Vittorio Veneto (1818) by Giuseppe Frizzi and Carlo Promis (who did the surrounding façades) one recognizes again contemporary French influences. At the top of the piazza is Ferdinando Bonsignore's church of Gran Madre di Dio (1818), a thank-offering for the end of the French occupation and yet another Pantheon-like Romantic Classical edifice. Among the elegantly designed houses of the new quarter with their well-designed 'syncopated' iron balconies, a local Turin feature of the time, are two more domed churches – the Sacramentine (1843) by Alfonso Dupuy, and S. Massimo (1845) by Carlo Sada.

Development was a continuous process in nineteenth-century Turin. The Piazza Vittorio Veneto was followed by Lombardi and Frizzi's Piazza Carlo Felice (1823), buildings again by Promis, while, to balance the former, at the end of the Via Po the Piazza dello Statuto was laid out in 1864 by Giuseppe Bollati. The Piazza dello Statuto reflects the influence of the Baroque architect Juvara, thus exemplifying the tendency for effects to become richer as the century advanced. But generally French influence predominated and by the 1860s this meant the somewhat pretentious Second Empire style. The limits to which excess could go in the second half of the century, however, may be judged from Alessandro Antonelli's Mole Antonelliana (1863) and domed spire for S. Gandenzio (1875). So often with works of this period such offence as they give is increased by their large size.

At one end of the Piazza Carlo Felice was built the fine railway station of Porta Nuova (1866) by Alessandro Mazzuchetti and Carlo Ceppi, terminating the central axis of the city at the other end of which is the Royal Palace of Savoy. Architecturally the station is a form of Romantic Classical *Rundbogenstil* much favoured in south Germany somewhat earlier.

Genoa became a great industrial seaport in the nineteenth century but its best architectural work was the enlargement of the sixteenth-century Palazzo Marini (by Alessi) to serve as the Municipio when Lucca Beltrami gave it a new façade (1888) in Alessi's version of Mannerism.

Planning work influenced by the Second Empire was also done at Florence in the 1860s when for a short time it was the capital of Italy. Following Hausmann's scheme in Paris, Giuseppe Poggi laid out some broad streets and piazze on the old fortifications; but much more modestly than those which inspired them. The Piazza della Repubblica, however, illustrates the increasing tendency to heaviness and elaboration as the century wore on.

By the mid-century most architecture in Italy was Renaissance Revival of some sort such as the decent Palazzo del Comune, Alatri (1862); but from then on, as a result either of the elaborate pomposity just noticed in the Piazza della Repubblica and at Turin or a certain uninspired academic dullness, much of it failed to accommodate itself either decently or adequately to earlier and usually better work by which it found itself so often surrounded. Domestic architecture was open to the contemporary influences of historicism and stylistic fashion, the emphasis being on romantic interpretations of national themes, rather than foreign borrowings, understandable as an expression of the new nationalism, but it is a pity there was nothing comparable in quality to the products of

Verdi's genius that set the imagination of a people alight at this time.

In Rome, under Pope Pius VII, Giuseppe Valadier developed the Piazza del Popolo (1813) from a design going back to 1794 and subsequently modified in Napoleon's time. But his architectural work was rather dull and lacking in character. Perhaps his best work in Rome was the façades of S. Pantaleo (1805) and S. Andrea della Fratte (1826).

The Teatro Argentina is an essay in the Roman manner by Pietro Camporesi who assisted Pasquale Belli and Luigi Poletti in their reconstruction of the old fourth-century Early Christian basilica of S. Paolo fuori le mura (1825). In a sense an archaeological exercise, the finished church nevertheless has something of the hard, cold, precise feeling of French classic churches, as if contemporary influences were consciously or unconsciously at work also.

Rome has not much of consequence to show from the middle years of the century but after becoming capital of the new united Italy in 1870 much expansion took place, such as the laying-out of the Via Nazionale and the Via Venti Settembre in which is the Ministero delle Finanza (1870) by Raffaelle Canevari. Like the Ministero della Guerra it is a somewhat flat production, lacking imagination and feeling.

But an exception among the academic revivalists was Gaetano Koch whose large and impressive Esedra di Termini (1885) with its bland curving arcaded façades and grand fountain by Guerrieri is the best piece of late nineteenth-century town design in Rome. Koch also did the Palazzo Margherita (1886), now the United States Embassy, in an equally dignified and unobtrusive academic manner, and the more monumental Banca d'Italia (1889). A similar Neo-Renaissance design is the Palazzo della Belle Arti (1882) by Pio Piacentini which shows how preferable this style was to some versions of Second Empire Neo-Baroque represented by the vast heavily rusticated, not to say vulgar, Palazzo di Giustizia (1883) by Giuseppe Calderini. The most over-lush, over-scaled, extravaganza is, of course, the notorious monument to Victor Emmanuel II (1884) at the top of the Corso. A pretentious and decadent piece of Classicism to dominate any city, let alone Rome, it was the work of Giuseppe Sacconi, though other architects including Koch and Piacentini also worked on it. Apart from this

VITTORIO EMANUELE II MONUMENT, ROME

assertive display of nationalist aspirations in white marble the Tempio Israelitico (Synagogue) (1904) by Armanni and Casta shows to what depths Italian architecture could now sink.

Gothic Revival, which in various forms played such an important role in British architecture in the nineteenth century, is not surprisingly rare in Italy, the home of the classical tradition. The Palazzo 'der Villa', Florence (1850), is a stylistic exception in the indigenous tradition. Two others are by the English architect G. E. Street and both are in Rome. They are St Paul's American church (1873), a very striped affair with open arcading and a campanile-like tower (as much Romanesque as Gothic) and the High Victorian English Church of All Saints (1880). The first is one of Street's best, and well able to hold its own with the 'originals'. Prominent native Gothicists were Niccolo Matas who did a new front for S. Croce, Florence (1857), and especially Emilio de Fabris who completed, with greater success, the polychrome façade of the Duomo in that city (1866). The wine and cheese warehouse at Codisotto shows that Italian Gothic, as in Britain, could be the inspiration of commercial architecture; but built in 1900 it shows how much later in time the mode was capable of affecting Italian architecture. The great English Edwardian architect Edward Lutyens produced a fine classical design for the British School in Rome in 1911.

The most original structures in the second half of the nineteenth century were the products of the new and enterprising cast-iron

PALAZZO 'DER VILLA', FLORENCE

and glass technology which had been developed, notably in Britain with the Crystal Palace (1851), and which was also employed in the great new railway stations of Italy. These structures were huge glass-roofed shopping arcades or galleries which were appearing elsewhere in Europe at this time, representing a splendid contribution to the business of urban living.

The best in Italy is the Galleria Vittorio Emanuele II, Milan (1865), designed by Giuseppe Mengoni and built by an English firm. The great cruciform structure with its curved glass and iron roof, 'triumphal arch' portal, octagonal crossing, and richly and elegantly detailed arcaded Renaissance elevations is most impressive, as well it might be since it is of the largest of the species in Europe. Another very large one is the Galleria Mazzini, Genoa (1871), whilst the Galleria Umberto I in Naples (1887) is rather less successful.

These examples of architectural work, using entirely new materials and expressed in an idiom without precedent, despite the concessions to tradition in the elevations, are portents of the

GALLERIA VITTORIO EMANUELE II, MILAN

future – of the several forces coming together towards the end of the nineteenth century to create a completely new architecture different from that of any other period in human history.

There is one other influence besides engineering architecture which made itself felt in Italy about 1900 and with which it is appropriate to close this chapter – Art Nouveau, or, as it became known in Italy, the stile Liberty or stile floreale. Already architects in other European countries had become aware that the academic tradition had become moribund or run to seed in an overgrown tangle of eclecticism – C. R. Mackintosh in Britain, Gaudi in Spain, and other architects in Belgium and Vienna – and each was contributing to an original, anti-historical style in which a new and quite remarkable flowing style of decoration, somewhat *fin de siècle* in character, was being evolved.

Some Italian architects were not unresponsive to these developments, as may be seen from Giuseppe Sommarunga's weird Gaudi-cum-Baroque Palazzo Castiglione, Milan (1900). Raimondo d'Aronco in his building for the Turin Industrial Exhibition of 1902 produced a strange concoction of French, Belgian, and Viennese elements of Art Nouveau and from the early 1900s date the house in Pesaro by Giuseppe Brega, Ernesto Basile's Casa Basile, and the Casa Frassini in Palermo. Both architects, however, regressed to Classical Revival and though Art Nouveau made,

EXHIBITION BUILDING, TURIN, 1902

therefore, only a rather negative contribution to the formation of the modern style in architecture, by asserting its originality and refusing to continue the old traditions it did in the long run have a quite important effect in Italy. Certain aspects of it, notably its preference for plasticity and the sculptural modelling of rather flowing architectural forms, did impress later architects. The Italians have always shown a marked feeling for these particular qualities. Once again, partly owing to the stile Liberty, they have become a prominent element in much modern Italian architecture. But the element of fantasy in Art Nouveau is one which, being opposed to reality, could lead astray and therefore it needs to be handled with discretion.

12 Galleria Vittorio Emanuele, Milan (1865): engineering and architecture: a huge glass and iron roof of nineteenth-century technology curving above rich Renaissance Revival façades.

13. Palazzo Olivetti, Milan (1954). Despite its assertiveness this office building by Bernasconi, Fiochi and Nizzoli is essentially in the tradition of *architettura razionale*. Makes great play of the aluminium sun-breaks on its main front.

CHAPTER TWELVE

The Twentieth Century

As in other European countries the seeds of what was to become 'modern' architecture, as distinct from that of all other periods and styles, were sown in Italy before the First World War when Neo-Baroque and the rhetorical bombast of works like the monument to King Victor Emmanuel (not completed until 1911) and the Borsa, Genoa, were dominating the architectural scene.

But in a catalogue of an exhibition of revolutionary designs at Milan in 1914 the young Antonio Sant' Elia declared that 'since the eighteenth century there has been no architecture'. Like all manifesto statements this is a gross exaggeration, but it recognized that Italy had produced little during that period to set against the products of a glorious past and up to that moment, unlike other countries such as Britain and America, she had played no part in preparing the foundations of the modern movement in architecture beyond an excursion or two into Art Nouveau. Italian architects had been content generally to maintain a tradition of academic Revival and to follow in the paths of their more original colleagues abroad.

Perceiving the need for a radical reform Sant' Elia attempted to show in his designs what the architecture of the future might be like, starting from first principles. To some extent he was influenced by the Viennese School (Otto Wagner and his disciples Olbrich, Hoffmann, and Loos) who had rediscovered logical planning and sought to adapt it functionally to new social needs. They relied on geometrical shapes and bare forms which accepted the machine aesthetic and the new technology which provided fresh structural opportunities and materials. These they welcomed and believed should be used frankly and 'honestly'.

All this marked a fundamental break with the architecture of the past, except perhaps in its basic rationalism, and was antithetical to the fashions of the abortive Art Nouveau. As an anti-traditionalist, Sant' Elia was obviously in sympathy with such views, yet his Città Nuova project was in some respects a romantic conception. Here is the metropolis of the future with its tower blocks, curved fronts, and multilevel bridges depicted in what were then strange plastic and dynamic forms. But it was never more than a project and the only Sant' Elian structure is the cenotaph on Lake Como, an angular dipylon with sloping buttresses, a somewhat monumental adaptation from some of his drawings by Terragni and Prampolini, two younger men who were stimulated by his work.

Sant' Elia, if the most prophetic architect at this time, was not a lone voice in Italy. The 1914 exhibition was the first of the Nuove Tendenze group of avant-gardists who were bent on creating a revolutionary architecture in tune with an urbanized and industrialized society. Only this way, they argued, could art hope to recover the vigour and vitality it had shown at the Renaissance.

It was at this point that the ideals of the Nuove Tendenze architects fused with those of the Futurists, poets like Marinetti and artists like Boccioni, who had already rejected an art based on the past and advertised their ideas at home and in Paris, at the Futurist Exhibition held in 1912. Their chief spokesman shared with Loos an admiration for modern engineering design, glorifying such things as racing cars, seeing it as the desirable result of pursuing practical, functional ends.

The Futurists had theories of 'plastic dynamism' which favoured forms not dissimilar to Sant' Elia's and they laid stress on a concept of space that was articulated by objects within it. Though their concept was not the only one to bear on the philosophy of modern architecture it did direct attention to spatial problems with which modern architecture was to be much concerned.

There was enough common ground between these two revolutionary groups for Marinetti to gain the commitment of Sant' Elia and the Nuove Tendenze group to Futurist objectives and prevail upon Sant' Elia to reissue his introduction to the exhibition catalogue as a specifically Futurist statement. It is difficult, however, to assess the importance of Futurism in architecture. There were few works executed of any merit, apart from a number of exhibition pavilions and a few villas, and interest in it lapsed until the late twenties when the Fascists, who shared its aggressive nationalism and love of violence took it up and realized something of its aims in the work of Fillia. Erich Mendelsohn's expressionistic Einstein Observatory, Potsdam (1920), owes something of its plastic qualities to Sant' Elia and the Futurists. It certainly had a powerful influence on industrial design of the inter-war years with its 'aerodynamic' streamlining and contributed to the ideas of Le Corbusier.

But at any rate, from now on, the modern architecture of Italy was already embarked on its career. The break with tradition had been made, once and for all, and if for the time being it was not the Futurists and their plastic dynamism who were to lead but the international 'rationalists' with their austere geometry, it was Sant' Elia more than anyone who had made Italy aware of the potentialities of modern architecture and prepared the ground for the Movimento per l'Architettura Razionale, as it came to be known, of the inter-war years. Though he was killed early in the First World War his ideas persisted. How many saw his projects at the time is another matter since some have only recently been published.

After the war the principal foreign influence was still that of the Viennese joined now by the Germans Walter Gropius and Ludwig Mies van der Rohe who were developing their ideas in architecture and industrial design both in their buildings and at the Bauhaus, that important centre where rational architecture, applied arts, and new technologies came together with such fructifying results. But already Italy was in the grip of Fascism and before carrying forward the story of 'modern' Italian architecture we must look now at how this movement affected architecture generally.

Mussolini came to power in 1922 and in view of the imperialistic yearnings of the Fascist movement it was natural that he should be drawn to a form of Neo-Classicism of whom the chief exponent was Marcello Piacentini. An early work was the Triumphal Arch at Genoa (1923) and in the mid-twenties he built the Teatro Quirinetta and the Albergo degli Ambiasciatori in Rome. These were followed by an Olympic sports centre, Foro Mussolini (now Italica), the smaller Stadio dei Mormi being particularly pretentious with huge distorted statuary.

Pincentini's best work may be seen in the new buildings erected in the thirties for the Città Universitaria of Rome. The various faculty buildings are by other hands, but the spacious general plan and administration building are his. The style is vaguely classical but free of the overblown rhetoric of official buildings in some other countries at this time, notably Nazi Germany. Proportions are classical but all is square cut and without bases, capitals, mouldings, etc. It is thus often imposing without being pretentious and makes fine use of marbles in the traditional Italian manner. But Piacentini and other official architects of the time, such as Muzio in Milan, were content to ignore new developments in technology and design except for this preference for smipler, plainer rectangular forms and to continue building lictoral towers, colonnades, and arcuated structures such as the ungainly Palazzo della Civilita Italiana which Piacentini built for the 1937 Esposizione.

Fascist town planning was ambitious and sometimes successful. Piacentini's plan for Rome in 1931 made provision for an increasing amount of motor traffic that was beginning to clog the city's circulation and yet to respect and tidy up the relics of antiquity, thus making the best of both worlds. This is best seen in the Via dei Forti Imperiali. But the attempt to bring to completion a centuries-old plan by extending the Via della Conciliazione (1934) was a piece of arrogance that came to disaster and serves as a warning to modern planners dealing with long-established areas. There were also several reasonably planned if rather dull new towns, owing something to the garden city idea, created in the drained lowland of the Campagna – Latina, Pontinia and, the most successful, Sabaudia.

Though all this building work of Piacentini and his colleagues constituted the bulk carried out in Italy between the two wars it was not, as history has shown, to be in the mainstream of twentieth-century development and even during the period when it was dominant it did not enjoy a monopoly of Fascist patronage.

When the Fascists took over a decade earlier than the National Socialists in Germany, they found no established modern architecture as the latter did. Consequently there was no feeling that here was a left-wing inspired movement whose ideals challenged their own. Instead they saw an opportunity of taking it over at its inception and using it as a symbol of their revolution and of modern Italy. Even before the war Futurism had shown more than a tincture of Fascism. 'We are out to glorify war,' wrote the dangerous Marinetti. All this meant that in Italy modern architects were given encouragement and not expelled as they were from Germany when the Nazis closed down the Bauhaus. But by its origins and nature modern architecture was not adapted to serving the authoritarian state and Fascist modernism was not very successful, with a few notable exceptions.

In 1927, the date of S. Matté-Trucco's somewhat Futuristic Fiat Motor Car works at Turin (with a race track on its roof), a group of seven architects, mainly from that city, exhibited as Gruppo 7 at the Biennale at Monza. They took their stand mainly on rationalist principles such as 'sincerity, order, logic, and clarity', and the rejection of all historicism and discredited ornament. But they also stressed the need for a national version of the modern style based on regional characteristics (rather a paradox this, since 'rationalist' architecture was essentially international in its sympathies) and in this they were reflecting Fascist aspirations. Two of the group, Luigi Figini and Gino Pollini were destined to make great reputations for themselves later on, as we shall see, but for the present the architect who did most at this time to re-link modern Italian architecture (*architettura razionale*, that is) with the 'International Style' was Giuseppe Terragni.

The Novecento Italiano was a cultural movement aligned with Fascist politics. If Piacentini was the chief of the 'ancient Roman' element there is no doubt that its modernist leader was Terragni. Before he died in 1942 he was to produce the best buildings in the early idiom in Italy, and as a propagandist for the movement helped to create a climate of thought in which modern architecture could grow.

Terragni's best early building dates from 1927, the year of Gruppo 7's exhibition. The Novecomum is a block of flats at Como where he did most of his work. Belonging to the 'white architecture' of the period and owing something to Berlin and the Constructivist work of Soviet Russia, this rather self-conscious design was a source of cliché for the pseudo-modernist on the look-out for new ideas. Constructivist and Functionalist elements were present at the Exhibition of the Fascist Revolution in Rome (1932) to which Terragni contributed.

Functionalism based on the concept that 'form follows function' was much in the air at the time. It was obviously an extension of the earlier admiration of the machine and the rejection of the 'hypocrisy' of much nineteenth-century façade architecture; but it

CASA DEL POPOLO

developed to the point where it provided an aesthetic for the architect. Terragni no less than Le Corbusier was affected by the idea.

The modern Novecentist masterpiece is Terragni's elegant Casa del Fascio (now del Popolo), Como (1936). Its four storeys are arranged round an internal court, its frame construction functionally expressed in its beautifully proportioned open-grid elevations, quite free of ornament but displaying the dramatic contrast of solid and void apparent in the Novecomum. Both buildings have the austere purity of their period but the Casa del Fascio has an innate classicism in its calm static feeling and use of fine marble.

Functionalism was never as pure as devotees of machine form believed and just as Terragni tended to lay more emphasis on plastic rather than surface effects compared with the Internationalists he admired, so also was he capable of introducing more personal feelings into architecture than extremists among functionalists would allow. Again, he is like Le Corbusier in this.

Thus in his infants' school, Asilo Sant' Elia, Como (1937), though there are the open frames resembling the Casa del Fascio, there is also a new breadth and warmth, a new lightness and delicacy in keeping with its more humane purpose. This lucid and attractive work is one of the best schools in modern Italy which has not, unfortunately, been too successful in this building type. Also far from 'automatic' purely functionalist works are the Casa Pedraglio infants' school, Como, and his villas at Como, Rebbio and Seveso. Yet if Functionalism has since done much harm among commercial developers, at that time it was still a valuable discipline for modern architects, feeling their way towards a new style and it is one of the most valid criteria today.

Terragni's Casa Giuliani-Figerio (1939) near Lake Como, shows in its rectangular integration of bare vertical and horizontal planes, balconies, and cantilevered roof edge a complex development of ideas germinated in Rietveld's famous Schröder House in Utrecht. But there is also a move away from the earlier emphasis on geometrical volume towards a freer spatial planning. It was a design that was to produce many imitations in Italy but none as distinguished as the original.

Terragni was an architect whose work was of European stature. He lived to regret his connection with Fascism and his premature death was a great loss to Italian architecture.

Meanwhile Gio Ponti, probably the best-known Italian architect today, had been pursuing his early career. He favoured a graceful rationalism with Neo-Classic motifs, but though he kept aloof from revolutionary factions like Gruppo 7, he did give the rationalists one of their best opportunities when he invited them to contribute to the Fifth Triennale (1933), Milan, for which he was responsible. Figini and Pollini, already mentioned as members of Gruppo 7, achieved success with their house there – 'international' but with a distinctly Latin feeling.

The next year saw the beginning of the new railway station in Florence by Giovanni Michelucci and his associates. The most progressive station in the world in its day, it demonstrates how the *architenttura razionale* was given a free hand by the Fascists. It would have been impossible at that time in Germany. Michelucci also did the Geology Department for the Città Universitaria, Rome.

In 1928 Ponti had founded the journal *Domus*, an important forum of ideas in architecture, interior and industrial design. In the latter he himself with his multi-faceted talent has been very successful. Italians generally have shown a remarkable ingenuity and flair in designing fittings and furnishings for modern buildings and this has had the salutary result of raising the standard of public taste to a high level, besides gaining prestige abroad.

During the thirties Ponti became a fashionable and at times facile architect who designed industrial buildings, flats, churches, and the Mathematics Institute for Rome University, but not until 1936 did he really break with Neo-Classicism. In that year he built the first of his two Montecatini office blocks in which rationalism was modified by Novecentist plasticism to produce one of his best works, personal, and well ahead for its time.

Ponti's career straddles the Second World War, but before following its development further we should consider the important work begun at Ivrea in the Val d' Aosta to the north-west of Turin. One of the best patrons of modern Italian architecture was Adriano Olivetti, the head of one of the most successful manufacturing organizations in Europe and a man particularly alive to the implication of the new architectural ideas and the possibilities of applying them to industrial needs. In 1939 he commissioned Luigi Figini and Gino Pollini to design the main Olivetti plant at Ivrea. Its long repetitive imperonal glass fronts are in the now established tradition of rational architecture (e.g. Gropius and Mies), but the factory is not just an isolated piece of industrial architecture, rather the centre of a continuously developing urban scheme to which have been added workers' housing, further extensions to the main factory and a social service building by the original architects, a precise and elegant foundry (1952) by Annibale Fiocchi, now the resident architect, and most recently a fine complex of social and recreational buildings on a landscaped site (1959) by Ignazio Gardella. Another factory and study centre is the work of Eduardo Vittoria.

The company's offices in Milan, the Palazzo Olivetti, were built in 1954 by Bernasconi, Fiocchi, and Nizzoli who have given it a somewhat Latin-American aspect with the aluminium brise-soleils as a prominent feature of its main front. The latter have also been used at Ivrea too and are a small return for the inspiration modern

PALAZZO OLIVETTI

Italian architecture has afforded Latin-American countries. Also in 1954 a smaller Olivetti factory was built at Pozzuoli near Naples by Luigi Cosenza, a more articulated plan with lavish social service complex. Pleasantly landscaped overlooking the Bay, it shows what can be done to make industrial buildings less inhuman and more acceptable.

Gardella's best work has been done at Alessandria, between Turin and Genoa, beginning with his T.B. clinic (1936), a rationalist conception of considerable achievement, yet showing early his characteristic willingness to accommodate his designs to local environment and tradition. In the fifties he produced at Alessandria buildings as varied as a children's hospital, a vocational school, the Borletti factory, and a block of workers' flats (1952) in which, over a ground base of elegant rationalism, he reveals a personal melodic style. His work in Venice includes a house on the Grand Canal and an apartment house on the Zattere degli Incurabili. The former adjusts to a critical setting with impeccable taste, and the second is a witty rendering of a vernacular theme in the contemporary idiom. They show one way of treating with respect the architectural traditions of a place like Venice without being subservient to it.

The Second World War produced a building pause and resulted in the destruction of many old buildings; but because the Fascists had not suppressed modern architecture it was there when hostilities ended as an established tradition ready to begin the process of reconstruction. This is one reason why Italy moved rapidly to the forefront of modernism in the late forties. Most architects subscribed to the rationalist aesthetic generally but were by this time ready to receive the fertilizing influence of the concept of 'organic architecture' originated by the American Frank Lloyd Wright earlier in the century and now given currency by Bruno Zevi, a younger man who had returned from the United States and built several blocks of flats in Rome. It was in Rome that the ideas of *architettura organica* were most followed in the fifties, notably by Eugenio Montuori, who had worked at Sabaudia. His great work (with associates) is the Termini Station, Rome (1950), the main feature of which is the huge concourse built across the front. Its vast canopy makes a grand sweeping entrance from the Piazza dei Cinquecento while the double curve of the roof echoes the piece of fourth-century Servian wall brought into the total design to emphasize Rome's cultural continuity. Behind the concourse a long office block rises five storeys, ingeniously increased to what seems like ten by doubling the fenestration strips to give greater scale. This is a long way from the 'honesty' of expression dear to early rationalists. Altogether this is a building of considerable panache and the best modern railway station in Europe.

Since the war, despite the poverty of the south (for which a fund was set up in 1950), Italy has become a rich country with new resources, such as natural gas, and a stable economy – the 'Italian miracle' in fact. This has been reflected in the outstanding work done in Milan during the forties and fifties. Among the best are the flats of the firm known as the BBPR after the initials of the partners, Banfi, Belgiojoso, Peressuti and Rogers. Before the war they had already made an international reputation with their Sanatorium at Legnano (1937) and they built the Central Post Office in Rome, but their most singular work in the last decade has been the Torre Velasca (1958) which owes something to the organic ideas propagated by Zevi and is infused with a new romantic feeling hitherto excluded by rationalists. The lower floors of this 26-storey building are offices; the upper projecting ones flats, so that the difference in social use is expressed formally. Its design is intended, too, to harmonize with the Gothic cathedral near-by and the rigid repetition of the fenestration pattern of most modern tower blocks has been avoided by the introduction of irregularities.

Other tower blocks in Milan are the Torre al Parco and the Torre Galfa but one of the best so far anywhere in the world is the Pirelli Building (1958) by Ponti and Pier Luigi Nervi, the structural engineer, and their associates. Ponti had built a second rather stern but attractively detailed office block for Montecatini in Milan in 1951 but mostly he had been engaged on projects elsewhere in Europe and South America until the Pirelli Company commissioned a prestige headquarters, once more in Milan.

On the basis of Nervi's tapering double vertebrate structure, from which the floors, without columns, are cantilevered out, Ponti conceived a narrow boat-shaped envelope where to the satisfaction of the achievement of a unique finite form is added the subtlety produced by the fact that the planes of the 'bows' – triangular piers containing lifts, stairs, and ducts – never quite

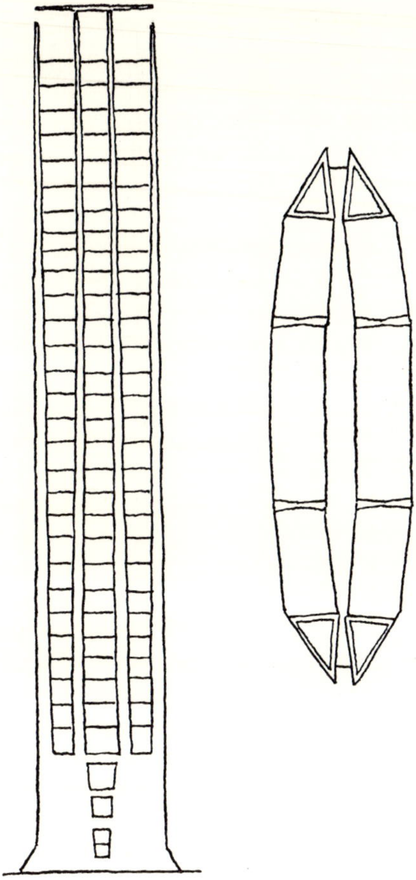

PIRELLI BUILDING

meet while the 'lid' of the building hovers above. This wonderfully unified and sophisticated office tower, its surrounding area also partly redesigned by Ponti on proper principles – raised forecourt over auditorium, canteen, etc. – is a far cry from the curtained wall boxes of much modern city architecture today with its dull repetitive façades and lack of that closed character required by a work of art. Without being assertive in any exceptionable sense it successfully dominates the Quatiere Direzionale and provides a fine, elegant, cohesive focus.

In 1961 Ponti became the first president of the International Museum of Modern Architecture founded in Milan and has gone

PIRELLI BUILDING

on to design the capital of Pakistan, Islamabad, and to build a new hospital in Milan.

Technically Nervi is an engineer but the modern cult of the engineer goes back to Functionalism and beyond, as we have seen, and Nervi had used mathematics not just for structural ends but to obtain aesthetic effects of high distinction. Always he has laid stress on the need for an intuitive vision to select from several practical possibilities the best aesthetic alternative. In an age of 'technological' architecture this makes Nervi an architect while the scale of his talents make him a great one.

His career matured slowly at first but using his chosen medium of reinforced concrete he gained an outstanding success with the Stadium, Florence (1930). In this he dramatically exploited an exposed scissor structure and introduced intertwined flying stairs and a curved and cantilevered roof of new expressiveness.

As an engineer Nervi's main problem has always been roofing

large spaces and he experimented in a series of aircraft hangers (Orbetello), Spa buildings (Chianciano), and industrial plant such as the Gatti wool factory, Rome (1951), finding different ways of doing this. The former were great vaults growing increasingly lighter as he learned from his experiments and study of shells in nature how to obtain 'strength through form' within the surface itself. But the factory has columns supporting a slabbed roof on which a strong pattern of ribs is moulded creating a spatial effect, something like a late-medieval vault. Nervi has a sculptural feeling for concrete and this can be seen not only in, say, the massive tapered columns of the Istituto di Cultura (1961) where they, rather than the ribs, articulate the interior space, but also in the corrugated and reticulated treatment he gives his wide arching vaults where structural requirements are capitalized to produce imaginative effects. The circular 'helianthemum' grid vault at Chianciano is particularly beautiful.

Yet these efforts were only made possible by Nervi's technical innovations. He invented his own system of pre-stressing concrete, a new type of movable shuttering, and uses small-scale lightly-reinforced prefabricated concrete elements made up on the site, techniques which permit precision, speed, and economy, and such flexibility as to rival the introduction of the frame system in the fresh possibilities which they open up to imaginative minds.

These concrete techniques may be studied in the Turin exhibition hall (1948), the best since the Crystal Palace. This is really two contrasting structures, one less grand, more personal, and more easily comprehended than the other. But in the vast flexible Italia 61 Pavilion, Turin (1961) he used steel for the first time in a major way with great cross-sectioned palm-like piers and ribs independently supporting discontinuous steel roof sections through which light falls. The effect internally is impressive while on the exterior façades are brise-soleils.

The Palazzetto dello Sport, Rome – with A. Vitellozzi – (1959) is perhaps the most beautiful sports building in the world. Its shallow dome, made up of precast concrete coffers in many sizes, has a rib pattern that carries the thrust outwards to the surrounding ring of Y supports, characteristically exposed. The rippled eaves line is both structurally and aesthetically successful. The larger arena built with Piacentini for the 1960 Olympics, the Palazzo dello Sport, seating 16,000, has less charm and a less

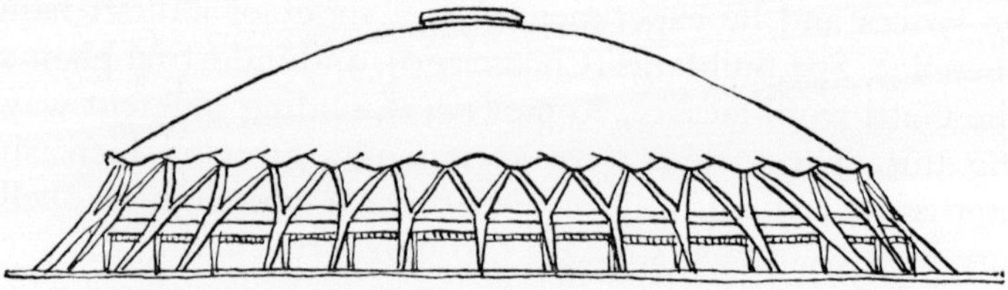

PALAZZETTO DELLO SPORT

effective exterior but again a superb web-like dome of prefabricated unit ferro-concrete and 'sculptured' roof supports display the typical Nervi blend of bold engineering and imagination.

G. Baroni had built a hyperbolic paraboloid shell vault for an iron foundry in Milan in 1934 and an upturned-umbrella-shaped one for a warehouse in Ferrara four years later, but Nervi's use of curved concrete in tension derives ultimately from the Swiss engineer Maillart, of course. Like Felix Candela of Mexico he has developed it to the extent that the term 'structural acrobatics' can be understandably applied to some of his most compelling roof structures. At the same time can be recognized the serious aesthetic impulse to create new forms that lies behind the witticism. Architects now have the means to create a plastic architecture that goes far beyond the sculptural freedom of Baroque.

Riccardo Morandi who designed the Automobile Pavilion, Turin (1959), an underground hall able to hold its own next to Nervi's exhibition halls already described, was the engineer of the Leonardo da Vinci Airport, Rome (1960), a splendid example of a twentieth-century type, the international airport. Especially effective is the huge central building, strong and original in form. The work of several architects it exemplifies the almost invariable modern practice to design in groups.

Franco Albini, an early and consistent rationalist noted for his elegant and sensitive designs, has worked steadily from the 1930s onwards. Interesting recent work are his two museums in

WAREHOUSE NEAR PADUA

Genoa dating from the fifties, the Palazzo Bianco and San Lorenzo, works subtly adapted to the objects displayed, and the Rinascente department store in Rome (1961). Italian architects have made museum building and remodelling unsurpassed elsewhere. Other examples are Gardella's Museum of Modern Art, Milan (1953), and Carlo Scarpa's at Verona and Palermo.

Scarpa was a convert to organic architecture and one of the results of Zevi's infusion of such ideas has been a reappraisal of rationalism like Albini's and a search for new ideas. Hence the revival of interest in Art Nouveau from the early years of the century has produced Neo-Liberty (a more expressive, freer approach to form) and there has been an attempt to create an Italian form of New Brutalism. Vittoriano Vigano's Istituto Marchiondi, Milan (1959), a remedial school, is a craggy, dramatically massed, and roughly finished concrete building that for all its tough, bleak appearance seeks to avoid a closed prison-like atmosphere and still has echoes of Terragni. Whether or not its 'spiritual' function is right for its purpose, it has been one of the most influential structures of recent Italian architecture. A striking example of modern representational building is the new British Embassy in Rome, by Sir Basil Spence.

In general with exceptions, such as the Parioli district of Rome, domestic architecture in Italy has been very successful from smart multi-storey city blocks, such as Luigi Moretti's, to minimal-cost housing for small communities that takes account of different social needs and local cultures – e.g. Olivetti housing at Ivrea. A great deal has been done by INA–Casa. Notable developments may be seen at Cesate, just north of Milan (Albini, Albricci, BBPR, Gardella), and in Naples (Cosenza and Carlo Cocchia).

The modern successors to the old Roman roads like the Appian Way are works like the Autostrada del Sole between Milan and Florence, and the route between the latter and Bologna, with their modern architectural shapes. The curving concrete Vainot Dam on a tributary of the Piave river is the tallest in the world and an apt symbol of the new technological Italy of Ferrari, Olivetti and Necchi, who also foster good industrial design.

So far all the twentieth-century buildings in this chapter have been typical of its diverse and secular character, from Nervi's exhibition halls to, say, the Carcare viaduct on the new Ceva–Savona highway. Let us now refer to two modern churches. The

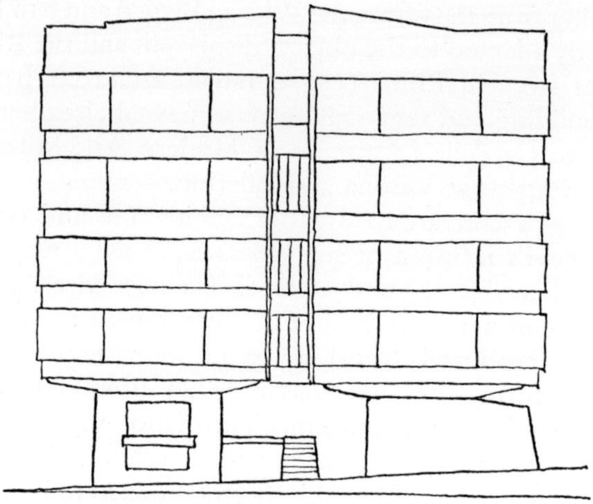

CASA DE GIRASOLE: FLATS, ROME

church of the Madonna dei Poveri, Milan (1952), by Figini and Pollini is somewhat brutal in its raw, exposed appearance but at the same time expresses realism and integrity. There is a dramatic contrast in lighting between the subdued nave and brilliant sanctuary; in both the light enters mysteriously and indirectly.

The church at Baranzate, Milan (1957), by Angelo Mangiarotti and associates also has its contrasts: the dark crypt and sacristy in the 'plinth' and the calm clear light of the main body of the church above, with its translucent and insulated glass walls. The original structure which supports the roof is quite independent.

Because modern Italian architecture over the last twenty years has been so dynamic, vital, varied and undoctrinaire, it is one of the most stimulating for designers all over the world to study. Once more, after nearly two hundred years, Italy is in the van of architectural advance. If one has to select two qualities which more than any others are outstanding in her architecture and from which other countries have most to learn, they would be its imaginative resourcefulness and the value it attaches to qualities, materials, and craftsmanship – its use of marble and mosaic finishes, for example, that not only taps a long native tradition but also produces a richness rare in modern architecture. Creative originality and a sense of continuity – it is a formidable combination that looks well for the future.

14*a* Palazzo dello Sport, Rome (1960); its shallow, reticulated dome of prefabricated concrete units typifies P. L. Nervi's boldly imaginative engineering.

14*b*. Marchiondi Institute, Milan (1959). An expressive and dramatic Brutalist design by Vittoriano Vigano showing the recent move away from more rational 'classical' modern architecture. A very influential work.

15. Torre Velasca, Milan (1958), by BBPR. A striking tower-block which owes something to *architettura organica* and the new Romanticism. Avoids the rigid fenestration pattern of most tower-blocks, and the bracketing-out of the upper storeys reflects a functional division.

GLOSSARY

abacus: the flat slab on top of a capital.
acanthus: a conventionalized leaf in classical decoration.
acroterion: a plinth for an ornament (or both together) set at the apex and corners of a pediment.
aedicule: the frame of a niche or opening in classical architecture consisting of two columns supporting an entablature and pediment.
agora: the central open space in a Greek town, cf. Roman forum.
aisle: the lower division of a basilica or church parallel to the nave, choir, or transept from which it is divided by pillars.
ala: a small side apartment in a Roman house.
ambo: a raised stand from which the Epistle and Gospel were read in Italian medieval churches. Replaced by the pulpit in the fourteenth century.
ambulatory: an aisle round an apse or circular building or across the east end of a church.
amphitheatre: an oval or elliptical building with an arena surrounded by tiers of seats.
apse: the semi-circular or polygonal end of a basilica, church, or side chapel.
aqueduct: an artificial water channel, usually elevated on a brick or stone structure.
arcade: a range of arches carried on columns or piers; 'blind' if attached to a wall.
architrave: the bottom member of an entablature.
archivolt: an architrave moulding following the line of an arch.
arcuated: of a style of architecture in which a structure is supported on arches, cf. trabeated.
ashlar: masonry of smooth squared stones set in regular courses.
astylar: of a classical façade without columns or pilasters.
atrium: in Roman domestic architecture an open but often colonnaded entrance or central court; in Early Christian churches the forecourt before an entrance.
attic: a low storey above a main cornice.
aumbry (ambry)**:** a small cupboard set in a wall.
baldacchino: a canopied structure (usually over an altar) supported on columns.
balustrade: a row of balusters supporting a coping.

barrel vault: an arched stone covering running the length of a building or an apartment.

base: lower part of a structure; a flat circular moulded slab supporting a column in a classical order.

basilica: a Roman public hall or Early Christian church based on its plan; by extension, a medieval church with aisles and clerestory.

bay: a vertical unit of a wall or façade; also a compartment of a nave or aisle.

bema: a raised platform sometimes introduced between the main body and apse of Early Christian churches; extended outwards it became a proto-transept.

brise-soleil: a 'sun-break' of fins or baffles to shade windows in a sunny climate.

buttress: a projecting vertical mass of masonry stiffening a wall or resisting an outward thrust.

flying buttress: an arched prop of masonry resisting the lateral pressure of a wall or vault.

calidarium: the hot room of Roman thermae.

campanile: a bell tower in Italian architecture, often detached.

cancelli: the barriers or screens separating the nave from sanctuary or presbytery in an Early Christian church, cf. chancel.

candelabrum: a large ornamental candlestick.

cantilever: a projecting beam or slab held down at the wall end by a superincumbent weight or in some other way.

capital: the moulded or carved block on top of a column.

casino: originally a small ornamental pavilion or garden house.

cella: the central enclosed portion of a Roman temple, excluding the portico.

chancel: the eastern part of a church reserved for the clergy and choir.

channel: a groove or fluting in a plain surface or column.

chevet: the east end of a medieval church which consists of an apse surrounded by an ambulatory and sometimes by radiating chapels.

choir: the portion of a church set aside for clergy and choir, divided off from the rest by a screen.

ciborium: a baldacchino.

clerestory: the upper part of a wall with windows, as in the nave of a church above the aisle roof.

cloister: a covered walk in a monastery or college arranged round a square court.

coffering: panels sunk deeply into the surface of a ceiling.

colonnade: a range of columns.

colonnette: a small column.

column: a vertical member in classical architecture consisting of base, round shaft, and capital designed to carry an entablature or arch but also used non-structurally.

console: in classical architecture a bracket in the form of an S-shaped scroll.

corbel: a projecting stone bracket. **corbelling:** a series of corbels extending progressively farther forward, one above the other.

cornice: the projecting upper portion of an entablature or any projecting top course.

cortile: an internal court surrounded by a colonnade in Italian architecture.

Cosmati work: marble ornament with coloured inlay of stone, mosaic, and glass. Found in Italian Romanesque architecture of the 12th and 13th centuries, especially round Rome and Naples.

crenellation: battlements.

cresting: a run of repeated ornament along the top of a roof or wall, often pierced.

crocket: a curved leaf-like ornament in Gothic architecture.

cruciform: cross-shaped.

crypt: a space under a building, usually under the chancel of a church and used for burial.

cubiculum: a small apartment for sleeping or resting.

cubiform: cube-shaped.

cupola: a spherical roof over a square, circular, or polygonal apartment.

cyclopean: a term used loosely to describe masonry of very large polygonal blocks.

dais: a platform at the end of a hall.

domical vault: a webbed vault, over a square or polygonal apartment, resembling a dome.

dosseret: in Romanesque and Byzantine earchitecture a high block above a capital to support arches above, cf. the similar use of an entablature block in Roman architecture.

dwarf gallery: a small arcading on the outside of a building, especially in Italian and German Romanesque architecture.

echinus: a rounded projecting moulding supporting the abacus of a Doric capital.

entablature: the horizontal top part of a classical order consisting of architrave, frieze, and cornice.

entasis: the swelling of a classical column to correct the optical illusion of concavity.

exedra: in classical architecture a recess or alcove, semi-circular or rectangular, fitted with seating; also applied to the niche or apse of a church.

façade: the face or front of a building.
fluting: vertical channelling on the shaft of a column.
foliate: leaf-like.
forum: a space for assembly and market at the centre of a Roman town; surrounded by public buildings and colonnades.
fresco: a wall painting; properly one executed 'fresh' on wet plaster.
frieze: the middle member of an entablature or, in a room, the space between the top of the panelling and the cornice or ceiling.
frigidarium: the cooling room of Roman thermae.
gallery: the upper story above a church aisle and opening on to the nave; also called a tribune and sometimes, erroneously, a triforium.
Greek cross: cross with all four arms of equal length.
grille: grating, usually of intersecting iron bars.
groin: an edge formed by intersecting vaults.
hypocaust: a chamber below ground level heated by hot air from a furnace; the Roman system of heating a building or important room.
impluvium: a shallow tank to collect rainwater in Greek and Roman houses, usually in the courtyard.
impost: a course or moulding from which an arch springs.
insula: Roman tenement-like living block.
intercolumniation: the distance between two classical columns, measured in diameters.
Latin cross: a cross with one of the four arms elongated.
lintel: a horizontal member spanning an opening.
loggia: a covered gallery behind an open arcade or colonnade.
machicolations: floor openings in the stone parapet of a crenellated wall.
martyrium: a chapel containing the relics of a martyr or to mark the site of a martyrdom.
mausoleum: a magnificent tomb.
metope: a panel between triglyphs on a Doric frieze.
module: the measure of proportion by which the parts of a classical building are regulated; in modern practice a convenient unit upon which all the dimensions of a building and its components are based for economy and ease of construction.
mosaic: decorated surfaces on floors and walls formed by setting in mastic small cubes (tesserae) of stone, marble, and glass in Roman and Byzantine architecture.
mouldings: contours of projecting members.
mullion: a vertical division between the lights of a window.
naos: the sanctuary or chamber of a Greek temple containing a cult statue.

narthex: a porch in front of the nave and aisles of some churches.

nave: the main division of a church west of the chancel arch or crossing, with or without aisles.

necropolis: a 'town of the dead', a cemetery.

nymphaeum: a 'temple of the nymphs' in classical architecture, i.e. a building where plants, running water, and sculpture provide a pleasant retreat.

oculus: a circular opening.

oecus: a reception room in a Roman house.

opus Alexandrinum: ornamental paving of variously coloured marble inlay in geometrical patterns.

orchestra: in a classical theatre the circular space for the chorus in front of the stage.

order: in classical architecture, a column (consisting of base, shaft, and capital) with the entablature it supports, proportioned and decorated to an accepted mode. In medieval architecture, a ring of voussoirs in an arch.

orientation: the positioning of a building in relation to the points of the compass. Most churches are aligned east-west with the altar at the east end but Early Christian churches were 'orientated' westwards like St Peter's, Rome.

palazzo: an Italian 'palace' or large and imposing town house.

pedestal: a base supporting a column, obelisk, or statue in classical architecture.

pediment: the triangular end of the moderately pitched roof of a classical building above the top of the entablature or cornice. A similar but smaller form used over doors or windows, sometimes segmental.

pendentive: a concave spandrel marking the transition between a square or polygonal apartment and a circular dome, cf. squinch arch.

peripteral: of a classical building having a surrounding row of free-standing columns.

peristyle: a continuous colonnade surrounding a classical building or court.

piano nobile: the main floor of a palace or villa when the principal reception rooms are above a ground floor or basement.

piazza: a formal open space or square surrounded by buildings in a town.

pier: the solid support of a pair of arches in an arcade.

pilaster: a rectangular column usually engaged with a wall but projecting from it.

pile-dwelling: a prehistoric lake dwelling resting on piles or posts.

podium: the platform on which a building is raised or the lowest part of a pedestal.
porphyry: a red and white crystalline rock.
portal: an elaborately designed, often recessed, doorway.
portico: a roofed space open on at least one side and enclosed by a range of columns supporting the roof.
postern: a concealed exit or sally port in military architecture.
prostyle: having a portico of free-standing columns.
prothesis: a part of a church where the elements of the Eucharist were set out.
prothyrum: the entrance passage from the street in a Roman house.
pseudo-peripteral: of a classical building having a surrounding row of pilasters or engaged columns only.
pulvin: *see* **dosseret.**
quoins: the corner stones at the angle of a building, especially when rusticated.
reredos: a decorated wall or screen behind and above the altar in a church.
revetment: a retaining wall or a facing to a wall or embankment.
rib: a stone arch on the groin or surface of a vault.
rose window: a circular Gothic window with tracery in a radiating pattern.
rotunda: a circular building, usually domed.
rustication: stonework of large freestone blocks (rough or smooth) with recessed joints.
salone: a large reception room in an Italian palazzo or villa.
sanctuary: specifically the holiest part of a church, i.e. the presbytery portion of the chancel.
sarcophagus: a large ornamental stone coffin.
scroll: an ornamental motif in the form of a partly unrolled parchment.
squinch arch: a small arch across the inner angle of a compartment making the transition to a circular dome or polygonal structure above, cf. pendentive.
string course: a projecting horizontal band along a wall.
stucco: plaster applied to a wall or ceiling surface; usually moulded decoratively when used internally or smoothed and painted externally.
stylobate: the platform of a classical temple, usually of three steps.
swag: a festoon of fruit, flowers, and foliage.
tablinum: in classical houses a room with one side open to the atrium; the master's apartment.
tepidarium: the warm room of Roman thermae.
term: terminal figure, or sculptured bust, to a pedestal or pillar.
terracotta: a burnt clay material harder than brick.

tessellated: of a cement surface in which tesserae are set.
tesserae: small cubes of marble, or stone, or glass used in mosaic work.
thermae: Roman baths-cum-social centres.
trabeated: of a style of architecture in which a structure is supported over openings by beams or lintels, cf. arcuated.
transept: either arm of the transverse part of a cruciform church.
tribune: the apse of a basilica or rostrum; also the gallery of a church.
triclinium: in a Roman house, a dining room with couches on three sides.
triforium: a wall passage above the arcade and open to the nave.
triglyph: a block with three vertical grooves between metopes in a Doric frieze.
trulle: a primitive Apulian stone hut of beehive form in recessed stages.
tunnel vault: *see* **barrel-vault.**
tympanum: in classical architecture the triangular area within a pediment and the space between the base and cornice of a pedestal. Otherwise, the area between a lintel and the arch over it.
vault: an arched covering of stone.
velarium: a large awning supported on masts.
Venetian window: a semi-circular headed opening flanked by two narrow flat-headed ones; the Serlian motif.
vermiculation: ornament resembling worm tracks carved on masonry.
vestibule: an anteroom or entrance hall.
vestry: a robing room in a church.
villa: a large Roman farmstead or country house, the centre of an estate. From Renaissance times either a country house or a villa suburbana.
volute: the scroll of an Ionic or Corinthian capital.
voussoir: wedge-shaped blocks forming part of an arch.
wheel window: *see* **rose window.**
xystus: a long portico, open walk, or enclosure used for recreation or athletic exercise.

BIBLIOGRAPHY

Ackerman, J. S. *Architecture of Michelangelo*, 2 vols. (Zwemmer, 1961)
Ackerman, J. S. *Palladio*, Penguin, 1966
Alberti, L. B. *Ten Books on Architecture*, trans. by J. Leoni, ed. J. Rykwert (Tiranti, 1955)
Allsop, B. *History of Classical Architecture* (Pitman, 1965)
Allsop, B. *History of Renaissance Architecture* (Pitman, 1959)
Anderson, W. J. and Stratton, A. *The Architecture of the Renaissance in Italy* (O.U.P., 1927)
Ayrton, E. and Moulinier, S. *The Doric Temple* (Thames & Hudson, 1964)
Banham, R. *Theory and Design in the First Machine Age* (Architectural Press, 1960)
Bartlett, V. *Introduction to Italy* (Chatto & Windus, 1967)
Barzini, L. *The Italians* (Hamish Hamilton, 1964)
Bazin, G. *Baroque and Rococo* (Thames & Hudson, 1964)
Branner, R. *Gothic Architecture* (Prentice-Hall, 1962)
Briggs, M. S. *Architecture in Italy* (Dent, 1961)
Brown, F. E. *Roman Architecture* (Prentice-Hall, 1962)
Bumpus, T. F. *Cathedrals and Churches of Northern Italy* (Laurie, n.d.)
Burckhardt, J. *Civilisation of the Renaissance in Italy*, trans. by S. G. C. Middlemore, revised by I. Gordon (Muller, 1961)
Chastel, A. *Italian Art*, trans. by P. and L. Murray (Faber, 1964)
Chastel, A. *Golden Age of the Renaissance: Italy 1460–1500* (Thames & Hudson, 1964)
Clapham, A. W. *Romanesque Architecture in Western Europe* (O.U.P., 1936)
Collins, P. *Changing Ideals in Modern Architecture, 1750–1950* (Faber, 1965)
Conant, K. J. *Carolingian and Romanesque Architecture: 800–1200* (Pelican History of Art) (Penguin, 1959)
Davies, J. G. *Origin and Development of Early Christian Architecture* (S.C.M. Press, 1952).
Decker, H. *Romanesque Art in Italy* (Thames & Hudson, 1959)
Dinsmoor, W. B. *Architecture of Ancient Greece* (Batsford, 1950)
Fletcher, B. *History of Architecture*, revised by R. A. Cordingly (Athlone Press, 1961)
Focillon, H. *Art of the West in the Middle Ages*, vol. 1, Romanesque; vol. 2, Gothic, trans. J. Boney (Phaidon, 1963)
Fokker, T. H. *Roman Baroque Art*, 2 vols. (O.U.P., 1938)

Frankl, P. *Gothic Architecture* (Pelican History of Art) (Penguin, 1963)
Franklin, J. W. *Cathedrals of Italy* (Batsford, 1958)
Hamilton, J. A. *Byzantine Architecture and Decoration* (Batsford, 1956)
Haupt, A. *Renaissance Palaces of Northern Italy and Tuscany*, 3 vols. (Batsford, 1931)
Hay, D. *Italian Renaissance and its Historical Background* (C.U.P., 1961)
Hibberd, H. *Bernini* (Penguin, 1965)
Highet, G. *Classical Tradition* (O.U.P., 1949)
Hitchcock, H. R. *Architecture Nineteenth and Twentieth Centuries* (Pelican History of Art) (Penguin, 1963)
Hitchcock, H. R. *World Architecture* (Hamlyn, 1963)
Hoag, J. D. *Western Islamic Architecture* (Prentice-Hall, 1962)
Howarth, T. *Nineteenth and Twentieth Century Architecture* (Longmans, 1963)
Hughes, J. Q. and Lyaton, N. *Renaissance Architecture* (Longmans, 1962)
Hutton, E. *The Cosmati: the Roman Marble Workers of the Twelfth and Thirteenth Centuries* (Routledge, 1950)
Huxtable, L. *Pier Luigi Nervi* (Prentice Hall, 1960)
Joedicke, J. *History of Modern Architecture* (Architectural Press, 1959)
Krautheimer, R. *Early Christian and Byzantine Architecture* (Pelican History of Art) (Penguin, 1965)
Langlotz, E. *Art of Magna Graecia* (Thames & Hudson, 1965)
Lawrence, A. W. *Greek Architecture* (Pelican History of Art) (Penguin, 1957)
Lees-Milne, J. *Baroque Europe* (Batsford, 1962)
Lees-Milne, J. *The Baroque in Italy* (Batsford, 1959)
Lowry, B. *Renaissance Architecture* (Prentice-Hall, 1962)
Macdonald, W. L. *Early Christian and Byzantine Architecture* (Prentice-Hall, 1962)
Mâle, E. *Early Churches of Rome* (Benn, 1963)
Masson, G. *Italian Gardens* (Thames & Hudson, 1961)
Masson, G. *Italian Villas and Palaces* (Thames & Hudson, 1959)
Meeks, C. L. V. *Italian Architecture, 1750–1914* (Yale Univ. Press, 1966)
Millon, H. A. *Baroque and Rococo* (Prentice-Hall, 1962)
More, J. *Land of Italy* (Batsford, 1961)
Mumford, L. *City in History* (Penguin, 1966)
Murray, P. J. *Architecture of the Italian Renaissance* (Batsford, 1963)
Murray, P. and Murray, L. *Art of the Renaissance* (Thames & Hudson, 1963)
Pagani, C. *Italy's Architecture Today*, trans. by V. Fudge, and M. Gilenti (Tiranti, 1955)
Pevsner, N. *Outline of European Architecture* (Penguin, 1963)
Pevsner, N. *Pioneers of the Modern Movement* (Penguin, 1960)

Pica, A. *Recent Italian Architecture* (Tiranti, 1960)
Plommer, H. *Ancient and Classical Architecture* (Longmans, 1956)
Richards, J. M. *Introduction to Modern Architecture* (Penguin, 1956)
Richardson, A. E. *Art of Architecture* (E.U.P., 1938)
Rivoira, G. T. *Lombardic Architecture*, trans. G. M. Rushford (O.U.P., 1933)
Robertson, D. S. *Greek and Roman Architecture* (C.U.P., 1945)
Rogers, E. N. *Works of Pier Nervi* (Architectural Press, 1958)
Ruskin, J. *Stones of Venice*, ed. and abridged by J. C. Links (Collins, 1960)
Saalman, H. *Medieval Architecture: European 600–1200* (Prentice-Hall, 1962)
Scranton, R. L. *Greek Architecture* (Prentice-Hall, 1962)
Scully, V. *Modern Architecture* (Prentice-Hall, 1962)
Smith, G. E. Kidder. *Italy Builds* (Architectural Press, 1955)
Smith, G. E. Kidder. *New Architecture of Europe* (Penguin, 1962)
Smith. J. Sumner. *Architecture of the Italian Renaissance* (Batsford, 1965)
Stewart, C. *Early Christian, Byzantine, and Romanesque Architecture* (Longmans, 1954)
Stewart, C. *Gothic Architecture* (Longmans, 1961)
Summerson, J. *Classical Language of Architecture* (B.B.C., 1963)
Trevelyan, J. P. *Short History of the Italian People* (Allen & Unwin, 1956)
Tuulse, A. *Castles of the Western World* (Thames & Hudson, 1959)
Vasari, G. *Lives of the Great Painters, Sculptors, and Architects* (Dent, 1949)
Vitruvius, M. P. *De Architectura*, 2 vols. (Loeb, 1934)
Walker, D. S. *A Geography of Italy* (Methuen, 1967)
Wheeler, M. *Roman Art and Architecture* (Thames & Hudson, 1964)
White, J. *Art and Architecture in Italy, 1250–1400* (Penguin, 1966)
Wittkower, R. *Architectural Principles in the Age of Humanism* (Tiranti, 1962)
Wittkower, R. *Art and Architecture in Italy 1600–1750* (Pelican History of Art) (Penguin, 1958)
Wölfflin, H. *Renaissance and Baroque* (Collins, 1964)

INDEX

References to illustrations are in *italic*